Developing Resilience for Social Work Practice

Edited by Louise Grant
and Gail Kinman

Individual chapters (in order) © Louise Grant, Gail Kinman and Richard Fountain; Gail Kinman, Almuth McDowall and Mariette Uys; Louise Grant and Becky Brewer; Siobhan Wray and Sacha Rymell; Kelly Alexander, Sara Henley and Kay Newman; Rose Parkes and Susan Kelly; Sarah Baker and Kathryn Jones; Gail Kinman, Isabella McMurray and Jo Williams 2014

First published 2014 by PALGRAVE

Palgrave in the UK is an imprint of Macmillan Publishers Limited, registered in England, company number 785998, of 4 Crinan Street, London N1 9XW.

Palgrave Macmillan in the US is a division of St Martin's Press LLC, 175 Fifth Avenue, New York, NY 10010.

Palgrave is a global imprint of the above companies and is represented throughout the world.

Palgrave® and Macmillan® are registered trademarks in the United States, the United Kingdom, Europe and other countries

ISBN 978-1-137-30249-6   ISBN 978-1-137-30250-2 (eBook)
DOI 10.1007/978-1-137-30250-2

This book is printed on paper suitable for recycling and made from fully managed and sustained forest sources. Logging, pulping and manufacturing processes are expected to conform to the environmental regulations of the country of origin.

A catalogue record for this book is available from the British Library.

A catalog record for this book is available from the Library of Congress.

Typeset by Cambrian Typesetters, Camberley, Surrey

This book is dedicated to all the hard-working social workers who seek to continue to maintain high professional standards and a commitment to relieving hardship and suffering in the face of highly challenging and demanding circumstances

Contents

List of illustrations

Practice foci

Acknowledgements

The editors and publisher would like to thank the following individuals and organizations for permission to reproduce copyright material:

Harry Venning for his kind permission to use his cartoon on p. xviii;

Workman Publishing Co. for their kind permission to reproduce material from M.B. Stanier, *Do More Great Work* (2010).

The editors would also like to acknowledge the help and support received from their respective families. They are also very grateful to Ashley Bennett and John Willett for their valued assistance in preparing the final typescript.

Notes on the editors

Louise Grant

Louise is a Principal Lecturer in Social Work at the University of Bedfordshire. Before that she worked as a social worker and as a manager in Children's Services. For the last seven years, she has taught qualifying and post-qualifying social workers. Her experience enables her to have a good understanding of the complexities of social work practice and its emotional demands, and the tools required to protect wellbeing and emotional resilience in practice. Louise has published several articles in high impact peer-reviewed journals (such as the *British Journal of Social Work*) and in the general social work press, and presented her work at national and international conferences. She is working towards a Ph.D. by published works.

Gail Kinman

Gail is Professor of Occupational Health Psychology at the University of Bedfordshire. She is a Chartered Psychologist with the British Psychological Society and co-chairs their Work–Life Balance Working Group which communicates evidence-based practice to organizations and employees. Gail has a longstanding research interest in occupational health psychology and has published widely in this field, with a particular focus on the wellbeing of people who work in emotionally demanding professions. She is currently involved in research projects at a national level with several occupational groups such as nurses, academics, prison officers, the police, and fire and rescue service personnel. She is currently working with health and social care professionals to enhance the personal resources that underpin emotional resilience to stress.

Contributors

Kelly Alexander
Kelly is a Senior Lecturer in Social Work at the University of Bedfordshire, specializing in mental health. She previously worked in forensic mental health services in London with a focus on women in secure care. Her research interests are in the areas of mental illness, risk assessment and identity.

Sarah Baker
Sarah is a Lecturer in Coaching Psychology at the University of Bedfordshire. She has developed and delivered peer-coaching workshops to a wide range of groups, including social workers. Her current research interests include developing mentoring schemes for improving wellbeing in helping professionals.

Becky Brewer
Becky is a Senior Practitioner in Workforce Development in Milton Keynes. Prior to this, she worked in Children's Safeguarding for over twenty years. In her current role, Becky has responsibility for running a range of learning and development schemes within Milton Keynes Children's Services.

Richard Fountain
Richard is a social worker with 36 years' experience working in Children and Families services in local authority settings as a practitioner and senior manager. Since 2010 he has been a Lecturer in Social Work at the University of Bedfordshire.

Sara Henley
Sara is a Consultant Clinical and Forensic Psychologist who has worked within the National Health Service for 24 years. Her current role involves running a busy psychology and therapy department within psychiatric services, in addition to teaching on university courses. She

has a particular interest in how CBT techniques can improve wellbeing in helping professionals.

Kathryn Jones

Kathryn is the post-qualifying lead for Social Work practice education at the University of Bedfordshire, where she has delivered the training for practice educators for the past seven years. Kathryn is a Practice Teacher Award holder with experience in supporting a wide range of learners to achieve their full potential.

Susan Kelly

Susan is an Independent Consultant and Mindfulness Teacher with over 25 years' experience in social work. She is particularly interested in the use of mindfulness practices in supporting people in the helping professions, with a particular focus on improving wellbeing.

Almuth McDowall

Almuth is Course Director for the M.Sc. in Occupational and Organizational Psychology at the University of Surrey, and works as an independent practitioner across the public and private sectors. Her particular interests include the development of work–life balance self-management competence.

Isabella McMurray

Isabella is a Senior Lecturer in the Department of Psychology at the University of Bedfordshire and a Chartered Psychologist. She undertakes consultancy and training in research methods and analysis with local authorities and charities, and conducts research with children and families, evaluating parenting programmes and exploring children's wellbeing and resilience.

Kay Newman

Kay is a social worker in Milton Keynes working in mental health services.

Rose Parkes

Rose is a Senior Lecturer in Community and Criminal Justice at De Montfort University. Prior to her employment in Higher Education, Rose was a Probation Officer. She has a particular interest in how practices such as yoga and mindfulness can improve employee wellbeing, and is undertaking research on the use of yoga in prisons to enhance the wellbeing of prisoners.

Sacha Rymell

Sacha qualified as a social worker in 1994 and has worked in Children's Services ever since. Since 2005, she has been the Head of Service for the Intake and Family Support Teams at Central Bedfordshire Council. Sacha has a particular interest in Child Protection.

Mariette Uys

Mariette qualified as a social worker in South Africa and has practised in England since 1997. She currently manages a front-line Social Care Team responsible for receiving referrals in relation to children and families in and out of hours. She also teaches on the Social Work course at Buckinghamshire New University.

Jo Williams

Jo is a registered social worker with 21 years' experience of working with children and vulnerable adults, initially in residential settings. Since 2005, she has worked in management roles within Local Authority Statutory Services.

Siobhan Wray

Siobhan is a Psychologist and Senior Lecturer in Leadership & Management at Sheffield Hallam University. She researches the impact of working life on employees and organisations, with a particular focus on wellbeing and productivity.

PART I

The professional context

CHAPTER 1

Social work and wellbeing: setting the scene

Louise Grant, Gail Kinman and Richard Fountain

CHAPTER OVERVIEW

Although social work is undoubtedly rewarding, practitioners frequently encounter situations that are emotionally demanding and potentially stressful. The stress experienced by social workers arises from a combination of occupational demands (such as managing a high caseload) and organizational constraints on effectiveness (such as working within bureaucratic cultures and coping with rapid change). This chapter sets the scene for the book by considering the context of social work practice and the demands that social workers face. A key aim of the chapter is to highlight the value of a perspective derived from positive psychology that aims to enhance wellbeing and resilience, rather than merely offer a range of tools to social workers to help them manage stress. While the emotional demands of social work require professionals to be personally resilient, it is emphasized that the responsibility for recognizing and ameliorating the causes of stress lies with the organization. The chapter concludes by outlining the aims of the book and introducing each chapter.

Stress: an overview

The terms 'pressure' and 'stress' are often used synonymously, but there are important differences between them. We need some pressure in our lives to help us meet the many challenges we encounter. Stress, on the other hand, occurs when the demands of work outweigh our ability to manage them and is likely to have negative effects on health, quality of life and job performance. The UK Health and Safety Executive (HSE) defines work-related stress as 'the process that arises where work demands of various types and combinations exceed the person's capacity and capability to cope' (HSE, 2009). This considers stress to be an imbalance between environmental demands (or stressors) and personal resources. The next section provides an overview of acute and chronic stress and their implications for the wellbeing of social workers and their professional practice.

Acute and chronic stress

Although stress has been conceptualized in many ways, essentially there are two types: acute and chronic. *Acute* (or short-term) stress is a reaction to an immediate demand, one that has occurred recently, or one that is anticipated in the near future. Examples of such demands within the workplace include rushing to finish a report, worrying about the outcomes of yesterday's case conference, or being concerned about a service user who is self-harming. Some intermittent demands, such as working towards a tight deadline, keep us alert, boost performance and can even protect us against disease (Emmons, 1986). Other types of acute demands, however, such as bereavement, divorce, job change and redundancy, can seriously impair wellbeing.

Early research findings demonstrated that the number and severity of life events experienced in a 12-month period were significantly related to several mental psychological and physical health conditions (Holmes and Masuda, 1973). It was generally argued that life events (even positive ones such as marriage and holidays) threaten wellbeing as they require social readjustment, and as adaptation to change is intrinsically stressful it depletes personal resources (Greene and Grant, 2003). Nonetheless, more recent research indicates that experiencing even the most severe life events can help us cope more effectively with future stressful situations (Kutilek and Earnest, 2001). The notion of 'stress inoculation' arising from such research is discussed further in Chapter 9.

Acute stressors can undoubtedly threaten wellbeing, but there is evidence that *chronic* (or long-term) stress is likely to be more damaging (Grant, 2012). The work-related demands described above may enhance health and performance in the short term, but if workload is *always* heavy, deadlines *frequently* unrealistic, case conferences *usually* emotionally demanding, and service users *often* a cause for serious concern, personal resources will be depleted over the longer term with negative implications for health (Green, Oades and Grant, 2006; Koeske and Koeske, 1989). Studies of social workers support this view, whereby 'daily hassles', or minor irritating events, annoyances and frustrations, are the most common sources of stress and the most likely to impair wellbeing (Green, Grant and Rynsaardt, 2007; Joyce and Showers, 1982).

The physiological response to stress discussed in Box 1.1 below accounts for the different ways that acute and chronic stress impact on health. It should be recognized, however, that the effects of stress are considerably broader, with serious implications for wellbeing and job performance. This is discussed in greater depth in Chapter 9.

BOX 1.1 THE STRESS RESPONSE

The physiological response to stress can account for the different impact of acute and chronic stress on health. Acute stress causes the release of stress hormones (such as adrenalin and noradrenalin), which instigates a chain of rapidly occurring bodily reactions including increased heart rate, blood pressure and respiration; muscle tension; sweating and suppression of the digestive system. People may also experience panic attacks involving sudden and intense anxiety which can lead to feelings of confusion and disorientation. This 'fight and flight' response is designed to be an adaptive reaction to short-term stress; when the threat recedes, the body will return to its normal state. Under conditions of long-term stress, however, physiological stress reactions can escalate from acute to chronic, resulting in persistent headaches, musculoskeletal problems, gastric disorders, generalized anxiety disorder and serious diseases such as hypertension and coronary heart disease (Jones and Bright, 2001). Chronic stress can also engender 'learned helplessness', where the individual perceives little control over the events in their life, gives up searching for solutions and may demonstrate a negative and defensive approach to work (Peterson and Seligman, 1984; Ladyshewsky, 2010).

Stress in social work

For several years, the UK Labour Force Survey (HSE, 2013) has found the highest prevalence rates of work-related stress amongst health and social care workers. This reflects the findings of studies of social workers conducted over the last twenty years or so that have observed high levels of stress and associated health problems in the profession (e.g. Jones and Ibbeston, 1991; Collings and Murray, 1996; Barak, Nissly and Levin, 2001; Maidment, 2003; Coffey, Dugdill and Tattersall, 2004; Stalker et al., 2007; Kinman and Grant, 2011; Ting, Jacobson and Sanders, 2011; Wilberforce et al., 2012).

The Health and Safety Executive (HSE) definition of work-related stress was provided earlier in this chapter. There are many potential stressors that can be experienced in the workplace but the HSE (2010) have identified the key sources of job-related stress as: excessive demands; insufficient support from managers and colleagues; role overload, conflict and ambiguity; poor workplace relationships; lack of control; and ineffective management of change. Like other professions, social work also has a range of more job-specific stressors such as high levels of bureaucracy (Hussein et al., 2013), frequent reorganization and revised policies and procedures (Storey and Billingham, 2001), tension between social work values and meeting targets (Lloyd, King and Chenoweth, 2002), poor public image of the profession (Collings and Murray, 1996; CPCSW, 2007) and threats of violence (Jones and Ibbeston, 1991; Wilberforce et al., 2012). Nonetheless, research findings indicate that stressors are more likely to emanate from the organization itself rather than intrinsic features of social work practice (Ramon and Morris, 2005). Like other public-sector providers in the UK, the recent austerity measures have led to increasing demands for social workers to do more with less, resulting in feelings of overload, job insecurity and anxiety (Collins, 2008; ADCS, 2013). Drawing on the HSE framework outlined above, the following section will consider the sources of stress in social work and the impact they may have in greater detail. Chapter 9 will further discuss demands and support in terms of their potential to alleviate the negative effects of work-related stress and build resilience.

Surveys typically find that *job demands* are the most frequent and potentially damaging sources of job-related stress (HSE, 2013). Social workers experience demands from different areas which have strong potential to conflict. They are required to adhere to social work values and ethics, fulfilling the needs of service users in a timely and compassionate manner whilst complying with statutory requirements and meeting externally imposed deadlines. Caseloads may be high and service users' needs diverse, requiring continuous reprioritization (ADCS, 2013). Moreover, high sickness and turnover rates and difficulties recruiting new staff can lead to a vicious circle of increased workload and longer working hours for the survivors(Van Heugten, 2011), with clear implications for wellbeing and the quality of professional practice.

Job control encompasses the flexibility of working time and the ability to take breaks, as well as autonomy over the pace and method of working. There is evidence that social workers who lack job control are more likely to experience work-related stress and burnout (Stalker et al., 2007; Kim and Stoner, 2008). Conversely, a strong sense of control can mitigate the negative effects of work stress and foster job satisfaction and commitment (Collins, 2008; Hussein et al., 2013). The damaging effects of a lack of *support* at work have been highlighted. A study of social workers in Romania found that low levels of perceived support from supervisors and colleagues, combined with excessive demands and time constraints, were key predictors of stress and burnout (Marc and Oşvat, 2013). In social work, support from managers is most commonly gained through supervision. Nonetheless, it is generally acknowledged that the supportive elements of supervision have been compromised in recent years in favour of a performance management approach. Research conducted by the British Association of Social Workers (BASW, 2011) highlights the variability in the quality and effectiveness of supervision. Although 40 percent of participants rated the supervision they received as 'excellent' or 'good', 70 percent claimed that they received insufficient emotional support in supervision sessions. The importance of reflective supervision and how this may be enhanced is discussed in Chapter 4.

Good working *relationships* underpin a healthy and resilient organizational culture (Ferguson, 2011). Bullying at work can have particularly powerful effects on wellbeing and quality of life (Nielsen and Einarsen, 2012). Indeed there is evidence that bullying behaviours (such as belittling comments, persistent and non-constructive criticism of work, and withholding resources or information) can be more harmful to employees than sexual harassment (Hershcovis and Barling, 2010). Employees need not be victims of bullying for them to suffer its negative effects. Daily diary research conducted by Totterdell et al. (2012) found that witnessing unpleasant interactions between colleagues tended to result in emotional exhaustion. The findings of a study conducted by Whitaker (2012) suggest that bullying may be a particular problem in social work. Fifty-eight percent of the sample reported being the targets of demeaning, rude, and hostile workplace interactions more than once in the previous year. There is a clear need for the social work profession to develop effective tools and clear guidelines to eradicate such behaviour, and build mutually supportive working relationships at all levels of the organization.

As well as evidence of incivility within the social work profession, a blame culture has arisen in recent years. It has become increasingly common for individual social workers, particularly within child protection, to be publicly castigated for 'failing to manage' high-profile cases which have had tragic outcomes. It could be argued that this approach to 'performance management' is principally driven by political imperatives that favour public demonstrations of assertive action (Ayre and Calder, 2010). Nonetheless, it fails to address the systemic failures in the 'social care machinery' that are typically responsible for such incidents. It seems that the first question to be asked when something goes wrong is 'who is at fault?', rather 'what can be learned from the situation?' As well as instilling a constant state of anxiety, a blame culture is likely to stifle innovative practice, as social workers fear making errors of judgement. Essentially, they are in a 'double bind' whereby taking pre-emptive action can be interpreted in a negative light (such as 'child-snatching' by the agents of a 'nanny state') or, if they fail to act, a tragedy could ensue for which they will inevitably be blamed (CPCSW, 2007).

The blame culture within social work has been promulgated by the media, which is extremely powerful in forming public opinion. Unsurprisingly, research indicates that public perceptions of social workers are generally poor (CPCSW, 2007) which, combined with views of social work as a stressful career, has had an adverse impact on recruitment (Eborall, Garmeson and Britain, 2001). The impact of these negative perceptions on social work students is well illustrated in a study conducted by the authors whereby 69 percent of a large sample of social work students considered that social workers were unfairly blamed when something goes wrong (Kinman and Grant, 2011). Other research highlights examples of stigmatization of the profession within students' personal communities and even within their own family (Clements, Kinman and Guppy, 2014).

The need to combat the stigma attached to social work has been recognized and advertising campaigns developed in an attempt to attract high-quality recruits (Sweney, 2009). Recognizing the potentially corrosive impact of a blame culture on social workers and service users, the Munro (2011) report recommended that employers must foster an environment where social workers feel supported by their managers and peers. Moreover, there is a growing understanding that a systemic approach will be considerably more effective than seeking to apportion blame in identifying the root causes of problems and how these might be best addressed (Munro, 2011). The development of a 'resilient organization' within social work is likely to facilitate such a culture change (see Chapter 10).

Research findings also indicate that *role stress* is a particular source of strain for social workers. Role stress comprises three elements: role overload (where an employee has too many roles, each associated with specific demands and expectations); role conflict (where the demands and expectations of one role make it difficult to fulfil those of another) and role ambiguity (where the expectations, responsibilities, tasks and behaviours expected of a particular role are unclear) (Kahn et al., 1964). Role conflict, in particular, can have wide-ranging negative implications (e.g. Fried et al., 1998). Research conducted by Kim and Stoner (2008) found that role stress was a powerful cause of burnout and turnover intentions in a sample of American social workers. The effects were particularly strong amongst those who lacked job control and social support. Role stress also has major implications for work–life balance, which is discussed in Chapter 3.

As people have an inherent need for predictability and order, it is unsurprising that *change* is a common cause of stress. Responding to major organizational change can deplete employees' resources and engender anxiety, fear and frustration, poor morale, a lack of confidence in their abilities and uncertainty about their future (Ferrie et al., 1998; Callan, Terry and Schweitzer, 1994; Dahl, 2011). Changes that increase job demands and reduce resources, in particular, can have serious implications for physical and psychological health, impair sleep quality and recovery, and increase sickness absence (Schaufeli, Leiter and Maslach, 2009; Greubel and Kecklund, 2011). Social workers have experienced numerous and wide-ranging changes over the last few years in response to political, economic, social and environmental imperatives. One of the most profound changes recently experienced in the public sector in the UK has been the adoption of private-sector management practices. The aim was to transform social services departments into managed services, where centralized management models of practice and decision-making are utilized, rather than relying on professional judgements of need (Chard and Ayre (2010) cited in Ayre and Preston-Shoot (2010)). An increased emphasis on administrative and prescriptive procedural systems has led to a devaluation of social workers' expertise and an erosion of their professional discretion and autonomy (Wastell et al., 2010). Social work practice was further transformed following the deaths of Victoria Climbié and, more recently, Peter Connolly. Recommendations of serious case reviews and inquiries led to the introduction of a raft of strategic and practice requirements which, combined with the increasingly managerialist approach to delivery of services, further constrained the professional autonomy of social workers (Ayre and Preston-Shoot, 2010).

It has been argued that the profession, similar to the health and social care sector in general, is collectively suffering from change fatigue (McMillan and Perron, 2013). Perceiving too many changes occurring at one time means that employees experience difficulties aligning their thoughts and actions to make sense of change (Bernerth, Walker and Harris, 2011). There is also evidence that the extent and pace of change have engendered a sense of professional devaluation in social workers which can compound the existing demands of practice (Lloyd et al., 2002). Change fatigue, therefore, has serious implications for job performance as well as personal wellbeing.

The intrinsic pressures of the role combined with the political, economic and environmental context of contemporary social work presents practitioners with many challenges. As discussed above, such working conditions can have wide-ranging negative consequences. Although employers have a legal and moral duty of care to safeguard the wellbeing of their staff, the organizational and occupational demands inherent in social work require practitioners to be emotionally resilient. Fostering personal and professional resilience that is sustainable over the longer term is crucial, not only for the protection of the individual social worker but also for the quality of the service they provide. This book provides the reader with a range of evidence-based techniques firmly grounded in the social work context to help them accomplish this.

Introducing this book

There are very many books available on how to manage workplace stress. This book provides an alternative perspective by drawing on the principles of positive psychology (Seligman, 2002; Froman, 2010). Without seeking to minimize the challenges faced by contemporary social workers, surveys commonly find high levels of satisfaction within the profession (Stalker et al., 2007). This book focuses on ways that social workers can develop their stress resilience rather than their stress management skills, therefore increasing the potential for job satisfaction. Stress is viewed as an intrinsic and inevitable part of social work practice that can be managed proactively by developing a personal toolbox of skills and techniques. Building on early work that examined its role in predicting the outcomes of adversity in children, resilience is increasingly recognized as a key stress resistance resource in the workplace. Research findings indicate that resilience is likely to be a particularly important quality in emotionally challenging jobs such as social work, as it can help professionals to not only manage the demands of practice more effectively but also thrive under such conditions (Collins, 2008; Howe, 2008; McAllister and McKinnon, 2009; McDonald et al., 2012; Beddoe, Davys and Adamson, 2013).

This book presents a range of tools and techniques that have proven potential to enhance the wellbeing and resilience of social workers. Coming from the different but mutually complementary backgrounds of social work and occupational health psychology, the editors have worked together for several years to develop practical evidence-based interventions to support social workers in the valuable but emotionally challenging job they undertake on a day-to-day basis. This approach was informed initially by curiosity as to why some social workers thrive under challenging conditions while others, who face similar demands, burn out and leave the profession. This led to an interest in applying the concept of emotional resilience to social work practitioners, based on the premise that it may help them adapt positively to stressful working situations and enhance their professional growth.

The research presented in the book clearly demonstrates that the benefits of resilience are wide-ranging; resilient social workers are more psychologically and physically healthy, experience less stress, and use more adaptive coping strategies (Kinman and Grant, 2011; Grant and Kinman, 2012). These findings, together with the emerging evidence that resilience is a quality that can be developed through carefully targeted interventions, inspired this book. Like other helping professionals, social workers tend not to prioritize self-care or indeed practice self-compassion (Figley, 2002; Bober and Regehr, 2006). Nonetheless, the overwhelmingly positive responses to the many training sessions the editors have delivered to trainee and experienced social workers on enhancing resilience, and the enthusiastic reactions to our research, indicate that social workers and their managers see the value in such an approach and are highly receptive to it.

While resilience is essential in a profession that is intrinsically emotionally demanding, it should be acknowledged that interventions that aim to enhance the coping abilities of individual social workers without addressing the structural causes of stress will undoubtedly fail. As mentioned above, employers' responsibilities for safeguarding the wellbeing of their staff are clear (HSE, 2010; Donaldson-Feilder, Lewis and Yarker, 2011). Individual resilience requires a resilient and supportive organizational culture to sustain it. The notion of 'environmental resilience' has recently emerged, whereby characteristics of the working environment can not only reduce stress, but also increase job satisfaction, wellbeing and commitment (Johnston and Paton, 2003; van Breda, 2011).

The positive psychological approach promoted in this book does not intend to let employers 'off the hook', nor do we argue that social workers are individually responsible for protecting their own health and wellbeing in the face of what can be excessive work demands. By developing tools and techniques to build their own resilience, we believe that social workers can manage the inevitable day-to-day challenges they will encounter proactively, enabling them to thrive rather than merely survive.

Introducing the chapters

This chapter has provided an overview of the current context of social work and the risk factors inherent to the job. The potential role played by resilience in protecting wellbeing and practice was highlighted. The next chapter (*Chapter 2*) explores the meaning of resilience and identifies the competencies that underpin it. Part II of the book presents a series of chapters that outline several evidenced-based strategies to enhance resilience in social work contexts.

The editors advocate the development of an individual 'toolbox', or set of resilience-building strategies which can be drawn upon in difficult times. Nonetheless, when delivering training, we have found individuals are often drawn to strategies that reinforce their existing skills or affirm their preference for a particular coping style. As mentioned above, and discussed further in Chapter 9, resilient social workers are those who possess a wide repertoire of coping techniques and are able to select the most appropriate strategy for the problem encountered. This book should therefore be approached with an open mind: we ask the reader to think carefully about whether some techniques which might not initially appeal may be the most effective in certain conditions. For example, if you are an action-oriented person, you may be drawn to the chapter on personal organization and time management (in which you may already have considerable expertise), whereas you would shy away from mindfulness, which could help you slow down and gain perspective. This book aims to enhance self-knowledge through a process of reflection. In order to accomplish this and identify which techniques are most appropriate to help you extend your repertoire, you may find it helpful to identify your personal profile of strengths and areas for improvement, and techniques for doing this are suggested in the final chapter of this book.

Helping professionals, such as social workers, tend to have particular problems maintaining a healthy work–life balance. This is a key factor in building resilience, as adequate opportunities for recovery are vital to sustain wellbeing and optimum professional practice. *Chapter 3* considers the ways in which work demands can 'spill over' into the non-work domain to impact on wellbeing, life satisfaction and personal relationships, as well as job performance. Ways by which social workers can maintain effective psychological and physical boundaries between their work and home lives to help them recover from work demands will be outlined.

In *Chapter 4*, the importance of developing positive supervisory relationships based on authenticity, respect and positive regard is emphasized. Also considered is how critical reflection can help foster emotional literacy and accurate empathy, which are fundamental aspects of resilience. Ways in which social workers can access appropriate supervision are identified and information provided for supervisors on how to promote effective supervision.

Chapter 5 considers ways in which personal organizational and time-management skills can support resilience. Several techniques are outlined to help social workers cope with competing demands, enhance their personal effectiveness, and dedicate sufficient time for respite and recovery. Tools are presented that can help social workers gain insight into their personal approach to time management and help them set realistic, achievable and sustainable goals. The behaviours that support or undermine the development of effective time management strategies are also examined.

Chapter 6 introduces the reader to cognitive behavioural techniques (CBT): a key problem-solving tool with strong potential to promote wellbeing and resilience. This chapter presents different ways to challenge negative thinking styles that can lead to self-blame and anxiety. CBT techniques can help social workers develop alternative strategies to manage emotional or behavioural concerns by identifying and confronting the ways in which they think about situations. In turn, this can help manage negative emotions and build self-efficacy and confidence.

Mindfulness, which is the focus of *Chapter 7*, has proven potential to foster resilience in social workers. Its benefits are wide-ranging: mindfulness practice can help people manage stress and anxiety more effectively and maintain boundaries between their work and home life, as well as enhance key social work competencies such as emotional literacy, self-awareness, critical reflection and active listening. Mindfulness can also help social workers focus on the present rather than ruminating excessively on past mistakes and fears for the future.

The importance of supportive peers in enhancing wellbeing and resilience has been highlighted in the research. *Chapter 8* therefore specifically focuses on how peer-coaching techniques can be used to enhance mutual support in social work contexts. More specifically, it explores how a problem-focused perspective to difficulties encountered by social workers can be changed to a more constructive, solution-focused approach, which is more conducive to building resilience. The importance of celebrating achievement and success rather than dwelling excessively on perceived failure is also emphasized. A fundamental component of emotional resilience is self-knowledge. Although this is highlighted throughout the book, it is a key theme of *Chapter 9*. The role played by individual differences that are key predictors of people's responses to stress is examined with a view to helping social workers gain insight into the aspects of the job that they find most stressful, their personal stress reactions, and the resources they have to help them manage stress and build resilience. Particular focus is placed on stress-resistance resources such as support and control and the implications of different coping styles and strategies for wellbeing and resilience.

Chapter 10 discusses the practical implications of the previous chapters for enhancing resilience at an individual level. The need for organizations to develop appropriate cultures and structures to support resilient social workers is also emphasized. A preliminary framework for a resilient workplace emerging from recent research is also identified. The chapter concludes by identifying future research priorities that have the potential to enhance insight into the features of resilience and how it can build a healthy and productive working environment over the long term.

CHAPTER 2

What is resilience?

Louise Grant and Gail Kinman

CHAPTER OVERVIEW

Much has been written about stress and burnout in social work and ways in which this can be managed. Although it is acknowledged that social workers need to be resilient to protect their wellbeing in an increasingly stressful profession, there is little guidance to help them accomplish this. This chapter introduces the concept of resilience and considers its relevance to the social work context. The advantages of adopting a strengths-focused perspective (that aims to identify the factors underpinning human fulfilment) over a problem-focused approach (that tends to dwell on the 'dark side' of organizational life) are considered. It is argued that resilience can explain why some practitioners who encounter profound difficulties not only fail to burn out, but frequently gain strength from their experiences. Drawing upon a range of approaches and perspectives, this chapter explores the meaning of resilience with particular focus on research that has examined social workers' views about the concept and the qualities that underpin it. Also considered are the potential benefits of enhancing resilience for personal wellbeing and professional practice. The chapter concludes by highlighting the need for social workers to develop a 'toolbox' of resilience-building competencies that is congruent with their circumstances and needs. These competencies are considered in greater depth in the chapters contained in Part II of this book.

Resilience: an exceptional quality or 'ordinary magic?'

Resilience seems to have become the new buzzword in caring professions. The need for social workers to be resilient is widely recognized, but what does resilience mean, and how can this important quality be enhanced? Resilience has been defined in a wide range of ways; Oxford Dictionaries and Waite (2012) characterizes it as 'toughness', 'springing back into shape' and the 'capacity to recover from difficulties'. Nonetheless, although the notion of 'bouncing back' after adverse experiences is a recurring theme, the qualities possessed by resilient people are considerably broader. Although resilience is undoubtedly beneficial for wellbeing, it should also be recognized that it is not a magical talisman that will protect people from all harm. This section explores the diverse meanings of the resilience concept emerging from the literature, its benefits and the qualities that underpin it.

Early researchers aimed to identify the positive qualities of resilient children and adults (for example, self-esteem and autonomy) that helped them adapt positively to adversity (Anthony, 1974; Jacelon, 1997). Others, however, focused on the aspects of the external environment that might support resilience (Masten and Garmezy, 1985; Werner, Garmezy and Smith, 1989). More recent conceptualizations typically see resilience as a dynamic interplay between personal characteristics and the effective utilization of supportive environmental features (Rutter, 1999; Collins, 2008). Research findings demonstrate that resilience can be enhanced through carefully targeted interventions to help people cope more effectively with minor stressors and serious life events (Fletcher and Sarkar, 2013).

In order to enhance resilience, it is essential to identify the underlying qualities of resilient people. The importance of adaptability and flexibility in fostering resilience has been widely recognized (Masten, Best and Garmezy, 1990; Luthar, Cicchetti and Becker, 2000). Pooley and Cohen (2010) consider resilience to be synonymous with resourcefulness, emphasizing the ability to utilize internal and external resources to respond to life challenges positively and flexibly, adjust to change effectively, and maintain a sense of control over the environment. (Collins, 2008), who has published extensively on stress and wellbeing in social workers, also considers the ability to manage change and sustain control and commitment in times of adversity to be fundamental components of resilience.

Although adaptability, control and commitment are undoubtedly key characteristics of resilient people, others have argued that the concept is considerably broader. Neenan (2009, p. 17) defines resilience as 'a set of flexible cognitive, behavioural and emotional responses to acute or chronic adversities which can be unusual or commonplace'. This indicates that resilience enables people to respond adaptively to novel as well as familiar problems. The emphasis placed on cognitive, behavioural and emotional competencies echoes Lazarus and Folkman's (1984) transactional approach to stress and coping, whereby an individual engages in primary appraisal (perceiving that a situation may endanger their wellbeing) and secondary appraisal (being uncertain whether they possess the appropriate resources to manage the threat) before selecting a coping strategy. The nature and importance of individual appraisals to building resilience is discussed further in Chapter 9.

A review of the literature (see Box 2.1) highlights the breadth of the characteristics that have been associated with resilience. In addition to the competencies discussed above, positive attitudes towards the self

BOX 2.1 CHARACTERISTICS OF RESILIENT PEOPLE

- Hardiness.
- Self-efficacy and self-esteem.
- Self-awareness.
- Emotional literacy (the ability to attend to, recognize and regulate moods in the self and in others).
- A positive self-concept and a strong sense of identity.
- A high degree of autonomy.
- The ability to set limits.
- Openness to experience and the ability to learn from experience.
- Advanced social skills and the social confidence to develop supportive relationships.
- Flexibility and adaptability in the use of coping strategies.
- Creative problem-solving and planning skills.
- Well-developed critical thinking abilities.
- The capacity to identify and draw on internal and external resources.
- Resourcefulness and successful adaptation to change.
- Enthusiasm, optimism and hope; an orientation towards the future.
- Persistence in the face of challenges and setbacks; the ability to recover rapidly.
- A sense of mastery and purpose.
- A sense of coherence: the capacity to derive meaning from difficulties and challenges.

and others, personality traits and behavioural tendencies, social skills and well-developed critical thinking, problem-solving and emotion-management abilities are also included. Many of these competencies have also been identified by Peterson and Seligman (2004) as key human strengths that underpin the virtues of humanity, justice, wisdom, temperance, courage and transcendence that underpin positive psychology.

As can be seen, the sheer breadth of these characteristics indicates that resilience cannot be easily defined. It may be more appropriate to consider resilience as a rubric or an 'umbrella' term, which encompasses a diverse range of competencies, capacities and behaviours that not only help people to manage adversity, but gain strength from such experiences. This perspective concurs with Ungar's view that what is considered 'resilience' will vary according to the type of demands people experience and the environment within which they operate (Ungar and Liebenberg, 2011). This highlights the importance of taking an approach that recognizes the role played by the individual and their occupational context in shaping resilience and its components rather than employing a 'one-size-fits-all' perspective. Such an approach is utilized in this book. The next section explores social workers' personal understandings of resilience and the characteristics that underpin it.

Resilience and social workers

Although few studies have yet been conducted, there is some evidence that more resilient employees tend to manage work-related stress more effectively and experience greater wellbeing. Studies of managers have found that resilience is positively associated with a variety of positive outcomes, such as psychological health, job satisfaction and job performance (Luthans et al., 2007; Youssef and Luthans, 2007). Furthermore, there is a general consensus that resilience is particularly important in 'helping' professionals, as they typically face complex, highly challenging and emotionally demanding situations. Nonetheless, until recently little was known about the nature of resilience, the personal characteristics that underpin it, or how it can be developed in the social work context. This section draws on research that has explored these issues.

Based on interviews with 21 experienced social workers in New Zealand, Adamson, Beddoe and Davys (2012) developed a conceptual framework with three elements: *the self* (comprising core attributes such as identity, autonomy, optimism, personal history, and internalized moral and ethical codes); *the practice context* (encompassing features of the organizational structure and culture) and *factors that mediate between the self and the practice context* (such as support from supervisors and colleagues, coping and problem-solving skills, effective boundary setting and developmental learning). This framework is useful in articulating how personal qualities of the social worker interact with the characteristics of their working context to predict individual vulnerability and protective factors.

Research conducted in the UK by Grant and Kinman (2013) investigated the personal representations of resilience of 300 qualified and student social workers. Perceptions of why social workers need to be resilient and the means by which this quality can be enhanced were also explored. The findings are discussed below.

What is resilience? Resilience tended to be conceptualized in either *reactive* terms (a quality that enhances one's ability to cope with stressful circumstances), or in more *proactive* terms (a protective resource that can be drawn upon to help people cope with future challenges). More specifically, social workers who saw resilience as reactive emphasized its role in helping people overcome current adversity without being unduly damaged by the experience, whereas those who perceived it in proactive terms typically referred to a quality that helps people identify and alleviate stressful experiences and have tools at their disposal to enable them to manage these before they become distressing.

Reflecting the range of qualities highlighted in Box 2.1, considerable variation in personal meanings of resilience was found. Social workers highlighted qualities such as adaptability, flexibility, perseverance, hardiness, self-reflection, self-knowledge and emotional literacy as being synonymous with resilience. Recognizing the important role played by experience in the job role, some key differences emerged between views expressed by social work students and more experienced staff. Students generally perceived resilience as an innate, fixed quality, whereas qualified social workers tended to emphasize the combined role of personal attributes and protective environmental factors.

Why is it important for social workers to be resilient? Resilience was generally believed to help social workers maintain optimum physical, emotional and cognitive functioning. Responses to this question were divided into two interrelated categories: (a) resilience increases job performance, as it helps social workers manage complex and challenging issues whilst ensuring that appropriate values and standards are maintained; and (b) resilience facilitates self-protection, as it allows social workers to manage the emotional demands of the job and avoid burnout. The role played by resilience in fostering perseverance, optimism and hope in the face of setbacks was also commonly highlighted. The implications of optimism for the wellbeing of social workers and service users are discussed further in Chapter 9.

What can be done to enhance resilience? Responses to this question were categorized into two broad themes which emphasized the dual responsibility of the individual social worker and their organization: (a) intrapersonal strategies (such as the development of reflective ability, self-awareness, effective coping skills and appropriate self-care) and (b) interpersonal methods (such as stress-management training, organizational resources and effective support and supervision). The importance of developing a wide supportive network was highlighted, as was the need to be proactive and assertive in accessing high-quality support and personal development opportunities from within the workplace.

This study (Grant and Kinman, 2013) yielded some interesting and useful findings. The views articulated by students can help social work educators develop fit-for-purpose interventions to build resilience at an early stage in their careers. The opinions expressed by qualified staff can also inform post-qualification training to refresh and revise social workers' self-care and resilience skills. It is, however, important to recognize the 'healthy worker effect', whereby people who are more robust tend to remain employed in high-strain jobs for longer (Li and Sung, 1999). This may mean that, like the interviewees in Adamson et al.'s (2012) study above, the social workers who participated were unusually resilient and not therefore representative of the wider workforce. Nonetheless, their continued survival in a stressful occupation means that the views expressed by both samples are particularly valuable in helping develop strategies to enhance resilience in the profession more generally.

The research discussed above has provided insight into social workers' conceptualizations of resilience, why it is important, and what can be done to enhance it. As argued previously, knowledge of the personal qualities that underpin resilience in the social work context and the extent to which it protects wellbeing is also required. Research conducted by Kinman and Grant (2010) found that social workers who are more resilient are those who are able to maintain positive and supportive relationships and access support from a range of sources. Resilient social workers are also those who express accurate empathy (take the perspective of service users and show concern for them, but avoid distress caused by over-involvement and over-identification). The ability to reflect constructively on practice, manage personal emotional reactions and those of others effectively, and utilize a range of context-appropriate coping styles was also found to underlie resilience. A key finding of this study was that social workers who were more resilient tended to be more psychologically, physically and cognitively healthy.

As well as protecting personal wellbeing, many of the factors found to support resilience in social workers and other working contexts (such as enhanced problem-solving skills and the ability to maintain appropriate interpersonal boundaries) are also likely to improve job performance. Although at the time of writing there is no supporting evidence, it could be argued that by protecting health and enhancing job satisfaction, resilience also has strong potential to reduce absenteeism and attrition. More resilient social workers will therefore provide a better-quality service to users.

Although social workers must take some responsibility for protecting their own wellbeing, it is recognized that organizations also need to be resilient, not only by diagnosing and addressing the structural causes of stress, but also in adapting to challenging times in a resourceful and emotionally intelligent manner (van Breda, 2011). As discussed in Chapter 1, employers have a legal and moral responsibility to safeguard the wellbeing of their staff by ensuring that working conditions are not intrinsically harmful. The fact that health and social care workers have significantly higher estimated prevalence rates of work-related stress than those employed in other sectors means that their wellbeing should be monitored with particular care. The frameworks developed by the UK HSE to help organizations diagnose and manage key workplace stressors and to identify the qualities managers should possess to protect the wellbeing of their employees will be discussed in Chapter 10.

Resilience: the underlying competencies

This section will explore further some of the competencies that have been found to support resilience: emotional literacy, reflective ability, accurate empathy and social skills.

Emotional literacy (or emotional intelligence)

Goleman (1996, p. 34) has defined emotional intelligence as 'being able to motivate oneself and persist in the face of frustrations: to control impulse and delay gratification; to regulate one's moods and keep distress from swamping the ability to think; to empathize and to hope'. The concept of 'emotional literacy' is similar to emotional intelligence but considered to be particularly appropriate to the health and social care context. It is defined as:

> the ability to understand your emotions; the ability to listen to others and empathise with their emotions; and the ability to express emotions productively. To be emotionally literate is to be able to handle emotions in a way that improves your personal power and improves the quality of life around you. Emotional literacy improves relationships, creates loving possibilities between people, makes co-operative work possible and facilitates the feeling of community. (Steiner and Perry, 1999, p. 11)

Emotional literacy, therefore, comprises two interconnected elements: *interpersonal* (such as social skills) and *intrapersonal* (such as self-awareness). Interpersonal emotional literacy helps people relate effectively to others and achieve instrumental goals. Intrapersonal emotional literacy encompasses the amount of *attention* that people give to their feelings (the ability to monitor and observe one's emotions), the *clarity* of these experiences (the ability to appreciate, and identify specific emotional experiences), and *repair* (the ability to recover from negative mood states or prolong positive ones). Many studies have found strong relationships between emotional intelligence or literacy and positive health-related outcomes (e.g. Schutte et al., 1998). Our own research (Kinman and Grant, 2011) found emotional literacy to be one of the most powerful predictors of resilience in social workers. Findings also suggested that social workers with stronger interpersonal and intrapersonal emotion-management skills are not only more resistant to stress, but also more physically and psychologically healthy.

The capacity to manage personal emotional reactions and those of others effectively – often in challenging care environments – is central to social work. Morrison (2007) has highlighted the importance of well-developed emotion-management skills in successfully fulfilling key social work tasks such as engaging with service users, assessment and observation, problem-solving, collaboration and co-operation and the effective management of stress. Moreover, research has generally found that people who are more emotionally literate tend to be more enthusiastic, optimistic and self-confident (Kotzé and Venter, 2011), which is likely to help social workers forge constructive and trusting relationships with service users. Emotional literacy has further implications for job performance, as it has been found to underpin well-developed decision-making abilities and communication skills (Jordan, Ashkanasy and Hartel, 2002). The practice focus example of Anna illustrates how emotional literacy can help in the social work context.

PRACTICE FOCUS 2.1: ANNA

Anna is a social worker in a Leaving Care Team. She is working with Jake, a 15-year-old boy who has sexually abused his siblings. When initially reading his file, Anna initially felt angry towards Jake. As an emotionally literate social worker, however, she was able to gain insight into her strong emotional reaction and recognized that this could, if unaddressed, affect her relationship with Jake. By identifying that she was experiencing anger rather than feelings of disapproval of his behaviour, Anna was able to explore the reasons for her powerful emotional response. Anna realized that she felt angry about the impact Jake's actions would have had on his siblings and began to consider what might have led to his actions. Appreciating that Jake had himself been sexually abused started to engender feelings of empathy; not condoning his behaviour, but enabling the beginnings of a relationship based on authenticity and understanding. Without this, Anna may not have been able to work towards addressing Jake's inappropriate sexualized behaviour.

Reading Anna's story, it might be helpful to think whether there have ever been situations at work where emotions have impacted negatively on your practice and what mechanisms can be adopted to ensure that these do not adversely affect social work practice. This is an area where supervision might be useful in providing a forum for discussion about emotions, which is covered in more detail in Chapter 4.

The attributes associated with emotional literacy (which Anna possesses) are desirable, if not essential for social workers. Professionals whose emotional literacy skills are underdeveloped are likely to experience a range of problems. They may find it difficult to develop appropriate boundaries and may also allow their emotions to influence decision making unconsciously due to the inability to interrogate their emotional experiences. Furthermore, they may also attempt to 'repair' negative mood states by engaging in potentially damaging behaviours such as comfort eating or excessive alcohol consumption (Riley and

Schutte, 2003; Zysberg and Rubanov, 2010). Indeed, a low level of emotional literacy may also encourage a social worker who is faced with hostility and lack of cooperation to escalate conflict by reciprocating in kind. Insight into one's personal emotional literacy profile and guidance on how this might be developed is, therefore, vital for enhanced practice as well as personal wellbeing. Several techniques introduced in this book such as CBT techniques (Chapter 6) and mindfulness (Chapter 7) are likely to be particularly effective. Self-knowledge and insight into personal coping skills will also be useful (Chapter 9).

Reflective thinking skills

By allowing social workers to gain insight into their practice, personal reflection skills have strong potential to enhance professional development and service provision. More specifically, reflection helps social workers consider how they might change their approach and/or method of intervention, or indeed adapt their skills to meet the needs of service users. Based on a model developed with physicians, Aukes et al. (2007) found it useful to consider three distinct, but interrelated elements of reflective thinking: *self-reflection* (for example, 'I want to know why I do what I do'); *empathic reflection* (for example, 'I am able to understand people from different cultural and religious backgrounds'); and *reflective communication* (for example, 'I am open to discussion and challenge about my opinions'). This is a useful framework that has strong potential to provide insight into social workers' individual reflective profiles to help them identify strengths and areas for development. The practice focus of Colin, who is a social worker in an older persons' team, illustrates the importance of reflective thinking skills.

In the practice focus of Colin, he was clearly able to reflect on his practice. It may be helpful to consider how supervision can develop reflective practice skills and to what extent reflection is seen as a vital component of effective professional social work.

Our research has found that reflection is a key protective resource for social workers, as those who are better able to reflect on their thoughts, feelings and beliefs can consider the position of other people, can draw on their reflective abilities to communicate effectively with others and tend to be more resilient to stress and experience better mental health (Kinman and Grant, 2011). Empathic reflection appears to be a particularly important factor in protecting social workers from empathic distress and psychological distress more generally (Grant, 2013).

PRACTICE FOCUS 2.2: COLIN

Colin has been working with Surinder for a couple of years. Surinder is a 70-year-old woman of south Indian origin who is the centre of a large and loving family who frequently turn to her for help and support at times of crisis. Surinder's husband died a year ago and she has just had a stroke which has affected her speech and mobility. Nonetheless, Surinder continues to cook for her extended family and still provides a listening ear. She has told Colin that she is coping well, but she often seems exhausted and is not prioritizing her own needs. Colin initially feels that he should be empowering Surinder to tell her family that she cannot cook for them any more and that her direct payment could be spent on having meals delivered to her home. Surinder is, however, extremely reluctant to take this course of action and became tearful when it was suggested. Colin uses *self-reflection* to consider why Surinder might have become so upset, realizing that food is not particularly important from his cultural perspective but, for Surinder, cooking may mean more than the provision of sustenance. Based on his *empathic reflection*, Colin decided to approach Surinder in a different way to explore her feelings about cooking for her family and the cultural significance of food. Surinder responds well to this approach and is able to explain to Colin the importance of feeding her family to her identity and an expression of love. He subsequently uses *reflective communication* in supervision to explain how his thoughts, beliefs and ideas have changed. Colin is responsive to challenges from Surinder and his manager, realizing that he needs to become more culturally aware in some aspects of his work. Colin's manager suggests that he uses the direct payment to pay for someone who is interested in developing her cooking skills to help Surinder. Surinder feels valued and respected and Colin feels that he has done a good job.

Accurate empathy

Empathy is a fundamental component of all helping relationships and critical to social work practice. While empathy is essential to forging effective relationships between social workers and service users, the job role frequently requires them to cultivate empathy in other people. An understanding of empathy and how it may impact on resilience and wellbeing is therefore vital. Many definitions tend to see empathy simply as the ability to 'walk in other people's shoes' (Trevithick, 2005): to adopt their perspective in order to understand their feelings, thoughts or actions. Although empathy is undoubtedly a key attribute for helping professionals, the risk of being emotionally over-involved with service users has been identified which can lead to compassion fatigue and burnout (Thomas and Otis, 2010). Like reflective abilities discussed above, it is helpful to utilize multi-dimensional models of empathy that encompass *perspective taking* (attempts to adopt the positions of other people), *empathic concern* (feelings of warmth, compassion and concern for others) and *empathic distress* (feelings of anxiety and discomfort resulting from the negative experiences of others) (Davis, 1983). This

PRACTICE FOCUS 2.3: KATHY

Kathy is an experienced social worker who works with adoptive parents and their children. She has been working with one couple, Jack and Megan, for some time and undertook their adoption assessment. Kathy really likes the couple and has a lot in common with them, culturally and socially. Megan and Jack's adopted children have attachment disorders and exhibit extremely demanding behaviour. On a visit last week, Megan told Kathy that she couldn't cope any more: she was beginning to dislike the children and frequently felt angry with them. She disclosed that, despite all they have done for the children, she feels that they give her nothing back in terms of love and affection. Megan was heartbroken and Kathy was touched by her experience. Kathy couldn't sleep after work that night and worried about what Megan was experiencing: thinking that she and Jack were such a lovely couple, and had so much love to give. The next day Kathy went into the office to discuss the case with colleagues and she found herself describing the children in derogatory terms and focusing on Jack and Megan's needs. A trusted colleague spoke to Kathy and helped her realize that she was over-empathizing with Megan and Jack due to their shared background, and was in danger of losing her child-centred focus. Kathy was then able to discuss this with her supervisor and explore how she had become empathically distressed by the situation. They considered her need for some reflective space to develop a more balanced and accurate empathic response in order to prioritize the children's needs. Kathy was subsequently able to develop a more accurate type of empathy which benefited her own wellbeing and that of the children and families she worked with.

perspective acknowledges the fact that empathy is not necessarily beneficial, which is illustrated above in the case of Kathy.

Our own research (Kinman and Grant, 2011; Grant, 2013) provides useful insight into the complex role played by empathy in the resilience and wellbeing of social workers. Empathic concern and perspective-taking appears to enhance resilience, whereas empathic distress tends to diminish it and is likely to lead to psychological distress more generally. This suggests that a certain degree of empathy is beneficial for wellbeing, but over-empathizing with service users may lead to over-involvement which, in turn, can result in burnout. 'Accurate' empathy (concern and perspective-taking) is vital in order for social workers to make genuine attempts to acknowledge and accept what their service users think and feel, and therefore enhances practice as well as resilience. Nonetheless, clear emotional boundaries are required to ensure that empathic concern does not 'spill over' into empathic distress, with negative implications for service users as well as social workers. It should be acknowledged, however, that emotional boundaries should be worn like a protective suit of armour, but should be 'semi-permeable': that is, flexible enough to permit feelings to freely flow in and out, otherwise empathetic connections with service users cannot be developed. As discussed above, empathic reflection is a key skill that can help social workers develop accurate empathy. Critical reflection and effective supervision (Chapter 4) are likely to be particularly helpful in fostering empathic and authentic connections with service users whilst maintaining clear personal and emotional boundaries. This technique will also help social workers explore situations in which they are most likely to become over-involved and ways to manage this.

Social skills

The importance of social skills in relation to interpersonal emotional literacy has been emphasized above. Like other professionals, social workers require well-developed communication skills, social confidence and, where appropriate, the capacity to be assertive. It is often assumed that people entering the helping professions already possess highly developed social skills, so little initial and post-qualification training tends to be made available (Morrison, Hathaway and Fairley, 2005). Nonetheless, our research has found considerable variation in levels of social confidence amongst social workers, indicating that some may require help to enhance their communication skills. This is particularly important, as social confidence was found to be strongly related to resilience and psychological wellbeing. More research is required, however, that examines specific social skills, such as cultural awareness or intelligence, as the ability to question cultural assumptions and adjust inner working models is fundamental to working effectively in multicultural environments (Campinha-Bacote, 2002). This was illustrated in the practice example of Colin above.

Social workers are often faced with challenging interpersonal situations, but being well-prepared can improve self-confidence and communication skills. Role play during supervision, as outlined in Chapter 4, or with a peer, can help social workers prepare for unfamiliar or challenging situations, such as emotionally challenging conversations with service users or court appearances. Acting out potentially difficult scenarios in a safe environment helps develop a compassionate and empathic but authoritative approach which can build confidence for handling real-life situations. Such techniques also provide important information about how other people may respond to us in particular situations and the strategies that may be most (and least) productive. This is illustrated by Sally's situation outlined below.

PRACTICE FOCUS 2.4: SALLY

Sally is a Newly Qualified Social Worker who has been allocated a child-in-need assessment. The family has been described as 'difficult to engage' and they are unhappy about social workers being involved in their lives. Sally feels anxious about her initial visit to the family and apprehensive about working with people who are so obviously hostile and angry. Knowing that this could affect her ability to engage with the family, Sally asks Chris, who is an experienced colleague, for advice. Chris offers to role-play the visit with her beforehand and to accompany her on the next visit in a supportive role. Sally is able to use these opportunities to practise her approach, which builds her confidence. The visit goes well and Sally feels more able to manage similar situations in the future. She recognizes that having the confidence to ask for help has enhanced her personal and professional development, as well as her personal wellbeing.

Social confidence is not only a key factor in facilitating effective relationships with service users, but it also helps build and maintain effective social networks with colleagues, friends and family. The support received from others can protect people against stress and build emotional resilience. Peer support and coaching (Chapter 8) and CBT techniques (Chapter 6) have strong potential to foster social confidence. Reflective supervision (Chapter 4) can also be valuable in helping social workers identify support needs and potential sources. The characteristics of social support as a key resilience resource are discussed further in Chapter 9.

Conclusion

This chapter has explored the many competencies that underlie resilience. As discussed, there is no great mystery to resilience: it is not an innate characteristic or trait, neither is it a talisman that protects people from all ills. Resilience typically arises from successful adaptation to everyday demands rather than unusual ones and from ordinary rather than extraordinary human capabilities. Resilience is a quality that can be developed, but a supportive and nurturing working environment is required whereby social workers are given sufficient time, resources and professional development opportunities. Being a resilient practitioner is an ongoing journey that will undoubtedly be challenging due to the many competing demands that social workers face. There will be days when we feel that we are not coping well or getting nowhere fast. There will also be times when we feel strong and ready to take on new challenges. This book aims to help you develop your personal resilience 'toolbox' that will help you navigate successfully through this journey. When considering the different strategies and techniques that are provided in Part II of this book, it important to be flexible and keep an open mind: what works for one person may not work for another and what works well in certain situations may not always work in others.

Developing techniques to build resilience

CHAPTER 3

The work/home interface – building effective boundaries

Gail Kinman, Almuth McDowall and Mariette Uys

CHAPTER OVERVIEW

Resilient social workers will be able to maintain a healthy balance between their work and personal life. The personal satisfaction gained from social work can enhance the quality of non-working life. Due to the nature of the job, however, social workers are at particular risk of work–life conflict and may struggle to replenish their physical and psychological resources sufficiently to function effectively. This chapter discusses the ways in which work demands can 'spill over' into the non-work domain to impact on wellbeing, satisfaction and personal relationships. The concepts of role conflict and time-based, strain-based and behavioural-based work–life conflict and their relevance to the wellbeing of social workers are explored. Particular focus is placed on how the emotional demands of social work practice can impact on the non-work domain. The importance of adopting a person-centred perspective is emphasized by highlighting individual differences in what is considered an 'ideal' work–life balance, and the diverse behaviours people use to juggle their work and non-working demands. The need for adequate respite opportunities to enhance wellbeing and job performance is emphasized. Several strategies are outlined that can help social workers achieve a work–life balance that meets their needs and consequently build resilience. Although it is crucial to develop effective personal strategies, the importance of organizational support in helping employees manage the demands of their work and non-working life is emphasized.

What is work–life balance?

Numerous books and articles have been written that aim to help people improve their work–life balance. The term 'work–life balance' is misleading, however, as it implies that 'work' and 'life' are independent, not interdependent, domains and that a 'perfect' balance is achievable. Even if an ideal balance were possible, this is likely to be a temporary state given that something is bound to happen in work or non-work life (or indeed both) to tip the scales. It may be more realistic to use terms like 'work–life fit' or 'work–life effectiveness' to acknowledge that an acceptable balance between work and other important aspects of life (such as family, friends, self-care and personal interests) will be different for everybody and priorities will shift over time to accommodate personal and professional commitments. Work–life fit relates to an employee's perception that their work life is balanced with their home life, and that they have sufficient resources to attend to work and home demands effectively (Voydanoff, 2005). Given that 'work–life balance' is so commonly used by employees and employers alike, this chapter will use this term and its opposite: 'work–life conflict'. As will be seen later in the chapter, however, the concept of work–life fit is particularly useful in helping people achieve a balance that meets their personal needs. The next section explores the implications of the roles that people take on for their work–life balance and wellbeing more generally.

Roles, work–life conflict and wellbeing

People take on many different roles in their work and non-working lives (such as spouse or partner, parent, or child of elderly parents) within the family, and several roles (such as manager, colleague and mentor) within the workplace. Additional roles outside the family and work domains, such as friendships, community responsibilities, and those related to hobbies and personal interests, are also likely. There is strong evidence that occupying different roles provides important psychological benefits (Baruch and Barnett, 1986). Multiple roles also facilitate social integration, which can protect wellbeing and foster resilience in the face of stress and adversity (Moen, 1997). Nonetheless, as each role brings with it a pattern of expectations, requirements, beliefs or attitudes, there is strong potential for roles to conflict. The term 'role conflict' refers to a 'situation in which differing role expectations result in incompatible role pressures, leading to psychological conflict for an individual as the pressures and role forces compete and conflict' (Korabik, Lero and Whitehead, 2011, p. 128). People experience role conflict when they feel pulled in different directions as they attempt to meet the demands of their various roles. Role conflict has wide-ranging negative implications for health and family life, as well as job performance, job satisfaction and retention (Kemery, Mossholder and Bedeian, 1987; Fried et al., 1998).

Role conflict takes two forms: *intra-role conflict*, referring to incompatible requirements within the same role; and *inter-role conflict*, which is a clash between the demands of two or more roles (Katz and Kahn, 1978). Intra-role conflict can arise in two ways. First, people's ideas of the requirements of a particular role can differ. For example, Anna's notion of being a 'good' social worker involves always being responsive to the needs of service users. Anna's manager, however, might think that a 'good' social worker prioritizes paperwork and meets externally-driven targets. These differing conceptions are likely to lead Anna to experience intra-role conflict. This type of conflict can also occur when an employee believes that the role *itself* has contradictory requirements and expectations. For example, Anna might feel that her role as a social worker requires her to be deeply engaged with service users' problems, while also recognizing the need to maintain an emotional boundary to protect her own wellbeing.

Inter-role conflict arises when the requirements and expectations of one role interfere with those of another. Work–life conflict is a form of inter-role conflict; this is defined as the degree to which participation in one role (e.g. family) is made more difficult due to participation in the other role (e.g. work) (Greenhaus and Beutell, 1985). For example, Mike will experience work–life conflict if he has to care for a sick child who is unable to go to school on a day when he has several urgent meetings scheduled with service users and other agencies. Sarah, who works in children's services and has a young family, will experience work–life conflict when she is expected to ensure a child at risk is settled in a foster placement out of hours.

The concept of work–life conflict draws upon resource-drain theory, which maintains that personal resources (such as time, attention and physical and mental energy) are limited and fulfilling demands emanating from one role will deplete the resources available to meet the demands of other roles (Edwards and Rothbard, 1999). Work–life conflict can be bi-directional: work-related demands can interfere with responsibilities and activities outside work (such as working rather than relaxing during evenings and weekends), and non-work responsibilities can hinder work obligations (such as in Mike's situation described above). Both work-to-home and home-to-work conflict can threaten wellbeing (Kinman and Jones, 2001), but work-to-home conflict is more common and potentially more damaging (Frone, Russell and Cooper, 1992). Nonetheless, one type of conflict can feed into the other, creating a vicious cycle that impairs people's involvement, functioning and wellbeing in both domains. Mike and Sarah are unable to fulfil the demands of their work and family roles simultaneously, which may have a longer-term impact on their job performance and satisfaction with family life.

Work has the potential to spill over into non-working life in three different ways (Netemeyer, Boles and McMurrian, 1996):

- *Time-based conflict* occurs when the time spent in one role limits that available for other activities. For example, a heavy administrative load will require long working hours, which will limit opportunities to spend time with family or on social activities. People who experience time-based conflict tend to cut down on breaks and commonly work during evenings, weekends and holidays in an attempt to fulfil work demands. Clearly, this will constrain opportunities for recovery and harm wellbeing over the longer term.

- *Strain-based conflict* arises when negative emotional reactions to work spill over into the non-work domain. Many people find it hard to switch off after work, but strain-based conflict can be a particular problem for helping professionals. Working on complex and emotionally sensitive cases and dealing with hostile service users can lead to social workers feeling anxious, distracted or irritable outside work. Concern about a service user's distressing circumstances might engender unhealthy rumination and emotional exhaustion. Feelings of powerlessness and inadequacy that can arise when managing a large caseload with limited resources can also threaten recovery. Moreover, a high level of interpersonal interaction at work (which is an intrinsic part of a social worker's role) can lead to people withdrawing from other personal relationships in an attempt to recuperate (Kanter, 1989). As social support is a key stress management resource, isolation from family and friends has potentially serious implications for wellbeing and resilience.

- *Behaviour-based conflict* is where conduct that is functional in one role is incompatible, or even counterproductive, in another. This type of conflict is generally more common in jobs that involve taking responsibility for others, and where employees are required to interact with uncooperative, hostile or aggressive people (Dierdorff and Ellington, 2008). As with strain-based conflict, social work has strong potential to lead to behaviour-based conflict. For example, a social worker is required to be assertive and task-oriented at work, but such behaviours are not always compatible with a harmonious family life! Moreover, an overly 'therapeutic' interaction style, which might be effective with service user, may not be productive when managing relationships with family or friends.

The impact of work–life conflict

Employees who experience work–life conflict may experience a range of psychological problems including depression, anxiety, emotional exhaustion and insomnia; they are also at increased risk of physical health problems ranging from headaches to cardiovascular disease (Kinman and Jones, 2001). Conflict between work and non-working life can also encourage negative health behaviours, which will inevitably impact on health over the longer term. People may increase their alcohol consumption to reduce tension after a bad day at work, and a lack of time and energy can increase the consumption of unhealthy foods and discourage physical activity (Payne, Kinman and Jones, 2012). Unsurprisingly, people who experience chronic work–life conflict are at greater risk of raised cholesterol levels and increased body mass index (Allen and Armstrong, 2006; Van Steenbergen and Ellemers, 2009).

Work–life conflict can impact on personal relationships as well as health. Employees who experience more conflict tend to be less satisfied with their relationships with family and friends (Kinman and Jones, 2001). They may also become argumentative or withdrawn at home, particularly when workloads are heavy or when they have experienced interpersonal conflict at work (Repetti, 1994). There is also evidence that an employee's job-related stress can 'cross over' to impair the wellbeing of family members. A study of dual-career couples conducted by Crossfield, Kinman and Jones (2005) found that the work demands experienced by an employee tended to increase their partner's level of distress. Although several explanations could explain the crossover process (such as mutual empathy and common life stressors), the study concluded that work-related discussions between partners were particularly important. Conversations that were more positive tended to improve the mood of partners, whereas those that were negative worsened it. These findings suggest that social workers who discuss traumatic incidents with family members, or who regularly complain about their working conditions, may feel better for 'offloading' their negative feelings, but risk 'transmitting' them to their loved ones – albeit unconsciously. This does not mean that social workers should put on a brave face and keep their emotional reactions to practice to themselves: indeed there is evidence that discussing uncomfortable feelings can enhance recovery in helping professionals (Moreno-Jiménez et al., 2009). Reflective supervision is likely to be a more appropriate environment, however, in which to explore and resolve such feelings than discussions with family and friends (see Chapter 3).

As well as threatening health and personal relationships, work–life conflict has serious implications for service users as it can impair the quality of service provision and the continuity of care. It has been linked to a range of negative work-related outcomes such as lack of commitment, absenteeism and turnover (Eby et al., 2005). Similar to work-related stress (see Chapter 1), conflict between work and home roles can also have a negative impact on performance by weakening cognitive abilities such as memory, attention and concentration (MacEwen and Barling, 1991). Such cognitive impairments typically stem from limited opportunities to recover from job demands and concerns. This is discussed later in this chapter.

Work–life conflict in social work

Research findings indicate that social workers may experience higher levels of work–life conflict than other occupational groups, particularly strain-based conflict (Aronsson, Astvik and Gustafsson, 2013; Lambert et al., 2006). A survey of 439 Australian social workers conducted by Kalliath, Hughes and Newcombe (2012) found high levels of time, behaviour and strain-based conflict which were linked to depression, anxiety and social dysfunction. The relationship between strain-based conflict and distress was particularly strong, suggesting that negative emotional reactions to work can damage mental health more generally. Respondents were invited to comment on the challenges they faced in managing the work–home interface. Three main themes emerged: work pressures (the nature of social work practice, workloads and high expectations of the organization and colleagues); family pressures (managing household tasks and providing care); and time pressures (limited time spent with family and on self-care). The role played by the expectations of self and others on wellbeing is explored further in Chapter 9.

Although work demands can undoubtedly conflict with non-working life, employment can also have many psychological benefits (Voydanoff, 2005). This is well illustrated in a study conducted by Kalliath and Kalliath (2006), who found evidence of work-to-life enrichment as well as conflict, which protected social workers' mental health and enhanced their family and life satisfaction. Clearly, enriching experiences at work can have many benefits for professional and personal life. Social workers who enjoy their work and who feel fulfilled by it are more likely to go home in a positive mood, which is likely to facilitate recovery, foster wellbeing, build resilience and enhance professional practice. Techniques that can be used to maximize gains and resources from work are explored in the chapters on mindfulness, peer support and peer coaching, and enhancing self-knowledge, coping skills and stress resistance.

There are several aspects of social work that may lead to work–life conflict. As discussed earlier in this chapter, the job encompasses many roles, the demands and priorities of which have strong potential to conflict. Heavy work demands can engender feelings of being overwhelmed by, as well as conflicted about, work and non-work roles. Employees may work longer hours in an attempt to manage their workload, leading to time-based conflict. Work–life conflict could also stem from role ambiguity, or a lack of clarity about the nature of the job and the expectations of others. Attempting to satisfy the demands of ill-defined roles is likely to be time-consuming and exhausting.

The emotional labour inherent in social work also has strong potential to lead to work–life conflict. Originally introduced by Hochschild (1983), emotional labour is defined as 'the effort, planning and control needed to express organizationally-desired emotion during interpersonal transactions' (Morris and Feldman, 1996, p. 987). Although all employees perform some degree of emotional labour, it is particularly common amongst helping professionals, as managing one's own emotional reactions and those of others is intrinsic to the job role (Zapf, 2002). The effort involved in suppressing genuine emotional reactions (which are incompatible with the job role) and displaying the 'correct' emotions (that may not be genuinely felt) can lead to strain-based work–life conflict (Kinman, Wray and Strange, 2011). For example, masking feelings of frustration with a service user and showing encouragement and positive regard can require considerable emotional effort and lead to feelings of self-alienation, emotional depletion and burnout. Critical reflection and effective supervision (see Chapter 4) can not only help counteract the potential harmful side effects of emotional labour but also help social workers improve their emotion-management skills and build resilience.

Job involvement is the degree to which an employee identifies with their work, actively participates in it, and considers their performance important to their self-worth (Robbins and Decenzo, 2004). Being involved in, and committed to, the job can enhance the quality of non-working life, but social workers are at risk of over-involvement. This may manifest itself as a failure to maintain emotional boundaries with service users or a tendency to over-empathize with their problems and can lead to compassion fatigue, burnout and work–life conflict (Koeske and Kelly, 1995; Thomas and Otis, 2010). An over-involved social worker may experience time-based and work–life conflict. There are only 24 hours in the day, so the time spent working will make it difficult to fulfil the requirements of other life roles. Preoccupation with service users' problems may lead to distraction or a failure to engage fully with family and friends. Both types of work–life conflict can seriously threaten recovery and quality of life. Box 3.1 gives some examples

BOX 3.1 EXAMPLES OF OVER-INVOLVEMENT AND BOUNDARY VIOLATIONS

- A *'special' relationship with service users*: the social worker feels as if they are the only person that can understand service users' problems and only they can help them; for example, a social worker may make more home visits than usual, take phone calls out of hours from service users and carers, or buy things for service users' children with their own money.
- *Preoccupation with service users and their problems outside working hours*; for example, the social worker worries about, or talks about, service users at home or when socializing.
- *Being overly protective of service users, or overly optimistic about future outcomes*; for example, the social worker may ignore risk factors and make a biased assessment, as they want a family to do well.
- *Excessive self-disclosure*; for example, the social worker discusses their personal problems, or aspects of their personal life with a service user.

of over-involvement and boundary violations. It should be acknowledged, however, that not all social workers would agree that these behaviours characterize over-involvement.

Reflective supervision (see Chapter 4) can help social workers explore the underlying reasons for over-involvement and feelings of accountability for service users. Techniques such as mindfulness (see Chapter 7) can engender accurate empathy and help social workers develop clear emotional boundaries between their work and other life domains. The implications of the 'rescuer syndrome', which is characterized by over-involvement, a strong sense of responsibility and a drive to maintain high standards of performance, is discussed in Chapter 9.

Individual differences in work–life balance needs

This section considers the role of individual differences in developing a balance between work and non-working life. As discussed earlier in this chapter, there is no 'one-size-fits-all' solution: what is considered an 'ideal' balance will vary considerably. One person may prefer to *segment* (where work and home life is physically and psychologically separate), whereas another will favour integration (where work and home life are blended, with no firm boundaries). It is therefore vital for social workers to: (a) consider the type of work–life balance they currently have and the 'fit' between this and their ideal situation; (b) the strategies they use to manage physical and psychological aspects of the work–home interface; and (c) the factors that might threaten or enhance their recovery and impact on their work–life balance.

Self-discrepancy theory (Higgins, Klein and Strauman, 1985) offers useful insight into work–life balance needs and priorities and the impact of social pressures. The theory distinguishes between three domains of the self:

- *The actual self:* the qualities that an individual believes they possess.
- *The ideal self:* the attributes that an individual would like to acquire.
- *The ought self:* the qualities the individual believes they should have which are imposed by the wider social group.

A discrepancy between the actual self and the ideal self can result in depression and shame, whereas divergence between the actual and the ought self can lead to guilt and anxiety. The theory maintains that people strive to reduce these discrepancies to achieve a closer fit between their actual, ideal and ought selves in order to enhance their wellbeing. This theory can be applied to work–life balance: for example, Hussein is a social work manager whose actual self works hard to fulfil the demands of his job, and consequently he has little time or energy left for his young family, friends or personal interests. Hussein's ideal self would prioritize family life over work, but his ought self feels that a good manager should be able to juggle the competing demands of work and family life effortlessly. The discrepancy between these aspects of the self leaves Hussein feeling ineffectual and unhappy with his job and his family life. The techniques outlined in the chapter on CBT (see Chapter 6) can help Hussein manage the unrealistic and punitive expectations of his ideal and ought selves, work towards self-acceptance and self-kindness, and achieve greater concordance between the selves.

Multiple discrepancy theory, an extension of self-discrepancy theory, provides an effective framework for social workers to assess the goodness of fit between their current work–life balance and their ideal state. This considers life satisfaction to be dependent upon discrepancies

---

PRACTICE FOCUS 3.1: JENNY

Jenny has just had a baby and returned to work in a Family Support Team. Before her pregnancy Jenny was a senior practitioner; she enjoyed this role a great deal. Feedback from her manager and colleagues indicated that her performance was of a high standard and they were looking forward to welcoming her back into this role. On her return to work, Jenny decided to go back to a social work role as she wished to prioritize the needs of her young baby. After settling back to work, however, she found that she missed her old role and felt unhappy and deskilled. Realizing that being a senior practitioner might be more demanding, but would actually make her happier at work and at home, Jenny started to think about how she could balance the competing demands of her parenting and professional roles. She also spoke to some colleagues who had managed effectively to juggle the competing demands of a young family with those of a senior role. Following discussions with her manager, Jenny was able to negotiate to work fewer hours at a higher grade. Jenny finds this work arrangement allows her to feel stretched and fulfilled at work and also lets her spend quality time with her baby, as she is leaving work earlier.

between what one has and: (a) what one wants; (b) what others have; (c) the best one has had in the past; (d) what one expected to have in the past; (e) what one expects to have in the future; (f) what one deserves; and (g) what one needs (Fouché and Martindale, 2011). Gaining insight into these factors will help people close the gap between the type of work–life balance they have and their ideal state. This process will also improve self-knowledge and resilience. The example of Jenny opposite illustrates how multiple discrepancy theory can be applied.

EXERCISE 3.1

Gaining insight into your personal work–life balance needs

In order to enhance work–life balance, it is important for people to think about the amount of time and energy they spend on the different aspects of their life, and consider how closely this is aligned to their personal values. Make a list of the most significant work and non-work elements in your life. These may include career; education, training or personal development; relationship with partner; relationships with children, other family members and friends; health, exercise and nutrition; fun and recreation; hobbies and interests; community activities; creative pursuits; emotional wellbeing and personal growth; and spirituality or religious commitments. Then plot each element on a wheel based on the amount of attention you currently give to each aspect, allocating scores of between 1 and 5, as illustrated in Figure 3.1, where the inner circles stand for low scores and the outer circles for higher scores. A low score (1 or 2) suggests that you are not giving much consideration to this aspect, whereas a score of 5 indicates that you give it a great deal of attention. It is important to show how you *actually* allocate your time and energy rather than how you think this 'ought' to be. Indicative scores are shown by the grey line in the example below.

The next step is to consider the level of attention you would *like* to give to each aspect of your life. Provide a second set of scores for each dimension on the same wheel: as above, a low score (1 or 2) means that this aspect is not very important to you, whereas a high score (4 or 5) indicates that it is very important. The example below shows these scores as a black line. Finally, compare any discrepancies between the

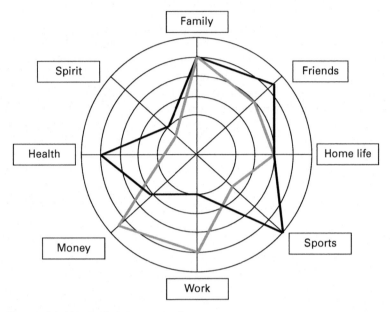

Figure 3.1 Work–life balance wheel

two sets of scores and ask yourself questions such as: 'Where are the biggest differences?', 'To what extent is my current work–life balance aligned with my personal values?' and 'Are there aspects of my life I wish to devote a considerable proportion of my time and energy to, but in which I am currently investing a small amount?' In the example you can see that the individual who is drawing up their wheel is spending considerable time and energy at work, and having sufficient money is also a key focus. Health and sports are getting much less attention than desired. Is this sustainable in the long term? What could they do to change this?

Although firm boundaries are often considered preferable, people vary in the extent to which they wish their work and home roles to be integrated or separated. Based on extensive research, Kossek and Lautsch (2008) have identified three boundary-management styles. Each style has a positive and a negative aspect, where people in one category feel in control of their situation and satisfied with their work–life balance fit, whereas those in the other category feel out of control and dissatisfied.

(a) *Separators* have firm physical and psychological boundaries between their work and non-work roles. The first sub-group, *Firsters*, make a conscious decision to prioritize work *or* non-work life and therefore feel in control over how they manage the work–home interface. Sasha is a Firster; she has two small children and at present her family life is more important to her than her career. Although she works hard, Sasha puts in a strict eight-hour day and avoids 'bringing work home' physically and psychologically. She tends not to worry about uncompleted work outside office hours, focusing her attention primarily on her home life.

Although Sasha has a young family, it should be emphasized that people with no caring responsibilities may prioritize their personal life over their job. The second sub-group of Separators are *Captives*, who are dissatisfied with their work–life balance. They feel 'forced' to focus on one aspect of their life to the detriment of the other. Terry, who is single, is a Captive. Several of Terry's colleagues have young children and, as he has no caring responsibilities or current partner, there is an assumption that he takes on the bulk of on-call responsibilities during weekends and public holidays. Terry enjoys his job, but his social life suffers from being on call so frequently and he has little opportunity to recover from work concerns. He sometimes feels resentful that his colleagues assume that, unlike them, he does not need much of a life outside work.

(b) *Integrators* find it difficult to set boundaries: they incorporate their work and personal life physically (in terms of time or location) and psychologically (in terms of their thoughts and feelings). Integrators are often highly skilled at juggling the competing demands of their work and non-working roles. The first sub-group, *Fusion Lovers*, choose to blend their work and non-working life. Abdul is an Fusion Lover; he prefers to work during evenings and weekends and holidays, and typically 'borrows' time during the working day to fit in personal commitments (such as shopping and going to the gym) in order to compensate for this. The second sub-group of Integrators, *Reactors*, also regularly shift between work and non-work activities. In contrast to Fusion Lovers, they do not multi-task out of choice, but to satisfy the demands of their work and non-work life. Reactors frequently spend their time 'fire-fighting'. Andrew is a Reactor; he cares for his disabled wife and often has to take time off work to take her to medical appointments. To compensate for this, he works at home during evenings and weekends but finds that this reduces the quality time he can spend with his wife. Andrew often feels overwhelmed by his joint responsibilities, and worries about work issues when he is at home, and vice versa.

(c) *Volleyers* alternate between periods of separation and integration, depending on their priorities and their work and personal circumstances. The first sub-group, *Quality Timers*, prioritize their work during busy times and their home life when work becomes less demanding. Saira is a Quality Timer with three young children. During term-time, her work comes first and her partner fulfils the majority of family responsibilities. During school holidays, Saira reduces her involvement in work and dedicates considerable time and effort to reconnect with her family and friends. Despite her shifting priorities, Saira feels in control of her work–life balance and is satisfied with both life domains. *Job Warriors*, on the other hand, do not enjoy volleying and have little control over when they switch between integration and separation. This may be because of unpredictable changes in work demands. For example, Frank works with looked-after children and sometimes travels long distances for statutory visits and reviews. He generally has little input over the scheduling of these meetings and it takes time away from his own family responsibilities.

Research has found that Reactors, Job Warriors and Captives (who have low control over boundary management) perceive a poorer work–life balance than Fusion Lovers, Quality Timers and work or family Firsters (who have high levels of control) (Kossek, Lautsch and Eaton, 2006). Nonetheless, each style has benefits and drawbacks for work and personal life. Gaining insight into personal boundary-management styles is required to enhance work–life balance fit. Whether people favour separation, integration, or a blend of the two, sufficient time should be given to recuperate physically and psychologically from work demands to protect personal wellbeing and job performance. The next section focuses on the importance of respite and recovery, and the ways in which social workers can develop 'corridors' between their work and non-working life to help them enhance recovery opportunities and foster resilience.

Recovery

As discussed earlier in this chapter, fulfilling work demands drain physical and psychological energy, which must be replenished, otherwise health and job performance will be impaired. It is therefore essential to dedicate sufficient time to relax and reconnect with family and friends in order to recover sufficiently. Sleep is probably the most valuable recovery strategy, but the type of activities and thought processes that people engage in outside work are also important. Answering the questions in Exercise 3.2 will give you some insight into how well you recover from work.

EXERCISE 3.2

How well do you recover from work?
Answer the questions below on a five-point scale where 1 = not at all and 5 = very much.
Do you feel very tired during the working day?
Do you feel physically tired after the working day?
Do you feel mentally fatigued after the working day?
Do you lie awake at night thinking about work?
Do you feel rested when you start work each morning?
Do you feel recovered when you return to work after the weekend and after holidays?

Now add up your score. If it is between *5 and 10*, you are generally able to recover from work very well, but it is important to watch out for any early warning signs that work demands are taking their toll and take pre-emptive action. If it is between *11 and 20*, you are experiencing some difficulties recovering from work demands. Think about how you could make more effective corridors between your work and home life to help you switch off (see below). If your score *is above 20*, you need to take action to protect your wellbeing and job performance. Try to be realistic in your personal expectations of respite and recovery. Most people (particularly those working in the helping professions) will occasionally experience difficulties recovering from the physical and emotional demands of work. The techniques set out in this and the other chapters in the book will help you gain insight into your personal work–life balance priorities and styles and the early warning signs that action is required.

Ruminating about work-related issues can threaten recovery processes. People frequently think about work during their free time, particularly during periods of high workloads, tight deadlines, or where

BOX 3.2 ICTS AND RECOVERY

Information Communication Technologies (ICTs) can help employees juggle the demands of their work and home lives, but they can also impair recovery. The use of ICTs for work activities during evenings, weekends and holidays can engender time-based and strain-based work–life conflict and also increase employers' expectations of the availability of employees outside 'normal' working hours (Major et al., 2006). This practice can also foster resentment and annoyance from family members and feelings of guilt in the employee (Middleton, 2008). Whether ICTs help or hinder work–life balance depends upon the extent to which employees feel in control of their use and their work–life balance management style (see above). Nonetheless, imposing some boundaries in ICT use outside work time is likely to enhance recovery opportunities for all. 'Rules of engagement' might involve the following:

- Switching work phones off during evenings and weekends.
- Providing service users with the 'out-of-hours' phone number and advising them that you will not respond to calls outside office hours.
- Not reading work emails at home, or reading them at specified times only.
- Not using your home computer for work, or placing a time limit on this.

interpersonal conflict has occurred (Cropley and Zijlstra, 2011). Research shows that helping professionals tend to ruminate about work problems more frequently than other occupational groups (Newsome, Waldo and Gruszka, 2012). By interfering with recovery processes, rumination can be counter-productive, as it can impair rather than enhance job performance. Rumination can also lead to psychological problems (such as depression and self-criticism), physical health symptoms (ranging from sleep disturbances to cardiovascular disorders) and damaging health behaviours (such as binge-eating and problem drinking) (Cropley and Zijlstra, 2011). Managing work-related rumination is therefore important in order to enhance wellbeing and resilience.

Thinking about work outside the work environment does not necessarily interfere with recovery: in fact, some types of rumination may enhance wellbeing. Cropley and Zijlstra (2011) have highlighted three aspects of work-related rumination: affective rumination; problem-solving pondering, and detachment. Affective rumination involves experiencing negative thoughts about work that are intrusive, pervasive and recurrent. Social workers may dwell on difficulties with particular service users or brood about arguments with colleagues. Such thoughts are synonymous with strain-based work–life conflict and are likely to lead to distress, emotional exhaustion and fatigue. Problem-solving pondering, on the other hand, is more constructive as it involves reflecting on work-related issues to solve difficulties. Work problems can sometimes be solved more easily outside the working environment when one has more 'thinking space'. For example, a social worker might set aside some time after work to think pragmatically about a problem experienced by a service user and reach a practical solution. Pondering differs from affective rumination in that it can generally be 'switched off' when not required and, as such, does not tend to impair work–life balance. Nonetheless, as with using ICTs, it is desirable to switch off from work issues entirely in order to recover effectively. The questions in Exercise 3.3 will help you consider the extent to which you engage in affective and problem-solving rumination and how well you detach from work-related concerns.

EXERCISE 3.3

Work-related rumination and detachment

Affective rumination:

Do you become tense when thinking about work-related issues during your free time?

Do you get annoyed when you think about work-related issues outside work time?

Problem-solving pondering

Do you find yourself re-evaluating something you have done at work during your free time?

Do you find solutions to work-related problems in your free time?

Detachment

Do you find it easy to unwind after work?

Do you leave work issues behind when you leave work?

(Cropley and Zijlstra 2011)

People often find that they need a 'corridor', or transition between their work and home roles to help them switch off from work. This may involve reading a book on the train home, or listening to the radio in the car. Other transitions include taking the dog for a walk, helping a child with homework, cooking dinner, watching a film, or going for a run. No one strategy is preferable to another; some people find that exercise helps them to disengage from work concerns, whereas others prefer more passive pursuits such as watching television or listening to music. As discussed throughout this book, social support is a key buffer against stress. As people are more likely to ruminate when they are alone than in the company of others, spending time with family and friends can be particularly effective in helping people recover.

To be effective in facilitating recovery, leisure pursuits require planning, prioritizing and active engagement: it is also vital to enjoy what you do. Activities that use different functional systems to those used at work are particularly effective in replenishing vital resources (Sonnentag and Fritz, 2007). For example, Jane has set herself a target of doing 'something different' at least once a month. She might have a spa day with a friend, do a sky-dive for charity or go to the theatre. Leisure pursuits that require challenge can enhance feelings of mastery and build personal resources that underpin resilience. Moreover, activities that require total absorption can lead to 'flow', which is particularly likely to boost recovery and wellbeing. Flow is a state of optimal experience where people are so intensely immersed in a task that they lose awareness of themselves, other people and even basic bodily needs (Csikszent, 1991). Mindfulness techniques, outlined in Chapter 7, can encourage flow experiences both at work and leisure.

The employers' role in enhancing work–life balance

This chapter has focused on the development of personal strategies to help social workers manage the competing demands of work and home. Nonetheless, as discussed in Chapter 1, employers have a duty of care to protect their employees' psychological wellbeing. They are also obliged to provide supportive work environments to help their employees achieve an acceptable work–life balance. Although lagging behind some other EU countries, the UK has legislation promoting so-called 'family-friendly' policies. There is a requirement for employers to consider seriously requests for flexible working arrangements from employees with caring responsibilities. Flexible working has the potential to help people balance the demands of their work and home life and is understandably popular amongst working parents, but the introduction of formal policies has had mixed success. Flexibility is likely to be most beneficial when employees can choose their own work schedules but, for many types of work, this is not feasible. Moreover, there are barriers to taking up flexible working policies, particularly amongst men, as employees tend to be concerned that this may demonstrate a lack of commitment (Coltrane et al., 2013; GEO, 2009).

Although flexible working options can be useful, more creative organizational approaches are required to help social workers improve their work–life balance fit. Support from supervisors has strong potential to protect social workers from the negative impact of work–life conflict (Kalliath and Kalliath, 2006). Research conducted by Hammer et al. (2007) has identified a number of supportive line-manager behaviours, such as *emotional support* (learning about personal work–life balance needs and listening to problems); *instrumental support* (helping employees avoid work-to-home conflict and vice versa); *role modelling* (demonstrating effective personal work–life balance behaviours) and *creative work–life balance management* (using novel options to reduce conflict between work and home demands). It is also vital for managers to recognize and disseminate the benefits for both the work and home domains. It could be argued that work–life balance competencies should be a key competency for social work managers. Supportive manager behaviours cannot work in isolation, however, and should be firmly embedded within a wider culture where all employees, regardless of caring responsibilities or life stage, are helped to achieve an effective balance between their work and non-working life and the benefits to wellbeing and job performance are recognized.

The final section of this chapter considers the ways in which work–life balance can be enhanced using techniques outlined in the other chapters of this book.

How can work–life balance be enhanced?

Reflective supervision (Chapter 4) can be used to identify the type of work demands that can threaten work–life balance, and explore strategies to manage these more effectively. Lack of opportunity to express emotional reactions to practice will hamper the recovery process and may lead to emotional exhaustion or self-medication behaviours such as problem drinking. Encouraging employees to discuss difficult emotions in a safe environment is likely to improve affective regulation skills, reduce strain-based work–life conflict and enhance wellbeing, resilience and the quality of professional practice.

Time management and personal organizational skills underpin an effective work–life balance. Techniques such as prioritizing, organizing and learning how to say 'no' can help social workers minimize time-based work–life conflict and maximize recovery time. Such techniques can also be useful in setting technological boundaries between work and home. Managing time mindfully and efficiently can help people gain perspective and increase opportunities for work–life enrichment via a sense of accomplishment and satisfaction. Similarly, using time management and organizational techniques in non-working life can ensure that people engage in activities that will bring them pleasure, rest and regained energy.

Cognitive behavioural strategies (Chapter 6) can help social workers recognize and take steps to reduce time, strain and behaviour-based work–life conflict. The type of thinking errors people commonly make can be identified and insight gained into how they can impact on the management of the work–home interface. CBT techniques can help social workers avoid negative self-talk (the punitive 'shoulds and shouldn'ts' and 'musts and mustn'ts') that can lead to unhealthy rumination and impair recovery. These strategies can also be used to identify and explore the 'voices' of the current, ideal and ought selves in relation to work–life balance and help people achieve congruence between these.

Mindfulness techniques (Chapter 7) can help social workers recover physically and psychologically by encouraging a focus on the present time, rather than unhealthy rumination about past events or fretting about the future. As discussed in this chapter, though people differ in the degree to which they wish to integrate their work and home life, some physical and psychological separation between domains is required for recovery. Mindfulness techniques can help people develop appropriate boundaries, facilitate flow experiences, and enhance acceptance and satisfaction with both the work and home domains.

Peer support and peer coaching (Chapter 8) can also help social workers enhance their work–life balance fit. Several strategies outlined in this chapter could be utilized within a peer-coaching relationship, to mutual benefit. For example, coaching partners could complete and discuss work–life balance wheels and boundary-management styles, explore personal strategies, vulnerabilities and strengths, and consider how work–life balance fit might be improved. The demands and resources within the work and home environment that might threaten or enhance work–life balance could also be discussed. Opportunities for work–life enrichment might also be considered through a mutual exploration of optimal moments. Over the longer term, a peer-coaching relationship will also provide mutual encouragement and support to help initiate and maintain change.

Self knowledge (Chapter 9) can help social workers become more aware of the personal beliefs, reactions and behaviours that can facilitate or threaten their work–life balance. Insight into personal risk factors and resistance resources emanating from the work and non-working domains is vital in developing an acceptable work–life balance. Knowledge of the positive and potentially damaging ways of coping with stress and the work-home interface can impact on work–life balance and how psychological flexibility can increase satisfaction with both domains.

ADDITIONAL RESOURCES

Gambles, R., Lewis, S. and Rapoport, R. (2006). *The Myth of Work–Life Balance: The Challenge of Our Time for Men, Women and Societies*. Chichester: John Wiley.

Jones, F. Burke, R. and Westman, M. (2006) *Managing the Work-Home Interface: A Psychological Perspective*. London: Taylor & Francis.

Kossek, E. and Lautsch, B. (2008). *CEO of Me: Creating a Life that Works in the Flexible Job Age*. Philadelphia, PA: Wharton School Publishing.

Major, D. and Burke, R. (2013). *Handbook of Work–Life Integration among Professionals: Challenges and Opportunities*. Cheltenham: Edward Elgar.

CHAPTER 4

Critical reflection and reflective supervision

Louise Grant and Becky Brewer

CHAPTER OVERVIEW

Supervision is a key opportunity for social workers to engage in reflection and learning. It is an environment in which they can discuss their practice and their emotional reactions to it, and plan for future intervention and their professional development. Reflection is fundamental to the supervision process, but this chapter focuses specifically on the role played by critical reflection and meaningful reflective supervision in enhancing emotional resilience in social workers. First, the chapter explores how critical reflection can help social workers manage their emotional reactions to practise more effectively. Secondly, it examines the role played by reflective supervision in fostering a relationship characterized by positive regard which, in turn, can build emotional resilience. Finally, it provides both social workers and managers with some skills and tools required to enhance resilience through the supervisory process. The chapter also describes some practical techniques for supervisors to use in supporting emotional literacy, accurate empathy and self-awareness, which have been found to underpin emotional resilience.

Critical reflection and emotional resilience

Managing emotionally charged situations and dealing with uncertainty and complexity are intrinsic to the social work role. It is therefore important for social workers to recognize and address the 'not knowing' elements of practice, and the fear and anxiety that this can evoke, in order to protect their wellbeing and maintain optimum job performance. The source of negative emotions such as fear and anxiety may not necessarily be recognized or managed effectively by the social worker, however, which can impair their job performance and lead to stress and burnout (Hewson and Shohet, 2008). Based on the early writings of Schön (1983) and subsequent research across the helping professions (e.g. Rolfe, Freshwater and Jasper, 2001; Ruch, 2005), critical reflection has emerged as an important learning tool to help employees manage complexity and ambiguity and cope effectively with situations where a straightforward technical solution cannot be found. The Munro (2011) report also emphasized the key role played by reflection in helping social workers manage the inherent tensions and uncertainties of their role.

The ability to critically reflect on practice is considered a key competency for social workers, as it underpins the acquisition, maintenance and enhancement of professional development (Collins, 2007; Ruch, 2008; College of Social Work, 2012). By facilitating insight into practice, critical reflection therefore has clear potential to enhance the professional learning of social workers and improve the service they provide (Yelloly and Henkel, 1995; Grant, Kinman & Alexander, 2014). Reflection can also help social work practitioners consider how they might adapt their practice to individual service users' needs and develop solutions to problems that might initially appear to be intractable. Furthermore, the development of holistic reflexive thinking skills can help social workers explore their emotional reactions, doubts, assumptions and beliefs, which can transform their self-understanding and improve practice (Ruch, 2007).

Having considered the role of reflection in social work and identified its many benefits for practice, it is important to consider how reflection is linked to wellbeing and emotional resilience. As discussed in Chapter 2, there is strong evidence that reflection is an important self-protective mechanism for social workers that can not only help develop the competencies that underlie resilience, but also enhance wellbeing (Kinman and Grant, 2011). This study also found that reflective ability is fundamental to emotional literacy, which encompasses the ability to reflect on thoughts, feelings and beliefs and consider those of others. Subsequent research conducted by Grant (2013) also found that social workers with stronger self-reflection skills who are able to communicate their reflections effectively tend to engage in more appropriate empathic interactions with service users.

It has been observed that social workers commonly attempt to cope with anxiety-engendered complex practice by adopting 'task and target' strategies rather than an emotion-focused approach (Ruch, 2008). While this might facilitate effective problem-solving, a problem-focused mindset does not encourage reflection and may engender a false sense of security. For example, a social worker might be tempted to 'cover their back' before going home for the weekend by sending a flurry of emails setting out the tasks they have accomplished rather than focusing on an underlying concern or issue. It has also been recognized that increasing workloads are likely to undermine opportunities to use reflective practice to enhance resilience and performance (Laming and Commons, 2009). Moreover, the danger of failing to acknowledge and manage the emotional demands of social work has been widely emphasized, as this increases the risk of emotional exhaustion and negative outcomes for service users (Cooper, 2005). It is, therefore, vital to create 'reflective spaces' (Ruch, 2008) where social workers have opportunities to critically reflect on their practice: supervision has strong potential to provide this space.

The role of supervision in promoting reflection and enhancing resilience

> Supervision provides a safe environment for critical reflection, challenge and professional support that operates alongside an organization's appraisal process. It includes time for reflection on practice issues that arise in the course of everyday work, and can help social workers and their managers to do their jobs more effectively. It enables social workers to develop their capacity to use their experiences to review practice, receive feedback on their performance, build emotional resilience and think reflectively about the relationships they have formed with children, adults and families. (Munro, 2011, p. 30)

Munro's view of supervision outlined above challenges the managerialist and bureaucratic agenda that has historically informed social workers' supervision. Her perspective places more emphasis on the importance of *reflective* supervision and its role in enhancing resilience, wellbeing and service quality. Reflective supervision is based on the notion that the supervisory process is a learning opportunity that enables the supervisee to gain insight about themselves and their practice, explore relevant theory and evidence, and use this information to consider how their knowledge and skills can be improved. This approach to supervision is influenced by theory about the reflective cycle in adult learning (Gibbs, 1988). Beddoe and Davys (2010) have drawn on this theory to develop a comprehensive and useful reflective learning model for supervision. They argue that reflective supervision based on Kolb's (1984) model of experiencing, reflecting, theorizing and conceptualizing provided within a supportive environment can promote resilience as well as learning.

As discussed in Chapter 2, resilience is a multidimensional concept which is underpinned by several interpersonal and intrapersonal competencies. Reflective supervision has the potential to enhance these qualities: that is, help social workers develop greater self-awareness, emotional literacy, critical thinking skills, persistence in the face of adversity, self-efficacy, experiential learning and an orientation towards the future. In order to get the best out of supervision, however, it is crucial that both social workers and their supervisors are clear about the role of supervision and its potential benefits.

A key element of professional supervision is support (Morrison, Hathaway and Fairley, 2005; Tsui, 2004; Beddoe and Davys, 2010). Research findings highlight the benefits of emotional support obtained through reflective supervision for managing workload stress and building sustainable resilience. Some (e.g. Hughes and Pengelly, 1997), however, maintain that an overt focus on the provision of support at the expense of other supervisory functions may lead to collusion between social worker and supervisor and detract from the needs of the service user. It should also be acknowledged that supervision has managerial administrative and mediation functions, as well as providing emotional support (Morrison et al., 2005). Nonetheless, although supervision should not be a therapeutic forum in which to dwell on personal problems, it is an appropriate environment to explore the emotions that social work practice can invoke, which can enhance practice (Children's Workforce Development Council, 2009). Indeed, there is evidence that supervisors who are able to nurture reflection through a combination of challenge, support and encouragement, and who recognize that the personal and professional will inevitably overlap, are likely to improve outcomes for both supervisees and service users (Grant, Schofield and Crawford, 2012). A framework of positive manager behaviours that can help employees manage stress is outlined in Chapter 10.

Social workers frequently experience strong emotional reactions to witnessing, reading about or discussing service users' negative or traumatic experiences. As mentioned above, this can cause anxiety and fear, but may also lead to a practitioner over-empathizing with service users and/or feeling emotionally manipulated. It is vital that social workers are aware of the need to reflect upon their emotional responses to service users in order to avoid negative outcomes such as empathic distress, compassion fatigue, vicarious trauma and burnout (Cunningham, 2004; Grant, 2013). Although little research has been conducted with social workers, there is evidence that the wellbeing of other helping professionals can be compromised in situations when supervision is not effective: for example, a study of psychiatry trainees found that those who were dissatisfied with the supervision they received were unable to cope with difficult client-related events (Kozlowska, Nunn and Cousens, 1997b) and also experienced psychological distress and feelings of despair (Kozlowska, Nunn and Cousens, 1997a). The crucial role played by supervision in exploring and making sense of conflicting emotional reactions to practice and enhancing emotion management skills for social workers is therefore an important area for attention.

To maximize its effectiveness and allow social workers to flourish, reflective supervision should create a 'safe space' for emotional thinking and reflection about ethical and practice-related issues (Ruch, 2007). It should be recognized, however, that social workers may feel unable or be unwilling to explore their emotional reactions within a supervisory context, which may create barriers to the genuine expression of feelings (Beddoe and Davys, 2010). There is also evidence that the foundations of emotional literacy are required in order to process emotional reactions and develop effective reflective skills (Grant et al., 2014). Some social workers may have a tendency towards alexithymia: a sub-clinical inability to identify and describe their own emotions (Larsen et al., 2003), which will clearly constrain their reflective abilities. More likely, however, is that supervisees may believe that emotional disclosure is not appropriate in supervision due to a fear of being considered weak, vulnerable and 'unprofessional' (Fook and Gardner, 2007). In turn, supervisors may worry about being overwhelmed by the emotions of their supervisees and concerned that they will be unable to manage and contain the feelings that are disclosed. For reflective supervision to be productive, social workers need to manage these barriers and prepare effectively for supervision; supervisors should also focus on the emotional needs of the supervisee as well as the more task-oriented aspects of practice. Above all, it is essential for both supervisors and supervisees to develop an appreciation of the ways in which emotional resilience, as well as performance, can be achieved through supervision. Reflective supervision can also enhance 'psychological capital' (Luthans et al., 2008). This is a multi-dimensional resource encompassing the ability to be confident (*self-efficacy*) in approaching challenging tasks with determination to succeed; to be positive (*optimism*) about success in the present and future; to have perseverance (*hope*) toward achieving goals and outcomes; and to be able to bounce back from adversity (*resilience*). The concept of psychological capital and the approach to resilience taken in this book are very similar. Both aim to delineate the resources that can be drawn upon during difficult times in order to remain healthy and thrive. As with resilience, psychological capital is malleable and there is evidence that the qualities underpinning it can be nurtured within supportive organizational relationships (Luthans et al., 2008; Duggleby, Cooper and Penz, 2009).

The supervisee's role: preparing for reflective supervision

A supervisee is not a passive partner in the supervisory relationship, and effective preparation is vital to maximize the potential of supervision for improving practice and enhancing resilience. Social workers will get the most out of their supervision when they are clear about its purpose, committed to making the supervisory relationship work, and well primed for any supervisory session. For supervision to be effective, social workers need to understand its function; this can be supported through a supervision 'agreement' which recognizes that it should not only focus on administrative and managerial issues, but also provide support and aid personal development. Supervisees should also consider supervision to be a joint process, which involves working alongside the supervisor to facilitate reflection on issues affecting practice in order to build expertise. This means being prepared to discuss the concrete and managerial aspects of the work, but allowing sufficient time and energy to reflect on personal strengths and weaknesses. At times this may be uncomfortable, but openness and honesty are intrinsic components of effective supervision. It has been recognized that social workers may need to be assertive in requesting good-quality reflective supervision, and newly qualified or less confident practitioners may experience particular difficulties in this regard (Grant and Kinman, 2013). Box 4.1 provides a list of trigger questions that could

BOX 4.1 QUESTIONS TO ASK IN PREPARATION FOR SUPERVISION

- What has gone really well this week that I am pleased about? Where and how have I excelled?
- What does this tell me about my strengths?
- What is the impact of my practice on service users?
- What have I found difficult in my practice? Where do these difficulties tend to recur?
- What areas do I feel stuck in?
- What am I learning about myself?
- What are my feelings and emotional reactions to cases that I am currently working with? Am I anxious, fearful, or over-confident, or am I proud and satisfied?
- If I only had to tell my supervisor three things about my practice, what would they be?

be used when preparing for supervision. When drawing up a written supervisory agreement, the requirements of both parties should be stated explicitly, as well as joint expectations of the gains that are anticipated. Particular emphasis should be placed on providing reflective space and developmental support and the role of supervision in enhancing self-knowledge, emotion management and resilience, as well as problem-solving capacity.

Practice focus 4.1 illustrates how a social worker who is aware of their own needs can utilize supervision to its best effect to promote their emotional resilience.

Emily's story demonstrates the importance of self-awareness in considering the impact that the work may have had physically and emotionally, and begin interrogating this in relation to real-life practice situations: for example, What happened? What emotions were experienced? What are the implications for herself and her practice? What patterns are emerging? This will help her facilitate future action.

Research findings show that written emotional disclosure in the format of a diary can be beneficial for social workers' health and well-being and help foster the competencies that underpin resilience (Grant et al., 2014). Emily's example also illustrates the benefits of keeping such a diary for personal development within the supervisory setting.

PRACTICE FOCUS 4.1: EMILY

Emily is an experienced social worker who is aware that she finds it difficult to contain her own emotional responses to challenging situations. In the past, Emily has sometimes been seen as a highly emotional and rather 'dramatic' person, who has a tendency to become over-involved with the families she works with. Emily was keen to become a much more reflective, emotionally resilient practitioner, but she initially struggled to identify the coping strategies needed to help her manage her emotional outbursts and develop a more contained professional persona.

In her third year of practice, Emily started to be supervised by a new member of staff. During the early sessions, Emily and her supervisor explored some of reasons behind why Emily might have found it difficult to contain her emotions. In order to facilitate this process, Emily's supervisor encouraged her to use reflective diaries to record and process her physical and emotional responses to difficult professional encounters. With professional maturity, Emily realised that this new supervisory relationship was an opportunity to be honest about her anxieties and to reflect on how they impacted on her ability to manage the complexity of her work.

Although it was not necessary for Emily to share all the contents of the reflective diary with her supervisor, reoccurring themes were quickly identified and explored within the supervisory relationship. During this process, Emily was initially surprised to note that the most subtle interaction between herself and others could trigger powerful emotional responses. Her skill was that she was able to identify that she needed support to become more emotionally resilient in order to protect her wellbeing and her enhance her practice. The skill of the supervisor was to provide Emily with the tools and the reflective space, and give her the permission she required to explore safely the impact of self on professional practice. After a number of sessions, Emily was able to: (a) recognize her own physiological and psychological responses to encounters and (b) monitor and contain her emotional responses in action.

Practitioners could consider keeping a reflective diary, where emotional reactions to practice experiences can be explored and reviewed prior to supervision and notes made on emerging themes.

For reflective supervision to be effective, it should be recognized that social workers need to be receptive to feedback as well as have the ability to reflect on this and its implications for future practice. It is particularly important to be able to share issues that have arisen during supervision itself; notice when there is a tendency to justify, explain or defend a position when receiving feedback and aim to move to a position where it is actively sought. Also there is a need to check that decision-making and assessments made during practice are based on evidence, rather than on prior assumptions or personal biases. A reflective diary can also help with this by identifying patterns of thoughts and actions that can subsequently be used as a basis for effective discussion during supervision. A social worker who has insight into their emotional reaction to a situation (such as feeling anxious, frustrated or angry after a particular interaction with a service user) will also recognize that this reaction is likely to provide insight into how that particular client is feeling. This emotional wisdom (Munro, 2002), which is a key aspect of emotional literacy, is a fundamental component of effective assessment and decision-making and also enhances self-knowledge and resilience.

Social workers will undoubtedly experience uncertainty and even make mistakes, regardless of their experience. Approaching supervision by being open to its possibilities and taking responsibility for personal learning is the first step to forging an effective supportive relationship and improving resilience. A positive attitude is also more likely to lead to enhanced learning and wellbeing. By approaching supervision prepared to reframe events positively and learn from mistakes and successes, a social worker will be able to cope more effectively and build resilience for the future (Collins, 2007). It should be recognized, however, that unrealistic optimism can encourage risk-taking behaviour and must be avoided. The role played by optimism and pessimism in resilience and wellbeing is explored in Chapter 9.

The role of the supervisor in promoting resilience

As mentioned earlier in this chapter, the Munro (2011) report found that supervision in social work typically focuses on the bureaucratic aspects of the work to the detriment of the reflective and supportive elements. As recognized by Beddoe (2010), there has been more surveillance than reflection. Some supervisors have become accustomed to providing supervision which focuses purely on case management, timescales and process, rather than developing space for open, reflective discussion. Such supervisors may minimize the importance of the

---

PRACTICE FOCUS 4.2: JASON

Jason has been a manager in an adult mental health team for over 15 years. He is finding it very challenging to supervise the 'new breed' of social worker who seem to demand a much more 'complex' supervision experience. Jason is currently struggling to supervise a member of staff who he perceives to be overly emotional and highly strung. He is finding it very difficult to contain the worker during supervision, and believes her emotional response to situations is having an impact on her ability to make informed, balanced and safe decisions.

Although Jason believes that it would be nice to spend time considering the impact that such challenging work has on each of his supervisees, he is more anxious to know: (a) if the worker is reporting back the whole story after meeting with the service user; (b) if all relevant key performance indicators have been met; and (c) whether all the potential risks have been identified and assessed by the worker. Jason thinks that talking about feelings is too time-consuming and a bit of a luxury in the light of the current work pressures. Several members of the team have recently left or taken time off sick with work-related stress, meaning that Jason feels more pressured to ensure he manages the work quickly and effectively. He thinks that if these social workers can't manage the heat of social work they are better off in a different job.

Tracy is an experienced social worker supervised by Jason. She feels that Jason is cold, unfeeling and insensitive. Tracy believes that the emotional impact of the work is generally ignored by Jason and is feeling more and more anxious prior to her supervision sessions. Although Tracy would describe herself as resilient and is usually quite assertive, she feels unable to tackle Jason and is under pressure to take on more work. The organization sees Jason as an effective manager, as all his tasks are completed on time and he is always up to date with her assessment targets. Tracy is considering leaving her current job, as she feels unsupported and her wellbeing is being adversely affected.

supportive element of supervision, and become fixated on checking and monitoring. As outlined earlier, supervision has many functions and, although case management is undoubtedly important, the effective support and development of staff are equally so.

Practice focus 4.2 describes a supervisor who is well and truly entrenched in a managerialist, task-focused style of supervision which offers little in the way of emotional support.

In the scenario above, Jason is unable (or unwilling) to see the detrimental effect of his supervisory style on Tracy. In order to enable Tracy to manage the work effectively and remain in a job she is good at, Jason needs to reconsider his supervisory style. There are clearly issues relating to trust and safety, and the supervisory relationship is not helping Tracy contain her feelings or manage the emotional impact of the work. This practice focus illustrates how a lack of reflective supervision could have an adverse effect on a social worker's ability to cope. In such situations, a supervisee who is struggling may be seen to have capability issues rather than merely requiring support. Unfortunately, in these situations, lack of support can lead to stress which, in turn, can impact on performance, making capability a self-fulfilling prophecy.

Organizations have a moral imperative as well as a duty of care to manage the wellbeing of their employees effectively. Failure to recognize the negative impact of the work on staff and not providing the support required could leave the organization open to claims for compensation for work-related stress (Cox et al., 2007). There is an expectation that employers provide good supportive supervision, and social workers who do not receive the support required for safe effective professional practice need to make their employers aware of this shortfall.

How can supervisors enhance resilience in the staff they manage?

The current context of social work was explored in Chapter 1, which highlighted the increasing tendency for social work organizations to emphasize key performance indicators and targets over the provision of support. Working in an organization with this focus, and/or one which embraces a culture of blame, will mean that social work managers will tend to focus on 'fire-fighting' and find it challenging to provide quality reflective supervision. Appreciating that workers need to be helped to develop the competencies that underpin resilience (such as emotion management, self-awareness, reflective ability and accurate empathy) is the first step in providing effective supervision. Supervisors can play a key role in enhancing the emotional resilience of the staff they supervise, even if the organizational conditions are not ideal.

Research has found that effective supervision can mitigate the effect of workplace stress and contribute to positive outcomes for employees. A meta-analysis of 27 research articles conducted by Barak et al. (2009) with a combined sample of almost 11,000 workers from social work, child welfare and mental health found that providing emotional and social support along with task-oriented supervision engenders a protective 'blanket' which enhances employees' stress-management abilities. Similarly, a study of mental health social workers conducted by Huxley et al. (2005) concluded that staff felt more valued and less stressed when supervisors were perceived to be supportive. Managing anxiety and uncertainty is a crucial task for supervisors. Acknowledging that these issues exist is the first step to enhancing resilience in supervisees. By helping social workers realise that there are rarely simple, straightforward solutions, an environment can be created in which challenging problems can be openly acknowledged and explored. Moreover, accepting that there will always be an element of uncertainty in making assessments and decisions can, perhaps counter-intuitively, engender self-confidence.

Research on resilience in children has found that the development of a 'secure base' with an attachment figure enables the subsequent containment of emotions (Ruch, 2008). The concept of containment draws on the work of Bion (1984), who argues that children require a consistent secure base to return to when experiencing a strong emotional reaction. The care-giver responds with 'reverie', which is the capacity to acknowledge the child's feelings and respond appropriately, thus enabling emotional containment to develop. If there are no opportunities to experience reverie, the child is overwhelmed with unresolved feelings and unable to manage emotional reactions. Although this perspective may appear overly deterministic, the notion of reverie can be a useful framework for considering how to contain relationships within supervision (Ruch, 2007). Indeed, Ferguson, emphasizes that 'social workers need to be emotionally held' and have space to be heard (Ferguson, 2009, p. 479). Containment and holding through supervision promotes a culture whereby social workers are enabled to feel safe and secure within a supportive professional relationship. The supervisor, who provides that secure base, can encourage a reflective stance that facilitates the processing of emotions with a supervisee, thus reducing the risk of psychological distress and mitigating the negative impact of unresolved emotions and distress on professional practice (Ruch, 2007; Toasland, 2007).

Effective containment requires the manager to do more than just hold the supervisee's feelings (Toasland, 2007). As discussed earlier in this chapter, supervisors are required to create an atmosphere of safety and challenge where supervisees are enabled to withstand the emotional content of the work and reflect on the implications of this for their practice (Gazzola and Thériault, 2007). A supervisor needs to develop a symbiotic relationship with the social worker to help them process and make sense of uncomfortable feelings. This is likely to help them develop the skills to manage such feelings more effectively in the future and enhance their professional judgement and decision-making abilities. It should be emphasized, however, that an overly supportive or 'permissive' supervisory style can undermine supervisees' feelings of confidence in their practice and impede the development of professional autonomy. This risk is emphasized by Lizzio, Wilson and Que (2009), whereby too much support can result in a perceived lack of competence, whereas too little can lead to anxiety. The skill of a supervisor is to enable supervisees to develop the skills required to manage the emotional content of the work autonomously, and to recognize when more support is needed.

It is also important for managers to understand transference: in other words, how social workers can project their anxieties and emotional reactions onto the supervisor (Mills, 2012). As well as helping their supervisees cope with the stress of the job, managers also have to contain their personal emotions and maintain their own wellbeing and resilience. Practice focus 4.3 explores the experience of one supervisor who is trying to establish the conditions necessary for an effective relationship, whilst recognizing the challenges that may exist.

This practice focus emphasizes the importance of a supervisor recognizing that there will be social workers who are not coping well with stress emanating from the personal and/or professional domain – or indeed at the interface between home and work (see Chapter 3). Newly qualified social workers in particular may be fearful about exploring the emotional impact of the work with a new supervisor; supervisors may need to be unequivocal in explaining that experiencing such feelings is normal and a

---

PRACTICE FOCUS 4.3: LEWIS

Lewis has currently taken over the responsibility for supervising Claire, a social worker who has been qualified for 18 months. Claire has just been allocated a new family, where all four children have recently been made subject of Child Protection Plans due to them regularly witnessing domestic abuse within the home.

Lewis is concerned that Claire seems unable to acknowledge that the parents might have the capacity to change. Indeed, she appears to be focusing predominantly on collating the evidence she requires to seek legal advice with a view to commencing care proceedings. Claire presents as very emotionally detached during supervision and appears reluctant to explore any other possible courses of action in this case. Lewis has noticed that, after supervision with Claire, he feels more anxious about her cases and does not feel he has gained any sense of what is influencing her practice.

Lewis has reflected upon what may be going on in this situation. He is aware that Claire had disclosed to colleagues that she had 'quite a difficult childhood' and came into social work as she felt she had something to offer the profession from these experiences. Lewis knows that he needs to prepare well for the supervision sessions and create an environment in which Claire's emotions can be explored, contained and reflected upon to ensure she considers how they might be affecting her work. Lewis is also aware that in supervision feelings can be transferred or projected from the worker to the supervisor, and that the anxiety he is feeling is probably that felt by Claire.

Lewis decides that the following issues need to be discussed in supervision to help Claire develop her understanding of self and, most importantly, how her personal experiences may be impacting on her practice. He is committed to building a supportive yet challenging environment for reflective supervision in order to accomplish this and help Claire build her emotional resilience.

---

sign of strength and competence (Children's Workforce Development Council, 2009), and that exploring them can have a positive role to play in decision-making and assessment. It is crucial that newly qualified social workers who are experiencing new demands, expectations and uncertainties are enabled to talk about the inevitable emotional burden and supported through this.

However, a note of caution is necessary. Supervisors need to be very clear about their role in helping supervisees acknowledge and manage their emotional reactions. The role of a supervisor is to offer staff support related to their job and occasionally discuss personal issues if these are impacting on practice. It is not their role to be a counsellor, or indeed to 'social work' the supervisee. If the need arises, supervisors will have to refer staff to their General Practitioner or Occupational Health specialist for personal counselling or treatment. If Emily from the earlier practice focus had been unable to process or contain her emotions, assistance may have been required from a counsellor. Seeking support for psychological distress is frequently stigmatized in the helping professions in general (Dickstein, Stephenson and Hinz, 1990; Gibb et al., 2010; Ting, Jacobsen and Sanders, 2011). Nonetheless, if a social worker is suffering from stress which is affecting their personal and work life, referring them for extra support is part of the employer's duty of care and could help them avoid burnout.

The next section provides some suggestions for how resilience may be enhanced through reflective supervision.

1. Role play

Morrison et al. (2005) have highlighted the usefulness of role play in enhancing the emotional understanding of practice situations in a safe and contained manner. 'Playing out' stressful and emotionally demanding situations, or those which can evoke fear and anxiety, in a secure and trusting supervisory setting can help workers process their feelings and grow in self-awareness and confidence. Using such techniques requires supervisors to have the ability to debrief workers and provide facilitative feedback. It should be recognized, however, that role play can create intense emotional reactions, and an understanding of projection (see above) is vital when using this experiential method.

Through role play the supervisee may also be able to move towards developing accurate empathy which, as seen above, supports resilience. Recent research on the use of mindfulness (see Chapter 7) has shown how mindful role play can enhance empathic understanding in psychotherapists (Andersson, King and Lalande, 2010). Using the 'empty chair' role-play technique (Houston, 1990) derived from Gestalt therapy (Perls, 1973) during supervision has also been found to increase empathic understanding and enhance the effective processing of emotions. This technique requires the worker to be facilitated to address the service user in the empty chair, and then inhabit the empty chair themselves 'as if' they were' the service user feeding back on their feelings, in order to improve awareness of self and others.

2. The use of silence
Silence can be an effective tool in supervision (Beddoe and Davys, 2010). Allowing short periods of silence can heighten self-awareness by providing social workers with the opportunity to recognize feelings and assumptions that may not be immediately brought to mind. It is all too easy to become action-focused in supervision, especially when time is short, and supervisors may attempt to process workers' own thoughts for them. Sitting in silence for short periods without awkwardness can create thinking space and opportunities for deep reflection.

3. Appreciative Inquiry
Some researchers have argued that an overt focus on what is not going well in practice can create dysfunction rather than improvement (Cohen, 1999). As emphasized throughout this book, optimism and hope are important aspects of resilience. Appreciative Inquiry (AI: Cooperrider, Whitney and Stavros, 2003) provides supervisors with an approach that can foster a positive outlook in their supervisees. AI differs from the more commonly utilized deficit model (what is going wrong and what can be improved), offering a strengths-based, optimistic approach which focuses on appreciating what has gone well and envisioning what might be, and what should be in the future. The AI model encourages workers to follow a four-stage process: first, consider what is going well; secondly, 'dream' about how things could be improved; thirdly, design a strategy for how these dreams could be applied; and finally, consider ways of delivering the change. This positive, compassionate approach permits people to explore their strengths, diminishes fear and anxiety and facilitates reflection for transformational learning. Research by Cojocaru (2010) found that improved service-user outcomes were found where social workers received supervision with an AI focus. Other authors have called for this approach to be used more frequently to ameliorate stress and build resilience (Onyett, 2011).

4. Open-question enquiry for reflective thinking
The use of Socratic, or open questions, during supervision can help social workers become more curious and critical of their own practice, allowing them to explore their feelings, reactions and plans for the

future and supporting self-confidence and autonomy. It is acknowledged, however, that knowing how to frame these questions in supervision requires expertise underpinned by effective listening skills (Beddoe and Davys, 2010). Supervisors who use these capabilities to reframe, clarify and ask expansive questions can facilitate deep reflection on the part of their supervisees. Questions beginning 'how', 'where', 'what', 'when' and 'who' tend to be more facilitative than 'why' questions as they encourage reflection and discourage defensive behaviour (Beddoe and Davys, 2010). This approach empowers workers to find the answers to their own questions and increases self-confidence, self-awareness and autonomy: all of which are linked to resilience.

Exercise 4.1 is designed to help supervisors prepare more effectively for supervision.

EXERCISE 4.1

**Questions to ask in preparation for supervision:
the supervisor's role**

- Do I ask my supervisees about their wellbeing?
- How can I facilitate a solutions-focused approach in my supervision?
- What are my supervisee's real strengths?
- How can I enable my supervisee to identify areas for development and set achievable goals?
- How can I move away from an over-emphasis on a managerialist agenda to a more reflective one?
- How do I deal with uncertainty and anxiety myself? What support do I have?
- What are my feelings and emotional reactions to cases explored in supervision? Am I anxious, fearful, over-confident or complacent? What might the impact of such feelings be on my supervisee?

Supervisors need supervision to build their own emotional resilience

To provide effective supervision and to protect their own wellbeing and resilience, it is important for social work managers to be provided with their own reflective space. They need to develop and sustain a supervisory relationship which fulfils the managerial, educative and supportive functions of supervision, as well as contain the emotional impact of the work with their supervisees (Ruch, 2012). Toasland (2007) acknowledges that this is a 'tightrope walk' where managers are required to simultaneously manage busy teams with increasing caseloads, avoid overloading staff, and provide space to provide effective supervision. Moreover, supervisors will need to develop their own competencies for enhancing resilience. Having a supportive supervisor themselves and knowing how to get the best out of these sessions will enable supervisors to manage others more effectively, as well as protect their own wellbeing and maintain their resilience.

Conclusion

Individual needs will vary considerably depending on experience, personality, and ability to manage the emotional elements of practice. Good supervision, however, requires a secure, collaborative relationship that allows supervisees to discuss openly the uncertainty, anxiety, doubt and other emotions engendered by social work practice. Supervisees should also be permitted to take risks and accept new opportunities. Such conditions will not only protect the wellbeing of social workers, but will also foster emotional resilience to enable them to manage future challenges more effectively. For supervision to be effective, supervisors need to be emotionally literate and recognize the importance of protecting their own wellbeing. They also need to carefully maintain their personal resilience toolbox and be supported by effective organizational policies and procedures. This chapter has provided some guidance on how effective reflective supervision might be accomplished to the benefit of supervisees, supervisors and service users.

Howe (2008, p. 187) has argued that organizations who fail to hold and contain workers are in 'danger of blunting, even destroying the most important resource they have – the emotionally intelligent, available and responsive social worker'. So enhancing resilience in social workers through supervision is not an added 'luxury' or a 'nice to have'; it is imperative if social workers are going to be able to thrive in a challenging profession.

ADDITIONAL RESOURCES

Davys, A., & Beddoe, L. (2010) *Best Practice in Professional Supervision: A Guide for the Helping Professions* (London and Philadelphia, PA: Jessica Kingsley).

Mathieu, F. (2012) *The Compassion Fatigue Workbook: Creative Tools for Transforming Compassion Fatigue and Vicarious Traumatization* (electronic resource) (New York: Routledge).

Morrison, T. (2005) *Staff Supervision in Social Care: Making a Real Difference for Staff and Service Users* (Brighton: Pavilion).

Shohet, R. (2008) *Passionate Supervision* (electronic resource) (London: Jessica Kingsley).

CHAPTER 5

Personal organization and time management

Siobhan Wray and Sacha Rymell

CHAPTER OVERVIEW

On a daily basis, social workers face competing demands from service users, managers, administrators and colleagues as well as people working for other agencies. Well-developed personal organizational strategies are required in order to survive, let alone thrive, in such an environment. This chapter considers ways in which these behaviours can be enhanced to help social workers cope successfully with competing demands, enhance their personal effectiveness and build emotional resilience. The behaviours that support or undermine the use of effective time-management strategies are explored. Also considered are ways in which personal needs and time shortages can be communicated effectively and interruptions managed to minimize disruption. Various tools and techniques are described that can provide social workers with insight into their personal approach to time management and help them set realistic, achievable and sustainable goals.

The social work role: managing competing demands

As discussed in previous chapters, social workers have many different roles, the demands of which can conflict to impair wellbeing and job performance. Managing the diverse needs of service users and their families, balancing competing demands from different professional groups and ensuring that key deadlines are met are frequently challenging. These demands regularly compete for precious time which is in short supply. Social workers are also required to balance the immediate demands of working in a client-facing but highly regulated profession, with longer-term needs such as updating skills and knowledge and engaging in personal development. Furthermore, the requirement to respond to emergencies means that social workers are expected to re-evaluate their goals and priorities on a daily basis, which compounds the pressure they experience. As discussed in Chapters 3 and 9 in particular, working in such a demanding environment limits opportunities for recovery, harms work–life balance and takes its toll on physical and psychological health. Well-developed time-management and organizational strategies are required in order to protect social workers' wellbeing and enhance personal effectiveness. These concepts will be discussed in the context of social work. Several exercises are presented that have the potential to help social workers improve their time-management behaviours at the individual and team level and facilitate the setting and achievement of personal and professional goals.

What is time management?

Many books have been written to help people improve their time management and personal effectiveness (e.g. Drucker, 1967; Macan, 1994; Covey, 1997). Time-management training courses remain ever popular in an era where organizations and employees are encouraged to 'do more with less' while ensuring optimum service provision. There is very little agreement, however, on what time management actually means. Claessens et al. (2004) have pointed out that the term is misleading, as time is an inaccessible factor and cannot therefore be managed. It may be more useful to consider 'time management' as the ways in which we manage ourselves to perform a range of tasks in a particular time-frame. It could also be considered as a type of self-regulation that enables people to improve their performance, develop professionally through learning, and achieve personal career success (De Vos and Soens, 2008). Through helping people manage competing demands more effectively and dedicating sufficient time for recovery, the potential for effective time management to enhance wellbeing and build resilience is also clear.

Time management has been used to refer to various processes that encompass determining needs, goal-setting, prioritizing and planning, and coping (Claessens et al., 2007). This chapter will use Claessens and colleagues' definition that time management refers to 'behaviours that aim at achieving an effective use of time while performing certain goal orientated activities' (p. 292). It will discuss key time-management *behaviours* rather than skills. Skills refer to techniques that we have learned, whereas the focus on behaviour used in this chapter allows consideration of what we actually *do* on a day-to-day basis. This approach, therefore, has greater potential to lead to more effective time-management behaviours and accordingly build resilience.

Time management and work: what's the use?

As discussed throughout this book, resilience is a key attribute for social workers. Managing a demanding and varied workload in a resilient manner requires people to work as effectively as possible whilst ensuring that their self-care is prioritized. As discussed in Chapter 9, the costs of failing to protect personal wellbeing can be serious, both for the social worker and the service they provide. For example, a study conducted by Aronsson, Astvik and Gustafsson (2013) found that 43 percent of social workers regularly failed to recover psychologically and physically from the demands of their work. Developing positive work behaviours to support recovery and work–life balance, such as effective time-management and personal organizational behaviours, underpins wellbeing and effective practice. Other ways to improve work–life balance are considered in Chapter 3.

As well as providing opportunities for self-care and recovery, personal organizational skills are also required to ensure that social workers dedicate sufficient time to reflective practice, supervision and professional development – all of which have been highlighted throughout this book as intrinsic aspects of resilience. There is also evidence that more resilient social workers tend to be more proficient at time and workload management, for example: setting realistic professional expectations; maintaining personal and professional goals; generating feelings of accomplishment and understanding their own limitations (Beddoe et al., 2013; Shier and Graham, 2011).

John's situation, described below, illustrates the importance of social workers developing effective time- and workload-management behaviours, as well as feeling in control of their work.

John is experiencing a form of paralysis brought on by a reluctance to try a new approach to help improve his personal organizational skills. The negative implications for his practice, as well as his wellbeing and work–life balance, are self-evident. John's situation will be revisited later in the chapter to illustrate how improved time management could enhance his professional development.

PRACTICE FOCUS 5.1: JOHN

John is a social worker in a Family Support Team and has been qualified for five years. He has a mixed caseload of Child Protection and complex Child in Need cases. Although John has a similar caseload to other social workers in the team, he generally feels busier than his colleagues. He is often observed rushing around the office and has confided to colleagues that he feels like he is continually 'chasing his tail'. John's professional and reflective practice activities are often not completed due to the time pressure he believes he is experiencing. He has a strong desire to remain service-user focused and often prioritizes direct casework above his other duties. John feels that he is achieving very little in his role, and is struggling to manage his workload. He often works late to try to catch up with his work, but never seems to feel on top of it. This is eroding his confidence and ability to do the job effectively, as well as his reducing the time available to relax and engage with family and friends. John could clearly benefit from developing his personal organization and time-management behaviours. He is reluctant to try anything new, however, as he believes that he does not have the time or energy to change.

Time-management behaviours and resilient practice

People who manage their time effectively have been found to possess specific attributes. These behaviours are examined below, together with suggestions for how they may be developed in the social work context.

Assessment of time

How quickly does an hour pass? The answer to this question often depends upon what we are doing. When engaged in conversation with friends, doing something we really enjoy or concentrating deeply on a work task, time often flies by, whereas waiting for a delayed flight or anticipating a difficult meeting can make an hour feel like a day. How we experience the passing of time depends on a wide range of factors that can differ from hour to hour, day to day. Our experience of time, therefore, has a psychological dimension. Although the ability to assess time accurately underpins effective time management and completing tasks successfully in both our work and home lives, we are not naturally very good at it. To illustrate our faulty assessment of time, Kahneman and Tversky (1977) proposed a 'planning fallacy', where individuals (and teams) typically believe that their projects will proceed as planned, even though they are aware that most projects do not. There is further evidence that people are generally overconfident about their ability to meet deadlines; particularly if are no serious consequences if they fail to meet them (Buehler, Griffin and Peetz, 2010; Buehler, Griffin and Ross, 1994).

Research findings indicate that people are generally poor at assessing how long tasks will take (Buehler et al., 2010; Burt and Kemp, 1994). More specifically, we are likely to overestimate the length of time needed to accomplish a task, if the task is new to us. For example, a social worker who has to write a court report for the first time may overestimate the time required to do this job. This is likely to cause anxiety if they are already pressed for time. We also tend to find it difficult to apply past experience when asked to estimate the amount of time a more familiar task will take (Roy, Christenfeld and McKenzie, 2005). This may be because we are overly optimistic about our abilities, or fail to recall the time it took us to complete similar projects in the past. In particular, there is a tendency for people to underestimate the time past tasks actually took and how long ago they took place: a phenomenon known as 'telescoping' (see Loftus and Marburger, 1983; Betz and Skowronski, 1997). Memory alone is an inconsistent and often faulty tool for time estimation: people will tend to think that familiar tasks will take less time than they do. For example, an experienced social worker may underestimate the time required to write up a court report, which then reduces the time available for other important tasks.

Developing a more realistic view of the time tasks actually take through a careful consideration of how long they have taken in the past can help people develop more effective time-allocation strategies. This is illustrated in the practice example below, where Nasreen develops baseline measures to help team members establish how long routine tasks should take.

There is a risk that baseline measures such as these can be used as a managerial tool for the purposes of surveillance. In this case, however, the measures were used to help social workers manage their time and their expectations of themselves and other team members more effectively. The collaborative manner in which the baseline measures were

PRACTICE FOCUS 5.2: JOHN (continued)

John's line manager, Nasreen, has noticed that he often fails to meet deadlines for writing up case assessments and this is having a negative impact on his performance. When reviewing John's workload, Nasreen noticed that his diary was filled with 'immediate/crisis work', which limited the opportunity for him to catch up with paperwork.

To help John rebalance his workload, Nasreen arranged a time-management supervision session. Despite his initial reluctance to discuss the problems he was experiencing, John disclosed to Nasreen that he was feeling increasingly annoyed with himself about his inability to meet deadlines. Whenever he starting thinking about writing up the assessments, he was put off as he felt overwhelmed by the amount of time the backlog would take to complete. John also mentioned that the worry this caused was also having a negative impact on his work and his home life.

John agreed to block off regular slots in his diary for writing up assessments. Nasreen emphasized that this time was not negotiable and that he would not be allowed to do further crisis work until the assessments were completed. Nasreen communicated this decision to the other managers. John found this new regime very effective – rather than worrying about preparing assessments for days, he did them in the allotted time and actually discovered that he wrote them up far more quickly than he thought he would.

PRACTICE FOCUS 5.3: NASREEN

Following Nasreen's work with John, she decided to develop some baseline measures for her team, which included estimating the time spent on some of the everyday tasks performed by team members. Nasreen consulted her team members when developing these measures and requested suggestions for innovative practice. This meant the team felt empowered to explore ways to improve their own practice. The baseline measures were considered during a group supervision session and, despite some challenging discussions, were accepted by all team members. They were subsequently adopted as an informal workload management tool.

developed meant that team members took ownership of them and felt motivated to use them.

The next section discusses the use of time diaries. These tools have great potential in helping people gain greater awareness of the time they spend on tasks and highlight potential for change.

Know thyself: using a time diary

The use of diaries to reflect upon emotional reactions to practice was discussed in Chapter 4. A time diary is a simple tool that can be used to examine how time is allocated on a day-to-day basis. It is an opportunity to record accurately the time spent on routine and novel tasks, meetings, travel and interruptions. To be a useful self-evaluation tool, however, a time diary should reflect *exactly* how you have spent your time on any given day, and include all aspects of your working life, including time worked outside standard hours (for example, working at home during the week or at weekends/rest days). You should endeavour to keep your time diary for at least one full week. Choose a week that is representative of your general working life (avoid choosing a week when you are doing unusual tasks, such as spending three days on a training course). Your diary can be handwritten or typed – whichever is most practical for you. It is important, however, to choose a method that can be easily accessed throughout the day; if you do not have access to a computer for much of the day a written diary will be best.

To begin your time diary, set up a page or word document following the structure given in Table 5.1. Split your day into 15-minute blocks, identifying the things you intend to do each day, including scheduled meetings, having lunch, etc.

At the end of each day, spend some time reflecting on how you have used your time and record your thoughts:

- Did you have any surprises?
- What went well during the day?
- What would you have changed?
- How did your actual day compare with your plan?
- Have you identified any personal behaviours that you would like to change?
- To what extent did your 'to do' list match the activities you actually undertook?

Table 5.1 Example of a time diary

Monday 19 April

List any tasks, meetings or activities that you have prearranged

Time	Tasks and activities	Comments
	Include any prearranged finish times. Activities – list all of the activities you have undertaken in the time-frame. Include all breaks and interruptions	Record any feelings, thoughts or actions related to your 15-minute slot
8.30	Arrived at office. Made coffee and discussed case X with J. Arranged handover for 2pm	
8.45	As above. Spoke with J for 20 minutes. Informal chat and meeting arranged	Emails not yet checked as planned, feel frustrated but conversation was useful
9.00	Finished conversation and logged on to system. 10 minutes spent checking and responding to emails	Still a number of emails left to check
9.15	Daily team catch-up. Scheduled 9.15–9.30am	
9.30	As above	
9.45	Finished catch-up 9.45am	Meeting usually overruns. This made me late for another meeting

Review and analysis

Continue to complete your diary for one full week. Arrange some time at the beginning of the second week to analyse your reflections. Make sure you schedule at least two hours' uninterrupted time for this activity.

1. Examine the core and routine tasks that you undertake daily, or every week (e.g. checking emails, writing weekly reports, attending team meetings). How long, on average, does each of these tasks take you in any given period (day or week)?
2. Give a time value to each task. What percentage of your week is given over to these routine or core tasks?

3. Examine the tasks that you have been involved in during the week that are not regular (for example, deputizing at a meeting, covering for a colleague who is off sick, being involved in an emergency home visit). How much time during your week is given over to these irregular activities? What percentage of these tasks have you initiated and what percentage has been initiated by others?

4. Examine the time that you have spent on other activities (e.g. travel, chatting with colleagues, lunch and other breaks, using the internet). How much of your time during the week was spent on these activities?

5. Identify the tasks that you did not expect to undertake. What types of task are they? Are you the most appropriate person to do them? Are they a good use of your time?

6. Compare what you have actually done with your original plan for each day. What are the similarities and differences? What types of task do you tend to do and what gets left?

Once you have completed your analysis you should be able to identify the following:

How long standard daily and routine tasks take. If it usually takes you 30 minutes to read and reply to emails in the morning, then you need to schedule 30 minutes for this activity. Often routine daily tasks do not get scheduled, or we underestimate how long they take. By accounting for this time accurately, you will be able to identify the time you have available to take on new projects or responsibilities.

Do routine meetings overrun? If the answer to this is 'yes', you need to schedule more time for them, or work with colleagues to improve time-keeping at the group level.

How long do you spend on unique tasks, unplanned meetings and other non-standard activities? How much of your time is spent on activities outside your core purpose? Do you need/want to be involved in all of these projects, or are there some you could pass on to others or step away from?

If little of your time is spent on project work, is there a particular task you would like to become involved in to enhance your professional development? With a clear understanding of how your time is currently utilized, could you approach your manager and discuss potential opportunities for this?

What are your 'time-stealers'? What do you do during the day that is not a good use of your time? Which behaviours use up your time in non-productive ways? Are these things that you want to change or not? What are the benefits of tackling time-stealers? How much time would you recover?

What was your time spent on? How much of your time did you spend reacting to new tasks or responding to immediate requests for information or help? Consider the tasks that are fundamental aspects of your role, and which are not. What percentage of your week was spent on these immediate, unplanned tasks? What percentage of your week was spent on planned activities that you see as core to your role? These two percentages will give you an approximation of the time you spend on proactive, planned tasks and reactive unplanned tasks.

Your percentage for proactive time will depend heavily on your job role. If you are a duty social worker answering calls from service users, then the majority of your working time will be reactive. If you are responsible for the preparation of policy documents, however, you may find that most of your time is proactive. This distinction is important – *you can only plan for your proactive time.* If your role requires you to react to incoming tasks for 50 percent of the time, then you can only plan for the 50 percent of the time that is proactive.

But all this will take too long to do and I am too busy

Completing and analysing a time diary in itself takes time, effort and commitment – but it is a worthwhile task. Many people complete time logs as part of their professional duties, including lawyers, accountants and architects: it is vital not to charge a client too little because the amount of time a task takes has been underestimated. The time diary is a tool to help you reflect accurately on the time it takes to do tasks. As discussed above, our ability to predict the duration tasks will take is much improved if we have feedback. The time diary is an opportunity for you to collect and analyse feedback. It will also help you to think about and prioritize tasks, schedule activities effectively, discuss your workload meaningfully and identify where you use time in a way that does not support your aims and priorities. The time that you commit to keeping the diary will help you make decisions about your schedule, communicate your workload to others, and ensure that you can make time for new projects and continuing professional development. It will also help you identify if and where you are overloaded at work, and the impact this might have on your personal recovery time and your work–life balance (see Chapter 3).

Planning behaviours, that is, setting goals and working towards them, are a key aspect of effective time management and personal organization. The next section considers them in more detail.

Setting and achieving goals

People set goals to achieve specific outcomes in life. A personal goal may be to run a marathon, learn a new skill, save for a holiday or plan for your career. The act of moving from a desire to a goal requires people to identify a difference between where they are (Point A) and where they wish to be (Point B), and to plan a course of action to get there. Very many studies have been conducted that explore the ways in which individuals set goals and how effective they are. Goal theory, developed by Locke and Latham (2006), proposes that challenging, specific goals will increase performance more than easy, vague goals. In other words, thinking that we would like to run a marathon one day is less likely to lead to change than entering a competition and training for this event. Planning behaviours (goal-setting and prioritizing tasks) are key aspects of time management (Claessens et al., 2004; 2007). Effective planning involves setting specific and challenging goals and considering how they can be met: that is, breaking large goals down into individual tasks and milestones.

The way in which people set goals and prioritize them is linked with the level of control they feel they have over their time and their ability to meet deadlines (Macan et al., 1990). As discussed in Chapter 9, research findings indicate that people who feel more in control of their time are healthier, less stressed, more satisfied with their work and have a better work–life balance. Moreover, there is evidence that feeling in control of when and how work tasks are done can help people manage a heavy workload successfully (Karasek, 1990). These findings reflect the work undertaken by Beddoe et al. (2013) and Shier and Graham (2011) which found that resilient social workers tend to feel more control over their ability to meet their personal and professional goals.

Setting goals in practice

Social workers' goals are often set by external stakeholders. Professional goals are also guided by personal ethics, values, and career aspirations. This means that, like many other professionals, social workers will be expected to achieve a combination of externally imposed and internally generated goals. Insight is needed, therefore, into the factors that can facilitate and impede the achievement of goals. Locke and Latham (2006) have highlighted several features in relation to this:

- Commitment to the goal.
- Feedback.
- Perceiving the goal as important.
- Situational constraints.

One of the main challenges in time management is balancing goals that are set by others with the goals that we have set for ourselves. For example, if you decide that you wish to train as a systemic therapist in the future, your personal career goals are unlikely to match the goals of your current social work employer. You may, however, be able to identify links between your personal goals and your professional ones; for example: 'If I am successful in my promotion I may be able to reduce my working week to four days to enable me to start training as a systemic therapist.' Commitment to professional goals and a sense of their importance may be hampered by situational constraints such as time, the need to engage in professional development and supervision, and the extent to which the person has the skills required to do the job to the standard required.

Effective professional goals are those that are to some extent aligned with personal goals. For example, some people may wish to develop their career in such a way that they can become a strategic leader within social work. The successful achievement of 'stretch' goals (that is, goals that are challenging but achievable) in a person's current role may help them appreciate the qualifications and experience required for promotion at that level and identify a network of people who can help them develop their personal profile. Personal development goals can be matched effectively to professional or work-based goals, strengthening commitment to the goal, enhancing its perceived importance and working within situational constraints. Such alignment is more likely to ensure that goals are achieved.

EXERCISE 5.1

Reviewing your goals

1. Write down three personal and three professional goals.
   Use the following questions to assess each goal on a scale from 1 =
   'not at all' to 10 = 'extremely':

   - How committed am I to achieving this goal?
   - How important is this goal to me?
   - How difficult is this goal to achieve?

2. For each goal identify three factors that may hinder successful
   completion of the goal and three factors that you can use to help
   you achieve this goal.

   Review your goals in light of your reflections. Consider whether these
   goals are effective for you and the resources you have available to help
   you meet them.

Defining and operationalizing goals

This section will focus on job-related goals, but the same techniques can
be applied to personal goals. As discussed above, effective goals are
challenging in their nature (that is, stretching, specific and considered
important). When defining a goal, it is useful to consider the SMART
framework to assess the goal and to facilitate its clear expression.

Specific: Specific goals are far more likely to be achieved than vague
ones. Write a specific goal statement. What will you achieve? For example, 'I will complete a post-qualifying social work course' is not as effective as 'I will do some research on the most appropriate post-qualifying
course to train as a systemic therapist.'

Measurable: How are you measuring success? How will you know
when you have met the goal? For example, 'I will become a systemic
therapist' is not a measurable statement, whereas 'I will research the
steps to becoming a systemic therapist and start the training within
three years' is measurable and allows you to assess success.

Attainable (but difficult!): As discussed above, goals should be
stretching, but not impossible. If goals are perceived to be too hard,
people can become overwhelmed. The way in which goals are framed
can make a difference to their achievement. Goals perceived as high in

challenge will improve performance, whereas those that are seen as threatening impair it, even when controlling for the actual difficulty of achieving the goal (Drach-Zahavy & Erez, 2002). It is important to bear this in mind when setting goals for others. So, for example, you may wish to become a Team Manager but, if you are a newly qualified social worker, this goal will need to be broken down into attainable steps.

Relevant and resourced: Goals that are not perceived as relevant are less likely to be achieved. Goals should relate directly to your work and your role. Setting a goal to become a systemic family therapist will only be relevant if this is something that is congruent with your current role, or may enable you to get a job in that field in the future. Goals require resourcing. Think about the time and support you need from yourself and others to achieve your goal and check whether this is realistic. If you cannot access the resources required to achieve a goal, then you are unlikely to succeed. So it will be important to ask yourself if you can afford to pay for training as a systemic therapist and work reduced hours for the duration of the training.

Time-bound: Goals should be time-limited. A goal to file your paperwork is far more likely to be achieved if you set a deadline for this task.

EXERCISE 5.2

Are my time-management goals SMART?
Revisit the goals that you recorded above, choosing those that you scored highly for commitment and importance. Check each goal statement against the SMART framework. Rewrite your goals to reflect the SMART elements.

Planning and monitoring: Planning is the action of breaking down goals into tasks to support their completion. As discussed above, this process allows people to focus on sub-goals or smaller components of a larger goal over shorter periods of time. Planning for the completion of goals, and monitoring success through reflection and feedback from others, support people in completing work goals, as well as ensuring that activities are planned for and milestones met. The act of planning can also help people evaluate their goal-setting behaviour.

Breaking goals down – planning tasks: once you have set your goal, agreed your measurement criteria, specified your resource requirements and identified a realistic time-frame to achieve the goal, you will need to set out and plan the activities you need to achieve the goal:

Operationalize your goal: Begin with your deadline – what will be completed by this point? Be specific: for example, will your report be complete and saved on your computer or will copies have been delivered to your colleagues? Include the time and date for delivery in your deadline.

Identify important milestones: Specify which major tasks need to be completed by when to ensure that you meet your deadline. This may include scheduling planning meetings, achieving print deadlines, setting dates for approval meetings, or specific external requirements. In general, milestones are not movable: to meet your deadline you must meet your milestones.

Plan for individual tasks: Working backwards from your deadline or milestone, identify the tasks that need to be completed (by you or others in the team) in order to meet each deadline/milestone. Include all tasks: for example, if you need to get your report reviewed by your line manager before you submit it externally you will need to plan for:

- Giving it to your line manager by an agreed deadline
- Receiving feedback from your line manager by an agreed time
- Acting on this feedback and resubmitting for approval (if necessary)
- Submitting the report.

Successful planning for such an activity requires scheduling time in your own diary and the diary of your line manager. By planning this in advance and blocking out sufficient time, you gain commitment from your line manager (and yourself) and, most importantly, identify any issues that may impact on your deadline such as annual leave or a competing priority. In other words, you identify bottlenecks from the start.

By planning tasks in advance, you are also able to test your deadline – is it achievable within the time-frame and with the resources that you have available? If not, you may need to reprioritize the task or change the deadline. For each goal, all identified tasks and milestones should be diarized. If you do not have enough PROACTIVE time available you may need to reconsider your goals.

EXERCISE 5.3

Planning to achieve your goals
Use one of the goals that you have identified above. Plan a timeline for completion of the goal. Identify your milestones and any activities that you may need others to do to allow you to meet your deadline. Work through the planning steps shown above (remembering to check whether you have enough proactive time available).

Is your goal achievable in the time-frame? If yes, put your tasks and milestones into your diary and diarize time with others if necessary.

If no, reconsider your deadline – can you move this? Is your goal too ambitious, do you need to review your SMART process? Try redefining your goal and testing again.

There is always too much to do

It is important to acknowledge that you are unlikely to be able to achieve everything you want to in a given time-frame. There are always competing objectives, tasks and other urgent issues. There are also likely to be factors outside work that may interfere with the achievement of goals, such as illness or family emergencies. The key to successful planning and completion of tasks is regular prioritizing and reprioritizing. This reflects the need for psychological flexibility that

EXERCISE 5.4

Review your time diary
Choose a day at random and make a list of all of the planned and unplanned tasks you completed in that day. For each task, give it a score of 1 = a low-priority task and 10 = a high-priority task (see the example below). Make a second list of the tasks that you failed to complete in the day and rank them in the same way.

What criteria have you used for the priority weighting of each task? Write these down.

Planned task	Score	Unplanned task	Score
Review weekly report	8	Support J with case X	9

has been highlighted as a key factor in enhancing resilience (see Chapter 9).

Urgency, importance and the presence of others

Unsurprisingly, tasks that are considered urgent tend to be prioritized above other important jobs. Tasks are more likely to be considered urgent, however, when they are allocated by a supervisor, or in the form of an interruption from a colleague (Bowers, Lauring and Jacobson, 2001; Alqahtani and Histon, 2012). In such scenarios, people are less inclined to follow their task plan and are more likely to undertake the new task even if they personally do not consider it important. Interruptions from colleagues and managers are often useful as they can communicate important information. Nonetheless, if an existing task requires deep concentration, interruptions can be distracting, hamper the achievement of tasks and goals and result in errors (Chisholm et al., 2000; Westbrook et al., 2010). It is unrealistic to expect to eliminate all interruptions, however, particularly in a team-based environment where people are expected to respond to the urgent needs of service users. It is important, therefore, to develop strategies to manage, assess and respond appropriately to interruptions from different sources. It is this act of assessment and decision-making that ensures the effective prioritization and reprioritization of tasks throughout the day, while ensuring that longer-term goals and commitments can be met.

The following section highlights strategies that can be used to manage interruptions effectively.

EXERCISE 5.5

Reviewing your priorities
Review your priorities list above. Re-code your responses based on their urgency and importance, using the definitions below:

Urgent – a task with an imminent time constraint.
Important – a task that has a strong impact on your work-related goals and is intrinsic to your role.

Examine your unplanned tasks. What made them important or urgent at the time? On reflection, were any of these tasks really urgent? Could any of them have been put off?

Strategies for managing interruptions

1. *Assess the requirement.* When faced with an incoming task or request for help or information, we often stop what we are doing and respond immediately. This is particularly true when we are asked to take on new tasks. A strategy for managing these scenarios more effectively is to seek further information. Ask the person who is requesting help:

   ■ What is the task?
   ■ What is the deadline?
   ■ What do you need from me to complete the task?

2. *Ask for some time to think about the request.* Agree a time to go back to the person with an answer. This gives you the opportunity to consider your existing workload and make a rational decision about your involvement in the task or project.

   If the task or request is one that you feel able to undertake, arrange a convenient time to discuss it and agree your contribution. All too often, a quick chat with a colleague can turn into a 30-minute conversation. Be clear about the parameters of your time and arrange to have the chat when you are able to engage fully with the individual without being distracted by competing tasks. Agree what you can and cannot help with and diarize the actions you will both take. Arrange to review the task once complete.

3. *Say no.* There are times when we are unable to become involved in other projects or tasks. Be prepared to say no if your involvement will impact negatively on your core tasks and goals, or unduly impair your work–life balance. It is appreciated, however, that social workers are frequently required to drop existing tasks to manage an urgent situation. Saying no often means we have to turn down the things we would like to do, while continuing to work on previously set goals that we may consider less stimulating. When you say no, be clear about why you cannot help at this time. You may be able to suggest colleagues who could offer support, or agree to help in the future. It is essential to be clear that we are saying no to the task rather than the person. Remember that it is usually better to say no to something at the outset, than to fail to undertake a task you have agreed to do without adequately considering whether you have the resources available.

4. *Managing supervisor requests.* As discussed above, a task can have implied importance if the person making the request is a supervisor

or manager. In this scenario, it is crucial that you are able to communicate your current workload and priorities clearly (this is where clear goal-setting and the diarizing of tasks is helpful). If a request will overload you, ask to discuss your workload with your line manager and request support in reprioritizing your current tasks. Clear communication will help you and your manager agree on the most effective work schedule for you in the context of the team priorities and goals.

Monitoring and feedback

Regular self-monitoring and feedback from others are critical to effective time management. Self-monitoring goals through review underpins the prioritizing and reprioritizing activities outlined above. People need to assess that their goals are still relevant and up to date, that they are making progress towards them, and that the completion of the goal will have the anticipated 'pay-off' in the work environment. For this reason it is vital to make time to review goals and progress periodically, consider the resources that are required and the relevance of the goal in a rapidly changing working environment, and make any adjustments necessary.

Self-monitoring of time-management behaviours through periodic use of the time diary can help people identify and manage behaviours that interfere with progress. Feedback from others is critical to professional development. Ask colleagues how they feel about your time-management strategies: are there areas which could be improved? Discuss your challenges and achievements with your manager informally and formally. Having a clear understanding about how you have spent your time and the goals that you have met forms the basis of a successful and meaningful professional development review. This could also form part of reflective supervision (see Chapter 4).

Conclusion

Time management undoubtedly takes time and effort, but the resources used to develop and maintain supportive behaviours have a high pay-off. Managing time is a behaviour set that is impacted by the individual and the team: in social work, it is inevitable that some days will be spent being entirely reactive rather than proactive. Nonetheless, through practice, you will begin to develop effective habits. Remember that successful time management is a journey rather than a particular skill set. Therefore, regular feedback, engagement and reflection are key to constant improvement, as is motivation and commitment to the process.

ADDITIONAL RESOURCES

Bird, P. (2003) *Time Management: Teach Yourself*. London: Chartered Management Institute.

Locke, E. & Latham, E. (2013) *New Developments in Goal Setting and Task Performance*. London: Routledge.

CHAPTER 6

Cognitive behavioural-based strategies

Kelly Alexander, Sara Henley and Kay Newman

CHAPTER OVERVIEW

Cognitive behavioural therapy (CBT) has long been established as an effective psychological intervention in the treatment of a variety of disorders, most notably depression and anxiety. However, there is evidence that cognitive behavioural strategies can be used to help people manage everyday difficulties more effectively. The principle of CBT is based on understanding key cognitive processes and how they impact on feelings and behaviour by identifying 'thinking errors', challenging and then modifying them to reduce their negative impact and therefore enabling a more accurate response to events and experiences. This chapter initially provides a brief description of the development and key principles of CBT. It highlights the impact of negative thinking, identifies thinking errors, and suggests strategies for challenging these based on personal strengths. Examples from practice are used to illustrate these principles and to highlight the utility of cognitive behavioural strategies in supporting social workers to manage challenging practice issues, thereby developing emotional resilience.

Emotional reactions to practice

As discussed throughout this book, dealing with the difficult, and sometimes traumatic, experiences of service users' lives can evoke strong emotions in social workers. These emotional reactions can range from minor feelings of stress and anxiety to secondary trauma responses, to more serious mental distress and, ultimately, burnout (Tobin and Carson, 1994; Huxley et al., 2005; Collins, Coffey and Morris, 2010). Many studies have found that helping professionals and trainees commonly experience anxiety in relation to their work (Menzies, 2000; Dziegielewski, Turnage and Roest-Marti, 2004).The emotional toll of the social work role can impact on practitioners regardless of whether they are located in the mental health field (Evans et al., 2005), within a children and families' context, or in other fields of social work practice (Bennett, Evans and Tattersall, 1993). Feelings of anxiety relate not only to the social workers' own sense of competence, but also from a sense of external threat. This can come from several sources: for example, government agenda, management practice, the media, complaints from service users and carers (see Chapter 1), as well as directly from practice. The stress caused by perceptions of threat can impact on social workers' confidence in making decisions (Munro, 2011; Parton, 1998). Social workers are often required to make difficult decisions in complex circumstances; the fear that negative consequences might stem from their decisions means that day-to-day practice (particularly for social workers in mental health or child-protection settings) can be fraught with anxiety. The potential threat to wellbeing is highlighted by Bennett et al. (1993, p. 33), who conclude: 'If the demands (at whatever level) exceed the perceived ability to meet them, the individual becomes under stress; that is, they experience stressful cognitions and emotions.' Appraisals of stress and their implications for wellbeing are considered further in Chapter 9.

Both trainee and experienced social work practitioners need to find a balance between recognizing their own anxiety and understanding what that anxiety is communicating in relation to a service-user situation, and becoming so anxious that they are unable to identify the barrier between their own and the service user's feelings. This can lead to over-involvement with service users, reduce accurate empathy and enhance empathic distress (Grant, 2013). Anxiety can emerge in response to a particular issue, case or service user. Negative feelings towards a service user or discomfort within a helping relationship can be a useful source of information about the service user's experience or the practitioner's capabilities, if they can be accessed consciously (Williams and Day, 2007). For example, when experiencing feelings of anxiety during a visit to a child it is useful to examine the source of these anxious feelings. It is important to ascertain if it is a reaction to the visit itself, the child's presentation, a current media focus on a particular child-protection case, or a personal concern about your own sick child. Appreciating the difference between useful anxiety and debilitating anxiety is essential to becoming an effective, reflective practitioner (Singer and Dewane, 2010) and avoiding the burnout associated with the emotional demands inherent in the social work profession (Lloyd et al., 2002; Hamama, 2012).

Exploring the emotions connected to stressful events, whether real and imagined, has been shown to be beneficial in reducing the incidents of intrusive thoughts and increasing self- compassion, thereby fostering self-efficacy and improved resilience (Greenberg, Wortman and Stone, 1996). CBT is a well-established approach which can facilitate a better understanding of emotions and help reduce negative anxiety and irrational thought, which can then free up the social worker to make more informed decisions.

What is cognitive behavioural therapy?

The use of cognitions in behavioural therapy developed during the 1950s and 1960s as a refreshing alternative to a strictly behaviourist model or psychodynamic model; neither of which focused on conscious cognitions (Grant, 2010). By the mid-1970s, cognitive work was becoming integrated into therapy, most notably in the work of Aaron T. Beck, supported by the major shift towards cognitive psychology in psychology in general (Rachman, 1997). This approach argued that it was the interpretation of events, rather than the events themselves, that had an effect on an individual's emotional wellbeing. In his seminal book *Cognitive Therapy and the Emotional Disorders* (1976), Beck described his theory particularly in relation to the treatment of depression. The emerging CBT approach was soon applied to anxiety and has subsequently been developed to provide treatment for a wide range of disorders and enable people to manage anxiety more effectively in a variety of contexts. The development of a central role for CBT, particularly in the UK, has continued, influencing psychological thinking and practice and many self-help approaches. It is highlighted as the current treatment of choice by the National Institute of Health and Clinical Excellence (NICE), giving guidance to practitioners, and is a well-evaluated, evidence-based psychological intervention (Hunot et al., 2007).

As mentioned above, CBT has been particularly effective in managing symptoms associated with a range of stress and anxiety-related disorders (Hofmann et al., 2012; DiMauro et al., 2013). CBT can help people increase their sense of control and mastery in situations that generate stress (Goldin et al., 2012). Padesky and Mooney (2012, p. 284) have emphasized a number of challenges to maintaining emotional resilience, including the danger of being emotionally worn down by multiple stressors. This is particularly relevant to social workers, who are expected to manage a range of tasks, each of which can exacerbate feelings of stress, such as: engaging with service users and carers; managing distressing information about service-user experience; keeping records up to date in the face of increasing bureaucratization; addressing risk; making decisions; and justifying actions in formal settings, such as in court.

Cognitive behavioural therapy explores how systematic thinking styles, particularly thinking errors, have a significant impact on how experiences and events are perceived. Thoughts are not errors in themselves; there are no 'wrong' thoughts, but the style of thinking will lead individuals to a particular interpretation. The objective of CBT is to recognize and test this thinking and generate the idea of alternative explanations. This is summed up effectively by Salkovskis (1997, p. 49): 'the aim is not to persuade persons that their current way of looking at the situation is wrong, irrational or too negative; instead, it is to allow them to identify where they may have become trapped or stuck in their way of thinking and allow them to discover other ways of looking at their situation'. CBT is collaborative, emphasizing personal engagement and responsibility, and therefore has an intrinsic appeal for self-help. This approach, therefore, has real potential for assisting social workers to develop an understanding of their own thinking styles and feelings, thereby enhancing coping skills and the competencies that have been found to underpin resilience.

Before discussing how CBT can assist in reducing stress and enhancing wellbeing, it is crucial to understand its key components. The central tenet of CBT is that cognitions (thoughts), feelings (physical sensations and emotions) and behaviour (actions) are inextricably linked and have a powerful impact on the individual (Salkovskis, 1997). It is the way in which events are experienced and thought about that governs the emotional reaction, and the tendency to act in particular ways. Logically, those thoughts that are the most strongly held will have the greatest emotional and physical impact, resulting in a behavioural response. Behavioural responses, in turn, further confirm the validity of the original thinking and the link between thoughts, feelings and behaviour becomes a perpetual, potentially vicious, cycle. Where cognitions are fearful or self-critical they are more likely to produce negative emotional and behavioural responses, particularly avoidance (Salkovskis, 1997). For example, a social worker who is struggling to fit in all the tasks allocated to them has also been asked to audit their caseload and number of direct client contacts. Their initial thoughts might be of concern as to how the figures will be viewed by the management team, despite feeling overstretched already; such thoughts can engender physical sensations of anxiety and avoidance, leading to reluctance to complete the audit and also reducing their cognitive ability to do so efficiently. Failure to complete the audit can engender further negative thoughts about how they will be judged, compounding the anxiety experienced and resulting in further avoidance strategies.

Intervention based on CBT principles can occur at any point in the cycle of anxiety. It is often most effective, however, when thoughts, feelings and behaviour are all attended to, but the thinking processes that are used are most influential, as it is not only the original cognitions that perpetuate the cycle, but how the resulting feelings and behavioural experiences are interpreted. Central to how CBT works is an understanding that thoughts and beliefs are not facts and can be changed. By challenging the initial thoughts in relation to the audit, the possibility of a different outcome emerges.

In seeking to help practitioners to manage stress and anxiety, the CBT model does not suggest people move to simple positive thinking, but the ability to assess experience in an 'accurate' way that promotes self-awareness and personal growth. The social worker who is able to rationalize the need for an audit of their work, rather than focus on thoughts that they will be judged negatively, will inevitably be less stressed; thus enhancing their capacity to cope with a potentially stressful and emotionally-charged role and, accordingly, emotional and professional resilience.

Using CBT to manage anxiety

Social workers may feel unprepared for the challenge of the social work role (Mathias-Williams and Thomas, 2002) and, as discussed in other chapters of this book, can experience stress in response to the demands of this role (Dziegielewski et al., 2004). They can also over-attend to perceived areas of deficit as opposed to their areas of expertise (Pines et al., 2012). The impact of automatic performance-related negative thoughts can be to further reduce confidence in personal capabilities, making poor performance a self-fulfilling prophecy (Bresó, Schaufeli and Salanova, 2011). For example, receiving a complaint from a service user can be an uncomfortable experience; this can have a more profound impact if the social worker questions their performance globally, rather than limiting it to this particular complaint. The impact of global, stable and internal attributions on wellbeing is considered further in Chapter 9.

A study that examined the frequency of secondary traumatic stress in social workers found that 25 percent of respondents identified intrusive thoughts, avoidance and difficulty concentrating as some of the consequences of working with service users in distress (Bride, 2007). Focusing on thoughts about the abuse of a child, for example, can engender a sense of hopelessness and reduced professional efficacy which can, in turn, impact on making decisions about what can be done now and in the future to protect that child. Of concern, however, are the findings of another study that revealed that just over half of the social work students surveyed stated that they would be unlikely to access individual counselling services for support in managing practice-related stress (Collins et al., 2010). There is an evident need, therefore, for acceptable, de-stigmatized interventions at an early stage of social workers' training.

Inexperienced helping professionals can over-focus on perceived areas of weakness, particularly when feeling challenged by or under pressure from those with more experience or authority. Such situations, and the lack of professional assertiveness that can accompany them, generate stress and anxiety. Recognizing their own skills and using these as a basis for assertive engagement in work-based interactions is linked with emotional resilience (Pines et al., 2012). A strengths-based approach, in which practitioners assess and value current skills and efficacy whilst identifying areas for development in relation to stress management, can therefore lead to greater role confidence and foster resilience. By identifying errors in thinking, CBT enables the practitioner to focus on skills and identify areas for development without becoming distracted and distressed by disproportionate negative and critical self-evaluation.

Recognizing the various ways in which stress manifests itself is an important part of reducing its impact (see Chapter 9). CBT techniques can enable social workers to identify, understand and manage work-related stressors more effectively, thereby reducing the potential for burnout (Dziegielewski et al., 2004). Psychological flexibility, that is, the ability to recognize thoughts and feelings in the here and now and utilize internal resources in order to manage emotions and take appropriate action in response, is also considered an essential tool for social work practitioners to manage stress (Brinkborg et al., 2011). Techniques derived from CBT have been found to enhance psychological flexibility in organizational settings (Bond, Hayes and Barnes-Holmes, 2006). The need for flexibility in coping styles is also discussed in Chapter 9.

There are other benefits of using CBT techniques; there is evidence that they can help people who have experienced work-related trauma to deal more effectively with initial symptoms and build a greater capacity to manage stress over the longer term (Lowinger and Rombom, 2012), which is clearly synonymous with resilience. Moreover, CBT can enable practitioners who have experienced long-term sickness absence to successfully manage their return to work (Lagerveld et al., 2012). Managing the conflict inherent in stressful interprofessional relationships within the helping professions can also be enhanced with CBT-based interventions (Brunero, Cowan and Fairbrother, 2008). In summary, CBT can offer simple but effective techniques to enable social workers to manage the everyday stress of their practice, avoid direct or vicarious trauma and develop sustainable resilience.

Application of CBT

People generally approach situations in their life with sets of assumptions about themselves and others, which are based on their previous experiences and established thinking styles. The following practice example uses Scott's experience as a mental health social worker who is attending a review tribunal to illustrate this point.

It is not Scott's ability that is the issue here, or even his experience at the last tribunal, but the way that he has interpreted this. For example, he might think the following: 'The solicitor could tell that I wasn't good enough and I was an easy target'; 'I felt flustered, which shows that I did not know what I was doing' and 'I'm no good at tribunals, so the next one will be a disaster.' Scott has had a number of negative thoughts about his performance that will inevitably lead him to feel anxious about his performance in similar situations in future. If he fails to identify and subsequently address these negative thoughts, his stress will remain unchecked, he is likely to make further negative interpretations from his performance in his next tribunal, and so a negative cycle

PRACTICE FOCUS 6.1: SCOTT

Scott will view this forthcoming mental health tribunal based on his experience of previous tribunals. At the last tribunal hearing he attended, Scott was strongly challenged by the solicitor representing the service user. Scott felt flustered and uncertain about his opinion and consequently felt that he had not performed well at the tribunal; he then made the broad interpretation that he was not good in tribunals. As the next tribunal hearing approached, Scott started to have intrusive and negative thoughts about his ability and how he would perform. This caused him to feel increasingly anxious and wish that he did not have to attend the tribunal at all.

becomes established. Eventually this can have an impact, not only on attending tribunals, but on Scott's overall effectiveness as a social worker and his ability to deal with complex practice situations. His wellbeing, resilience and job performance, therefore, are likely to be impaired.

Scott's experience illustrates how negative thoughts can be identified, which is a useful starting point in managing work-related anxiety. The following exercise may be helpful in identifying our own potentially negative thinking.

EXERCISE 6.1

Catching negative thoughts

Identify a work or placement situation that you feel anxious about. Make a list of the thoughts that you have about your performance in that situation, using Scott's experience to give you some ideas. You are looking for any negative thoughts about your own performance and abilities. Sometimes identifying or catching these thoughts can be a bit uncomfortable, but we will subsequently move on to strategies to manage anxiety.

Work situation	Negative thought
Challenged on my opinion by a solicitor in a tribunal hearing.	'I felt flustered and anxious.' 'I am not doing a good job.'

CBT shows that it is how a situation is approached that sets the tone for how it will be interpreted. That interpretation and consequent emotional reaction is then maintained by paying particular attention to factors in an event that confirm that interpretation. When Scott attends his next tribunal, he may well have a heightened awareness to any challenges or perceived critical comments of him that may occur. He may also over-attend to any physical discomfort he experiences, believing that he is visibly flustered. Scott then interprets this experience in the context of further negative thinking, which exacerbates anxiety and further inhibits his performance.

Negative thoughts tend to follow certain patterns or types of interpretation: these are effectively thinking errors. The next step in the CBT technique is to spot which thinking error is being used.

Thinking errors

As discussed above, cognitive patterns are crucial in determining how events are construed. They dictate whether an event is interpreted in a positive way (that supports resilience), or a more negative one (which is likely to engender stress). Cognitive distortions, or thinking errors, are the patterns of thinking that serve to reinforce a particular negative view of an individual's ability to function and cope, and lead to the expectation that it will *always* be the same, or perhaps even get worse. Identifying, understanding and challenging thinking errors are a critical part of the CBT approach to changing experiences of stress and fostering resilience.

Types of thinking errors are summarized in Table 6.1.

Returning to Scott and his difficult tribunal experience; when he was challenged in the tribunal setting he made several thinking errors. Scott believed that the challenge was personal to him based on his competency and performance = *personalization*; he over-attended to his experience of feeling flustered and interpreted this as meaning he was not performing well or doing his job properly = *emotional reasoning*; and he approached the next tribunal with the expectation that it would be difficult and that he would perform poorly = *over-generalization*.

Understanding which thinking errors are being used makes it easier to challenge them, so being able to spot those thinking errors is our important next step.

Having identified the thinking errors, the next step is to challenge the negative thoughts and generate alternatives. These alternatives are

Table 6.1 Thinking errors

Thinking error	Explanation
Catastrophizing	Imagining or believing the worst that can happen – 'making a mountain out of a molehill'.
All-or-nothing thinking	Polarized thinking, where things should happen 'always' or 'never', leaving no room for flexible interpretation; 'black-and-white' thinking that does not permit any uncertainty.
Jumping to conclusions: mind-reading/fortune-telling	Making decisions about what has happened or is going to happen, or what people are thinking, without gathering any evidence.
Emotional reasoning	Interpreting feelings as though they were facts.
Over-generalizing	Interpreting a single event, or aspect of an event, as an established pattern that will always have that outcome.
Labelling	Interpreting events or people in terms of negative labels, for example attributing a person's actions to their character instead of some accidental attribute.
Mental filtering	Filtering out contradictory or positive information that does not fit with a negative view, and selectively attending to confirming evidence.
Magnification/ minimization	Emphasizing the importance of some information and minimizing the importance of others.
Personalization	Taking responsibility for things that are not under personal control, or interpreting things in a personal way when they are, in fact, neutral.

less emphatic, more flexible and less judgemental and therefore less likely to result in an anxious response. It is important to bear in mind, however, that the original negative thoughts and thinking errors are well established and consequently easier to believe in than the new alternatives. The principle of practice needs to be applied to the new interpretations, so that they can become more established beliefs and assumptions.

In order to review and challenge established negative thinking patterns, it is vital to draw upon and augment already established strengths. Padesky and Mooney (2012, p. 284) emphasize the role of using existing strengths to develop a personal model of resilience. They suggest a 'Search for Strengths' approach which involves examining the activities that individuals already engage in, and how difficulties and obstacles are overcome. This technique was originally

EXERCISE 6.2

Spotting thinking errors

Using the situation set out in Exercise 6.1, review the negative thoughts you highlighted, using the table above to help you to identify which thinking error you are using.

Work situation	Negative thought	Thinking error
Challenged on my opinion by a solicitor in a tribunal hearing.	'I felt flustered and anxious.' 'I am not doing a good job.'	Emotional reasoning Social workers should not feel flustered – therefore if I feel this way it must mean I am not doing a good job.

developed for service users, but it is just as relevant for the social work practitioner who wishes to enhance their resilience. In order to identify established skills, it is important to look at behaviour that is well practised.

Returning to Scott's situation; as well attending tribunals, he also regularly writes applications for funding panels. He can use this experience to identify skills that can be utilized in a different setting. Identifying these strengths will enable Scott to challenge his negative thinking. In identifying strengths in order to overcome stressful obstacles, Scott is viewing such obstacles through a 'resilience lens' (Padesky and Mooney, 2012, p. 287). Emphasizing the importance of proactive resilience-building strategies (see Chapter 2), it is important to actively identify strengths in advance of the stressful situation, so they are readily available to challenge any negative thoughts. Spending time on this now will engender resilient approaches to stressful situations in the future.

We have now 'caught' the negative thoughts, 'spotted' the thinking error and 'noticed' the established skills. We are now ready to challenge negative thinking to develop alternative thoughts that more accurately represent the situation, are strengths-based, and minimize anxiety and promote self-efficacy. Without challenging his negative thinking, there is potential for Scott to generalize these thinking errors to other areas of his practice, for his level of anxiety to increase, and for him to act in

EXERCISE 6.3

Identifying strengths

Think about your role on a day-to-day basis, whether you are an experienced social work practitioner or student. Pay particular attention to the more complex tasks that are the most challenging to achieve. Write a list of the tasks you undertake, and the skills you use to achieve them. Here are some of the strengths that Scott has identified. Use these to help you identify your own strengths.

Writing funding applications	*Ability to extrapolate essential information*
Meeting funding panel deadlines	Ability to organize time

ways to try to avoid attending tribunal hearings altogether. If Scott evaluated his thinking errors he might generate these alternatives:

Personalization – 'It is the role of tribunal members to challenge the evidence that is presented to them. A robust challenge does not mean I am not doing a good job.'

Emotional reasoning – 'I might feel a bit flustered, but that does not mean that what I have to say is not valid.'

Over-generalization – 'Because that particular tribunal was difficult does not mean that they will all be the same in future.'

Scott has developed some good alternative statements that can be used to help him prepare for his next tribunal. Instead of feeling anxious and avoidant, he can approach the situation reminding himself of the skills that he possesses and, accordingly, feeling more competent and confident in his ability to perform. Exercise 6.4 is an opportunity for you to challenge negative thinking and generate alternate statements that are factual but not critical.

All four stages of the CBT technique have now been completed:

1. Catching negative thoughts
2. Spotting thinking errors
3. Identifying strengths
4. Developing alternative thinking

EXERCISE 6.4

Challenging negative thinking

Look at the table that you generated from Exercise 6.2. You have your list of negative thoughts and the types of thinking errors that you used. Drawing on your list of strengths, generate some alternative statements that are more realistic, have a different interpretation, and do not follow the typical thinking-error pattern.

Work situation	Negative thought	Thinking error	Alternative thought
Challenged on my opinion by a solicitor in a tribunal hearing.	'I felt flustered and anxious.' 'I am not doing a good job.'	Emotional reasoning 'Social workers should not feel flustered. If I feel this way it must mean I am not doing a good job.'	I am treating a feeling as a fact, but it is just a feeling. 'I might feel a bit flustered but that does not mean that what I have to say is still not valid.'

These are the tools to help us learn from difficult and stressful experiences and be prepared for the next challenge in a way that enables us to feel more competent, confident and resilient. As with any new skill, however, practice is required to make it reliable, so we will look at another case example to see how the technique works in a different situation.

At this juncture the scenario is all-too familiar. The struggle to put worrying thoughts out of our head is frequently unsuccessful. The notes take longer to write up as we are distracted and lack focus, and we are likely to take the anxious thoughts about the service user home with us. As an alternative, we will demonstrate how using a CBT approach could help Jenna to manage her thinking, focus on the task of record-keeping that she has set herself, and reduce her overall level of anxiety.

PRACTICE FOCUS 6.2: JENNA

It is 3.30 on Friday afternoon. Jenna has come back to the office having completed her home visits for the day. Before she leaves, she needs to document the information about her service-user contacts so that it is available for the weekend duty team. Jenna has just started to write her notes when she is handed a message that a service user has telephoned and needs to speak to her urgently. Jenna telephones the service user back and learns that he is concerned about a letter he has received about his benefit entitlement. The service user is emphatic in saying that he must see Jenna that afternoon. Checking her diary, Jenna realizes she is due to see the service user on the following Tuesday and feels that the current issue is not urgent. Jenna suggests to the service user that they could discuss the letter during Tuesday's appointment. The service user is well known to Jenna and has a history of self-harming and risky behaviour. He is upset and insistent on the telephone, but Jenna follows the established care plan of trying to help the service user to understand the difference between 'being' urgent and 'feeling' urgent, and she reassures him that she will go through the letter with him at his next appointment and help him consider its implications.

Jenna then turns her attention to her record-keeping, but finds that she cannot concentrate. She feels tired and wants to get her notes written so that she can go home, but instead feels inhabited by worrying thoughts about the service user. She fears that she will feel this way throughout the weekend.

Jenna identifies the following negative thoughts:

'What if I haven't made the right decision?'
'What if something happens between now and when I see the service user on Tuesday?'
'What if the service user makes a complaint about me?'

These do not seem unreasonable thoughts in and of themselves; it is the implied meaning behind them that engenders the anxiety. The next step is to explore these thoughts further by considering Jenna's potential answers to the question that she poses.

'What if I haven't made the right decision?' – 'Something awful will happen.'
'What if something happens between now and when I see the service user on Tuesday?' – 'It will be my fault.'
'What if the service user makes a complaint about me?' – 'My manager will think that I am no good at my job.'

The next step is to identify if there are any thinking errors taking place.

'Something awful will happen' – *Fortune-telling*
'It will be my fault' – *Personalization*
'My manager will think I am no good at my job' – *Mind-reading*

Having identified these as thinking errors makes it easier to offer a challenge and begin to develop alternatives.

'*Something awful will happen*' – 'I can't know what will happen; I have been certain that awful things will happen in the past and I have been wrong. Something *might* happen, but that is not the same as something *will* happen.'
'*It will be my fault*' – 'There are some things I am responsible for and some I am not. I can be responsible for making the best decision possible and following protocol. I have made my decision based on the care plan and the evidence we have about what is helpful for this service user.'
'*My manager will think I am no good at my job*' – 'My manager understands the difficult decisions that have to be made in practice. My manager gave me some good feedback about my work last week. If there was a complaint from this service user, it would not mean that I am not good at all – that is over-generalizing.'

By undertaking this process, Jenna is able to challenge some of her more extreme thinking and thus reduce her level of anxiety. Notice that Jenna also remembers receiving some positive feedback from her manager and uses that to help her challenge her thinking. By identifying strengths, Jenna's alternative thoughts become more powerful and therefore she is more likely to take notice of that thinking rather than the original negative thinking. The short-term impact of this is that Jenna is able to manage her discomfort at that point in time, and enable herself to focus on the task that she needs to undertake more effectively. It prevents her from overly attending to one potential source of concern and risk whilst potentially missing others; for example, there may be a greater risk to the wellbeing of service users in not leaving clear notes for the duty team. This process also facilitates learning from the situation, in that Jenna can more accurately reflect on her actions and discuss these with her supervisor without feeling overwhelmed by expectations of catastrophe and judgement. This learning is likely to enhance her psychological flexibility, her ability to manage stress and her emotional resilience.

Conclusion

This chapter has outlined the ways in which CBT can help social work practitioners enhance their emotional resilience. The core principles of CBT have been outlined and we have worked through a process that focuses on catching negative thoughts, spotting thinking errors, identifying strengths and developing alternative thinking. The case examples have demonstrated how following this process can challenge entrenched and negative cognitions to generate new thinking patterns and, more importantly, new behavioural outcomes.

A key element in making change is working through this process and then practising new strategies; undertaking the exercises in this chapter will help us to do this. Difficulties in applying this technique arise due to the well-established nature of our thinking patterns. We are very well-practised in interpreting events in a particular way so that alternatives can sound somewhat insincere or unconvincing. Repeating these exercises in different situations, however, will help to embed the technique so that avoiding thinking errors and developing alternative interpretations become an integrated strategy, not only to manage anxiety in specific situations but also to develop proactive resilient techniques.

Making any change requires sustained effort and practice which, for the busy and stressed social worker, may feel like an unaffordable luxury. The evidence-base for CBT is nonetheless compelling and it offers a realistic opportunity for social work practitioners to develop emotional resilience and enhance the service they provide.

ADDITIONAL RESOURCES

Bamber, M. (2006) *CBT for Occupational Stress in Health Professionals: Introducing a Schema-Focused Approach.* Hove: Routledge.

Branch, R. & Willson, B. (2010) *Cognitive Behavioural Therapy For Dummies*, 2nd edn. Chichester: John Wiley.

Greenberger, D. & Padesky, C.A. (1995) *Mind Over Mood: Change How You Feel by Changing the Way You Think*. New York: Guilford Press.

Neenan, M. & Dryden, W. (2004) *Cognitive Therapy: 100 Key Points and Techniques.* Hove and New York: Brunner-Routledge.

Padesky.com (http://padesky.com) for Mental Health Professionals.

CHAPTER 7

Mindfulness for resilience in social work

Rose Parkes and Susan Kelly

CHAPTER OVERVIEW

Mindfulness, the ability to focus one's awareness on the present moment while acknowledging and accepting feelings, thoughts and bodily sensations, has strong potential to build resilience. This chapter sets out some of the key concepts and practices that can be utilized to cultivate mindfulness, providing insight into how social workers can use it in their professional and personal lives. The chapter begins by offering a practical definition of mindfulness before outlining research findings that document its role in promoting resilience and its underlying competencies. Some of the main practices used in mindfulness meditation are subsequently outlined and their benefits in the social work context are considered. Also explored are the ways in which mindfulness training can used to expand awareness of the present moment which, in turn, can help social workers manage stress more effectively, improve their self-care practices, and notice and celebrate the positive elements of their work. Practice examples will be provided throughout to illustrate the characteristics of mindfulness practice and its potential benefits.

What is mindfulness, and why is it important?

In essence, mindfulness is the ability to actively pay attention to the present moment and acknowledge and accept feelings without judging them as 'good' or 'bad'. Over the last decade, mindfulness has become extremely popular both in the popular press and academic literature. Mindfulness practice has been found to have many benefits for personal and professional functioning such as greater self-control, objectivity and flexibility, improved mental clarity, concentration and memory, and the ability to relate to others and oneself with kindness and acceptance (Davis and Hayes, 2011). It can also enhance stress-management skills and promote psychological and physical health (Kabat-Zinn, 1994; Cohen-Katz et al., 2005a; Cohen-Katz et al., 2005b; Koszycki et al., 2007; Marchand, 2012; Ruths et al., 2013; Virgili, 2013). Indeed, the UK National Institute for Health and Clinical Excellence (NICE) now recommends the use of Mindfulness-Based Cognitive Therapy as relapse prevention for those who have previously experienced depression (NICE, 2009).

As well as in clinical settings, mindfulness-based training programmes are increasingly being used in the workplace as part of staff development and wellbeing initiatives. At the same time, there is an increasing interest in the potential for mindfulness to foster positive self-care strategies and compassion and other interpersonal skills in helping professionals (Gerdes and Segal, 2011). Mindfulness practice is likely to be useful, therefore, in supporting wellbeing in social workers by helping them develop the competencies associated with resilience, such as reflection, accurate empathy and emotional literacy.

The nature of mindfulness

Mindfulness has its origins in ancient Buddhist philosophy, but is increasingly used as a secular training programme in clinical settings, workplaces and the wider community. Although mindfulness has been defined above, like resilience, it is a complex term with multiple meanings. Put simply, mindfulness can be a trait ('John is a mindful person'), a state ('John was mindful of his decision') and a practice ('John is practising mindfulness meditation') (Shapiro and Carlson, 2009; Keng, Smoski and Robins, 2011). Levels of mindfulness have been shown to vary across individuals, but it is now widely accepted that mindfulness can be developed through training. This chapter will primarily consider how intentionally cultivating mindfulness practices may support social workers' resilience.

A widely recognized definition of mindfulness is offered by Jon Kabat-Zinn, a key founder of mindful practice, who describes it as the awareness that arises from:

paying attention in a particular way: on purpose, in the present moment, and non-judgementally. This kind of attention nurtures greater awareness, clarity and acceptance of present moment reality. (Kabat-Zinn, 1994, p. 4)

Puddicombe adds that mindfulness meditation:

isn't about becoming a different person, a new person, or even a better person. It's about training in awareness and understanding how and why you think and feel the way you do, and getting a healthy sense of perspective in the process. (Puddicombe, 2012, p. 15)

At its simplest, mindful awareness is about being fully *present* in life, knowing what you are experiencing while you are experiencing it, and relating to that experience in an open and receptive way, without judgement. In other words, it is the way in which a person takes note, makes sense of, or gives attention to their daily life (Brown, Ryan and Creswell, 2007). This is in contrast to the situation many of us find ourselves in, where the demands of a 'frantic world' (Williams and Penman, 2011, p. 7) may lead to living life on 'automatic pilot', lost in thought about the past or future, while missing moments of richness and choice in everyday life. Consider the difference between these two scenarios:

Scenario 1 – You go into the office and switch on your computer. It takes forever to start. Thoughts of how hopeless the office computers are come rushing in and then escalate into wider frustrations as you grit your teeth, clench your jaw and become increasingly annoyed.
Scenario 2 – You go into the office and switch on your computer. It takes forever to start. You notice that your jaw has clenched up and you realize that you are getting angry with an inanimate object about something you can do very little about. So you decide to look out of the window for a few minutes instead.

Both these scenarios take the same amount of time but, rather than reacting automatically, a more mindful response in the second scenario leads to a choice about what to do with the time. Mindfulness can be seen to be operating at several levels here:

1. Practising mindfulness can allow an increased awareness of body signals which may indicate stress for that individual (such as the clenched jaw in this situation). This simple awareness provides an opportunity to respond differently.

2. For an already busy social worker, deciding to try and deal with the computer issue in a team meeting rather than allowing it to impact negatively at that moment is a more helpful response than entering into escalating thought processes which may exacerbate stress.
3. Intentionally choosing to move your attention elsewhere (whether that is looking out of the window, focusing on your breath, or saying a few words to a colleague) is a more positive and mindful response and may make you feel more optimistic about the day ahead.

These are some of the benefits of being aware of life as it happens and acting consciously, based on this 'knowing what is happening now'. It does not exclude planning, reflecting on past cases, critical thinking or decision-making. Nor does it mean we should be walking around in some kind of blissful state. Hick explains mindfulness thus:

> This is not a passive resignation, but rather acceptance of that which is uncontrollable, or lack of resistance to that which is already happening. From this stance, we are in alignment with life and better able to face difficulties with more balance and options. (Hick, 2009, p. 4)

The concept of mindfulness has been introduced but, in many ways, it is best understood by its practice. The activity below will allow you to try out a simple mindful awareness practice.

EXERCISE 7.1

Taking a mindful pause
Place this book to one side, close your eyes and become aware of what is happening for you at this moment, having read the introduction to this chapter.

■ What thoughts are going through your mind?
■ Are there any emotions present?
■ Do you feel any body sensations?

Whatever you notice, there is no need to judge yourself or try to change anything. Maybe you are feeling distracted? Perhaps you are eager to get to the next part of the book? Do you find yourself thinking of anything else while you read through the introduction? Did any words or phrases trigger an emotional response or a particular thought? Whatever you notice, just allow it to be exactly as it is: resist the temptation to change how things are and instead only pay attention to your actual experience. You might even name it quietly in your mind as 'a sense of rushing is here' or 'feelings of distraction' or 'tense shoulders' are present. In doing this exercise, you are intentionally bringing awareness to your experience, at this moment in time, with a sense of acknowledgement and acceptance: this is mindfulness. This chapter now examines approaches to learning mindfulness and how they are linked to resilience and its associated competencies.

There are an increasing number of mindfulness-based approaches, the full breadth of which is beyond the scope of this chapter. Two of the most accessible approaches for supporting resilience in social work, however, are the eight-week secular mindfulness training programme known as Mindfulness-Based Stress Reduction (MBSR) and Mindfulness-Based Cognitive Therapy (MBCT). Both options offer intensive training in mindfulness meditation and are taught on the basis of evidence-based psychological and physiological models of stress and depression, respectively. Kabat-Zinn developed the first secular mindfulness course using MBSR in 1979 at the University of Massachusetts Medical Centre (USA), where he worked with people experiencing varying degrees of pain and distress as a result of chronic illness, with considerable success. MBSR courses are now offered in many countries and they have been the subject of extensive research. As mentioned above, they have been shown to be beneficial in supporting psychological health, empathy, self-compassion, satisfaction and quality of life as well as clinical outcomes (Kabat-Zinn, 1994; Cohen-Katz et al., 2005a; Cohen-Katz et al., 2005b; Koszycki et al., 2007; Marchand, 2012; Ruths et al., 2013; Virgili, 2013). In addition, studies have reported that MBSR can reduce stress, anxiety, depression and rumination (Keng et al., 2011; Marchand, 2012).

More recently, researchers in the UK and Canada (e.g. Teasdale, Segal and Williams, 1995; Segal et al., 2012; Williams and Penman, 2011) have co-developed MBCT, an integration of MBSR and some aspects of cognitive behavioural therapy (Chapter 6 provides more guidance on CBT approaches) as a targeted approach for people with a history of depression. The primary evidence-base for MBCT so far is in relation to its effects in reducing recurrent depression, but there is also increasing evidence for other benefits, including stress reduction (Crane, 2009). Mindfulness training consists of practices that are often categorized into 'formal', and 'informal' or 'everyday' practices. *Formal mindfulness practices* include meditations like sitting meditation, mindful walking and mindful movement such as yoga and Tai Chi. The less well-known *informal* or *everyday practices* involve bringing focused attention to everyday activities like eating, walking or brushing teeth.

EXERCISE 7.2

Drinking a cup of tea mindfully

1. Make yourself a cup of tea or another hot drink and find somewhere quiet where you can be undisturbed for approximately 10 minutes.
2. Start by holding the cup in both hands and imagine that you have never seen this object before. Notice its weight and any texture that you feel where your skin touches the cup. Tune into the warmth of the cup. Where do you notice this?
3. Now really look at the drink and notice the detail of what you see. As you do this, you might notice your mind has wandered off, or maybe you have judgements about the activity: this is all fine, and noticing the mind wandering off is part of mindfulness practice. Every time it does this, just quickly note where your mind has gone, then return your attention to the activity without judging yourself as 'doing things wrong'. The intention is just to notice whatever comes into your experience, whether that is the colour or shape of the cup or a thought about the rest of your day.
4. Now raise the cup to your nose slowly and see how close it has to be before you can smell anything – if at all. As you smell the drink, notice if there are any changes taking place in your mouth or stomach – any mouth-watering or other sensations? Explore this.
5. Now form an intention to take a sip and move the cup to your lips, very slowly, pausing to feel the temperature on your lips. Is it cool enough to drink? Explore this.
6. Now take a small sip and hold it in your mouth for about 30 seconds. Notice the flavours in your mouth as you swish the drink around. Really hone in on the fine detail – where on your tongue are you picking up any sensations? Are there any urges to swallow? See if it is possible to resist your usual pattern of drinking.
7. Then swallow and see if you can follow the sensations of the liquid as it moves down your throat.
8. Drink the rest of the tea mindfully.

These everyday mindfulness practices are based around activities which may already be a part of a busy social worker's day and offer the opportunity to pause and notice the quality of these activities as they are experienced. Whether these everyday activities, on examination, turn out to be pleasant or unpleasant, they offer the chance to 'shift mental gears' from a 'doing' mode of mind to a 'being' mode of mind, which is less goal-driven and allows the individual to be more fully present (Segal et al., 2012, p. 68). In cultivating this kind of refined and non-judgemental attention, experience can unfold in interesting ways. Through developing this ability to 'shift mental gears' flexibly and at will, social work practitioners can be better supported to manage challenging situations so that they can facilitate positive self-care in the midst of their busy working life.

Try out the activity outlined in Exercise 7.2 so that you can experience an everyday, informal action in a mindful way, focusing on the present. Try to make the activity like an experiment: see if you can bring your full attention to each stage by taking your time accomplishing each instruction.

Looking back over this experience of drinking mindfully, consider whether you noticed anything different about the drink, its smell, its taste, or the sensation in your mouth. The purpose of this exercise is to help us become intentionally aware of the present. Developing and practising intentional awareness through mindfulness practices can facilitate a greater understanding of bodily sensations in other situations which, in turn, can allow us greater insight into how our body responds to stress. This chapter now considers how we can respond to stress more effectively through mindful practices.

Responding to stress with mindful awareness

As outlined in Chapter 1, social work involves working day to day in challenging and often highly stressful situations. Mindfulness training can increase awareness of habitual reactions to these situations and enhance the ability to see them more clearly and through a non-critical lens. Bringing a quality of acceptance to present-moment experience, whether that experience is positive or negative, is central to mindfulness so that the *attitude* generated is that of compassion and non-judgement (Hülsheger et al., 2013). From this position of clear awareness of what is actually happening in any moment, the space for taking more skilful and appropriate action arises. The case of Rima, a social worker in a busy Children and Families team, illustrates this point.

Rima is in a case conference which has run over by more than an hour. She is becoming increasingly stressed as she knows that she will be late for her next appointment, which is a home visit to a young person. When the meeting is finished, Rima rushes to her car as quickly as possible and drives away, but soon finds herself stuck in traffic. She feels very anxious and starts worrying about whether the young person will wait for her or might leave before she gets there. If he does not wait, she realizes that she will have to make another visit, which makes her feel even more stressed, as she really does not have the time to do any more home visits with everything else that is currently going on. Rima wonders why she cannot seem to manage her workload as well as everyone else and whether she is really suitable for social work. She has always had this problem with managing her workload, right back to when she was at school. If only she could learn to focus clearly instead of always being late. As this train of thought continues, Rima becomes more and more agitated and tense, gripping the steering wheel hard. Her breathing becomes shallow and more rapid as she spends the rest of the journey worrying about how she can fit in another visit, and feeling irritated with herself for being late yet again.

When Rima arrives at the young person's home he is just returning from school. The visit goes ahead as planned, but Rima is uncomfortable as she finds it hard to concentrate and is distracted and anxious. She worries that this might affect her relationship with this young person negatively in the future.

Like Rima, it is often easy to become overly focused on unhelpful thoughts about the past or future, rather than what is happening in the present moment. Without the ability to bring ourselves actively into the present, much of our time may be spent thinking about the past or worrying about the future: reacting as if we are on automatic pilot. The reality here for Rima is that, in her present situation, there was very little she could actually do about the case conference running over time or being in stuck in traffic. She was unable to see this clearly, however, as she ruminated about her perceived deficiencies as a practitioner (making internal, permanent and universal judgements about herself and her abilities: see Chapter 9 for more details) and then her thoughts raced ahead to generate a 'worst-case' scenario. In the meantime,

Rima's anxious thoughts were manifesting a physiological stress response in the form of a 'fight or flight' reaction, adding another layer to her feelings of anxiety and irritability (Hanson, 2009), undermining her capacity to be fully present with the young person and engage in some useful work (see Chapter 9, for a discuss about the physiological response to stress and its implications for wellbeing). Mindfulness could help Rima to notice her rushing as she came out of the conference, and to take a more measured approach to her next steps.

The next activity is a mindfulness practice which may be useful to use in Rima's situation and in similar circumstances to both settle the mind and generate a clearer awareness. This practice was developed as part of MBCT and is now included as a core practice in most mindfulness training programmes. It can act as a bridge from more formal meditation practice to the 'real world', and can be practised anywhere at any time. This 'mini-meditation' is made up of three distinct steps or phases but, despite the title of the activity, it does not have to last for exactly three minutes. It is more important that you have a general sense of spending a little time on each of the three stages.

If Rima had completed this simple practice, she could perhaps have recognized that, no matter how much she rushed, she would still be late, and to consider a different response to the situation. A more measured approach would be to telephone the young person or parent/carer to explain the situation, so that she could drive to the appointment in a more mindful way. Instead of grasping the steering wheel tightly and worrying about the future consequences, Rima could have used awareness to bring about a different response. She could have sat back in her seat and softened the tense areas in her body while enjoying a few moments of peace in her car. This could have also helped her to prepare more effectively for the visit so that she could fully engage with the young person. In reading Rima's experience, you may recognize that you sometimes find it easy to become focused on the past or future and not fully engage with the present, which may cause you to experience stressful reactions; practising mindfulness can help you alleviate this.

Practising mindfulness can help us cope with life's demands in a positive and resourceful way, so that we maintain health and wellbeing in unfavourable and challenging conditions (McCann et al., 2013). It can enhance self-awareness and self-acceptance, which are key components of resilience. Mindfulness also has the potential to enable social workers to recognize and manage difficult emotions more effectively (Napoli and Bonifas, 2011). The next section considers this issue.

EXERCISE 7.3

The three-minute breathing space
Start by making a shift in your posture, whether you are standing or sitting, in order to indicate your intention to step into the present moment. You could sit upright, but in a relaxed manner and be aware of your feet as they touch the ground. Close your eyes, or lower and soften your gaze.

Step 1: Noticing and acknowledging
- Ask yourself 'What is going on with me right now?'
- 'What thoughts are here now in my mind?' There is no need to change them in any way, just acknowledge them. You might say to yourself, 'judging thoughts or worrying thoughts are here'.
- 'What feelings are present?' Just notice what you are feeling, without trying to push these emotions away or being critical of them.
- 'What bodily sensations am I experiencing?' Notice any areas of tension or other bodily sensations without trying to alter them in any way. See if you can just go along with your experiences as they are at this moment.

Step 2: Gathering
- Gently bring your attention to focus on the physical sensations of the breath in your body.
- Maybe you are aware of the rise and fall of your abdomen or chest.
- Perhaps you sense the air moving in and out of your nostrils or mouth.
- Deliberately focus your attention on each in-breath and each out-breath as they follow on from one another.
- There is no need to breathe in any particular way, or to hold your breath, just allow your body to breathe as it is.

Step 3: Expanding
- Expand your awareness so, in addition to your breath, it includes a sense of your body as a whole.
- Notice your posture and facial expression.
- Have a sense of the space around you.
- As this practice ends, see if you can take this sense of expanded awareness into the next moments of your day.

Recognizing and managing difficult emotions in social work

Although much research on mindfulness has examined its benefits for clinical populations (see above), some studies have begun to examine its potential to improve resilience (Hülsheger et al., 2013). Collard, Avny and Boniwell (2008) found evidence that mindfulness can foster wellbeing because it helps the individual to accept painful or difficult experiences in a non-judgemental manner. In essence, mindfulness encourages people to 'turn towards' difficult emotions with open interest, rather than denying or pushing feelings away (which is a normal human response in challenging situations). By facilitating self-knowledge and encouraging a focus on the present, mindfulness helps people gain insight into their reactions to challenging circumstances as well as their impermanent nature. Rather than mindfulness requiring concentration on one particular event or object, it is a liberating mindset that involves being receptive to whatever transpires, encouraging the viewing of circumstances in an objective and detached manner, thereby creating a more positive approach to life's challenges. Practice focus 7.2 considers the impact of the denial and suppression of difficult emotions on social work practice and then focuses on how mindfulness may be used to overcome this tendency.

PRACTICE FOCUS 7.2: LEON

Leon is a social worker in a mental health support service. He has been asked to complete some support work with a vulnerable adult, Mr Laynam, who is living semi-independently in the community after a long period in hospital. When Leon makes his first home visit to Mr Laynam, he is flooded with anxiety. Mr Laynam bears a strong resemblance to a previous service user who took his own life. He finds himself thinking back to what happened with this former service user and, feeling overwhelmed, ends the visit very quickly. Back at the office, Leon tries to push these thoughts out of his mind, but they just keep going around in his head. He does not want to mention his strong reaction to his supervisor as he knows it is not rational, and he feels anxious about being seen as unable to cope. As the weeks pass, Leon becomes more anxious at work and his sleeps begins to suffer. Leon telephones Mr Laynam, but never seems to find time to visit him and therefore feels very guilty.

Mindfulness practice offers a different way of relating to difficult emotions which might help Leon reduce his anxiety. He could, for example, use practices like 'sitting meditation' to allow his feelings to come out rather than being suppressed or denied. Developing this wider perspective through mindfulness meditation practices could, furthermore, enable Leon to notice when he is lost in thought or ruminating, so that he can step outside it and take a more skilful approach. This might include noticing his resistance to seek help in supervision in a non-judgemental manner, and recognizing that his thoughts about being seen as weak are just thoughts that are not necessarily accurate. This 're-perceiving' or meta-cognition (that is, the ability to see thoughts as mental events) is considered to be a key mechanism of mindfulness (Turner, 2009; Thomas and Otis, 2010). By observing thoughts and feelings as they arise, without criticism, the intensity and frequency of unpleasant feelings can be reduced, as greater tolerance to uncomfortable sensations is engendered (Brown and Ryan, 2003; Levitt et al., 2004). The recognized benefits for individuals adopting this approach, and for social work practice more broadly, cannot be overstated, as workers are able to relate to themselves and service users in a more considered and emotionally receptive manner.

Mindfulness and reflective practice

Mindfulness increases the capacity for non-critical self-awareness and reflection (Bolton, 2010), while supporting attempts to make sense of thoughts, feelings, values and beliefs. The resulting self-knowledge can foster greater compassion towards the self and others (Chaskalson, 2011; Napoli and Bonifas, 2011; Gerdes and Segal, 2011). Indeed, Kessen and Turner (2012) argue that it is impossible to be non-judge-mental and empathize with others unless a high level of self-awareness has been attained. Similar observations have been made by Doxtdator (2012), who reports that the increasing evidence-base for the effective-ness of mindfulness has led to its growing acceptance by those in the secular field and, equally, for those with strongly held religious beliefs. It is worth pointing out that the use of some meditative approaches like yoga have been considered problematic by several faith groups (Driscoll, 2011; Russell, 2012) and, where mindfulness is associated with religious practices, there has been resistance to its use (McGarrigle and Walsh, 2011). As both MBSR and MBCT are entirely secular evidence-based programmes, however, such concerns are misguided.

Mindfulness, emotional exhaustion and job satisfaction

As discussed in previous chapters, social workers commonly experience high levels of job-related stress which can, in turn, impair personal wellbeing and professional functioning (McGarrigle and Walsh, 2011; Grant, 2013). Mindfulness training has strong potential to foster wellbeing by improving self-care and encouraging the worker to develop appropriate coping strategies to deal with the stress and the emotional impact of their work (Cunningham, 2004; Berceli and Napoli, 2006). Mindfulness can also help regulate negative moods by reducing rumination on tense or fraught encounters which, ultimately, engenders feelings of self-efficacy and wellbeing (Koszycki et al., 2007).

As well as decreasing stress, mindfulness training can also lead to a wide range of beneficial outcomes of relevance to social workers such as compassion satisfaction (Thomas and Otis, 2010) and enhanced feelings of personal competence (Shapiro et al., 2006). As discussed elsewhere in this book, helping professionals commonly experience compassion fatigue or vicarious trauma, where over-identification with service users' distress or emotional exhaustion may result in cynicism, withdrawal or avoidance strategies as a means of self-preservation. Thomas and Otis (2010) have argued that mindfulness helps practitioners to maintain appropriate emotional boundaries between themselves and service users, which is a key factor in developing accurate empathy and alleviating emotional exhaustion.

Like other helping professionals, social workers are frequently required to perform 'emotional labour' (Hochschild, 1983), which is the requirement to manage a discrepancy between the emotions they are required to display and those that they actually feel. For example, a social worker may need to appear outwardly calm and engaged in a threatening situation, whereas inwardly they might feel distress or fear. Although often necessary and desirable for effective practice, this type of emotional regulation can result in feelings of inauthenticity, emotional exhaustion and job dissatisfaction (Hülsheger et al., 2013). Mindfulness practice may be useful in such circumstances, as it engenders self-compassion (Birnie, Speca and Carlson, 2010).

Other benefits associated with mindfulness

Mindfulness training can bring many benefits to the social worker and their professional practice. Research findings indicate that mindful individuals are more likely to work in an anti-discriminatory manner because of their openness to others and non-judgemental perspective (Napoli and Bonifas, 2011). More specifically, Brown et al. (2007) found that mindfulness helps to reduce prejudice because the mindful practitioner is required to step back from their perceptions or interpretations of events (which are shaped by pre-existing schemata and past experiences) in order to see their perceptions for what they are: *an interpretation of reality*. By entering into this process, the individual is able to see that their interpretation is one of many possible perspectives, which enhances their cultural competence. This reduces depersonalization and cynicism and fosters an appreciation of the perspective of others (Cohen-Katz et al., 2005b; Kessen and Turner, 2012) which, in turn, builds job satisfaction, wellbeing and resilience.

Mindfulness can also enhance active listening skills by increasing awareness of the inner dialogue that occurs during the listening process (Goh, 2012). Often this 'inner chatter' can impede effective relationship-building, as the social worker's values and beliefs may prejudice their encounters and lead to service users being labelled. For example, feeling impatience, and acknowledging rather than denying this emotion, may enable a refocusing in the present moment. Indeed, through a gradual use of mindfulness and reflection, practitioners are able to be consciously aware of their listening behaviours and their emotional reactions. This means that they can move away from habitual responses that get in the way of actively engaging with those around them.

Research has been conducted into the benefits of resilience for social work students as well as experienced practitioners. Mindfulness is not only helpful in reducing the challenges of training, but it can also reduce students' feelings of anxiety and self-consciousness during initial encounters with service users, helping them to regulate their emotional responses and preventing the occurrence of counter-transference (Gockel et al., 2013). Mindfulness can also benefit social work students by facilitating collaborative learning in the classroom, reducing unease around learning activities and, when issues surrounding discriminatory practice are discussed, promote greater tolerance and understanding of difference by moderating defensiveness (Gockel et al., 2013). Being able to observe thoughts and feelings rather than ruminating on them can only foster a more open and compassionate demeanour which will aid effective practice, enhance wellbeing and build resilience that is sustainable. It is essential for social workers to develop ways to maintain their resilience for the duration of their careers, as well as during their training. Mindfulness practices have considerable potential to facilitate this, with clear benefits for both personal and professional life.

Mindfulness training as a vehicle for developing self-care strategies in the workplace

The MBSR programme initially developed by Kabat-Zinn was developed to combat stress; he believed that when the body, mind and spirit become overwhelmed with anxiety, a separation can occur which impairs individual functioning. Sapolsky's (2004) work reveals that even the *anticipation* (our emphasis) of stressful events can impair health and wellbeing. When the mind is preoccupied with work problems, it can be easy to miss the physical signs of anxiety as feelings are typically suppressed in such situations. Through allowing people to regularly check thoughts, emotions and bodily sensations, mindfulness can help people gain insight into what wellbeing feels like and, conversely, anything that disrupts it. Indeed, mindfulness training courses like MBSR include specific work on developing awareness of stress warning signs and how to develop action plans which include nourishing activities which can be purposefully cultivated to improve the quality of life. Mindfulness training, therefore, is a powerful approach for stress reduction and enhancing resilience. The various ways in which stress can impact on wellbeing and individual functioning and how to detect the early warning signs of stress are discussed further in Chapter 9.

Practice focus 7.3 illustrates how increased self-awareness through mindfulness can enable a mental health worker to develop helpful strategies to protect her own wellbeing and self-care.

As Lisa learned, mindful practices are useful because they help develop self-awareness and empower us to identify appropriate solutions to challenging situations. A study by McGarrigle and Walsh (2011) found that the value of mindfulness lies in its ability to sustain appropriate coping strategies so that workers can deal with stress and the emotional impact of their role. If practised regularly in the work place, mindfulness enabled them to deal with their stress more positively as

PRACTICE FOCUS 7.3: LISA

Lisa is an experienced social worker based in a Children and Families team. Lisa's team has recently gone through a difficult reorganization and she now has a new line manager and colleagues. All of these changes have left her feeling somewhat depleted and, on the recommendation of a friend, she decides to do a mindfulness course to see if this can help.

During the course, Lisa spends some time reflecting on how she usually reacts when she is experiencing stress. She is able to identify that she buries herself in her work when times get tough. This means she does less of the things she enjoys, such as cycling and seeing friends, that help to keep her well in spite of the stressors from work. Lisa also realizes that, when she feels this way, she retreats into herself and avoids discussing work issues with colleagues because she thinks that, if she admits that she is struggling, her competence will be questioned. The mindfulness course enables Lisa to understand that, although this coping strategy is 'an old habit and familiar friend', it will not improve her situation and is likely to make things worse. She learns to reflect on this with a sense of humour and self-compassion, as she notes that other participants on the course have similar unhelpful coping strategies, and she is not alone in using avoidance as a way of dealing with stress.

On her return to work, Lisa decides to share some of the 'warning signs' she has identified with her line manager in their next supervision session. She is pleased at how interested her line manager is. They agree that, in future, if she notices Lisa is more self-absorbed than usual, she will ask if she is OK and will remind her that this is one of the warning signs that they have agreed she will look out for. This connection and sharing of the responsibility to 'watch out for my warning signs' helps Lisa to feel more contained and less anxious.

they became compassionate towards themselves. This study also found that developing an awareness of the physical sensations they experienced in response to stress, and using mindful practices to calm themselves down helped participants to make better quality decisions.

Many organizations now promote mindfulness practices to support the wellbeing of social work practitioners. This means that mindfulness could become embedded in everyday working life under the leadership and guidance of senior managers. If introduced into social work settings as part of a wider toolbox of measures, this approach has the potential to help employees manage stress and generate resilience, as well as enhance the services they provide. Nonetheless, as discussed in other chapters, sufficient time and organizational support are required if long-term improvements to wellbeing are to be achieved and maintained.

Conclusion

This chapter has explored the concept of mindfulness and its role in promoting resilience and its associated competencies. Practising mindfulness offers an opportunity, not to eliminate the inevitable stressful situations social workers will face, but to relate to them in a different way. Developing and cultivating mindfulness practice takes time and considerable effort, but may provide new ways for social work professionals to enhance their own resilience and their professional practice. In the first instance, it can encourage a person to become aware of their thoughts, emotions and habitual ways of dealing with difficult situations. Secondly, once this self-awareness is in place, the individual is empowered to make a choice about how to respond in future. Painful encounters do not have to be suppressed or avoided, but mindful breathing and awareness teach acceptance so as to lessen the harmful effects of stressful situations. Thirdly, the practice may enhance service provision: active listening, compassion and accurate empathy have all been found to emanate from those who regularly undertake mindfulness meditation. As discussed throughout this book, these qualities are essential for building resilience, wellbeing and enhancing practice.

ADDITIONAL RESOURCES

Websites

http://bemindful.co.uk
The Mental Health Foundation's Be Mindful website provides a searchable database of many mindfulness courses in the UK and gives some level of screening of teachers who provide these courses. It includes a postcode search facility. You can also access their online mindfulness course on the website and view videos from some of the leading teachers and academics in the UK.

http://mindfulnessteachersuk.org.uk
This website contains information about the UK Guidelines for Teaching Mindfulness Courses and links to Mindfulness Teaching Training Providers.

www.franticworld.com
This website accompanies the book by Penman and Williams (see below) and incorporates a forum and details of events and retreats, as well as links to meditations.

Books

Chaskalson, M. (2011) *The Mindful Workplace: Developing Resilient Individuals and Resonant Organizations with MBSR*. Oxford: Wiley-Blackwell.

Hick, S. F. (2009) *Mindfulness and Social Work*. Chicago: Lyceum Books.

Kabat-Zinn, J. (2004) *Wherever You Go, There You Are*. London: Piatkus.

Silverton, S. (2012) *The Mindfulness Breakthrough: The Revolutionary Approach to Dealing with Stress, Anxiety and Depression*. London: Watkins.

Williams, P. M. & Penman, D. (2011) *Mindfulness: A Practical Guide to Finding Peace in a Frantic World*. London: Piatkus.

CHAPTER 8

Peer support and peer coaching

Sarah Baker and Kathryn Jones

CHAPTER OVERVIEW

The importance of social support in enhancing the wellbeing of helping professionals has been widely emphasized. Friends and family can provide emotional support during challenging times. Many people find that support from colleagues is particularly helpful, as they can empathize and generate options for change that are firmly grounded in the organizational context. Peer coaching formalizes this type of support; it refers to a dyadic relationship based on sharing experiences and practices in order to enhance learning and problem-solving as well as to build stress-management skills. Its intrinsic focus on human strengths and flourishing also means that peer coaching has strong potential to enhance emotional resilience. This chapter initially outlines the development and key principles of peer coaching. It subsequently explores how the technique can enable colleagues to work together in a structured and focused manner to seek solutions, achieve specific goals and enhance the competencies that form the foundations of emotional resilience.

Peer coaching: the context

A body of evidence indicates that social support from the workplace has strong potential to help social workers manage work-related stress (Adamson, Beddoe and Davys, 2012; Collins, 2008). Nonetheless, as social workers may be reluctant to disclose any distress to their line managers due to fear of being judged negatively (Barlow and Hall,

2007), it is important to identify a means of support from within professional networks that may be considered less threatening. Research conducted in different occupational settings has found that support from co-workers can be particularly effective in reducing stress, enhancing job satisfaction and preventing burnout (Um and Harrison, 1998). Developing supportive relationships with peers (or colleagues of equal status) may encourage social workers to speak more openly and honestly about any problems and difficulties they are experiencing without fear of judgement.

Colleagues frequently share problems as a way of 'letting off steam' or gaining reassurance, but there may be little scope for resolution or personal growth from such interactions. Peer coaching provides a range of techniques to *formalize* supportive relationships with colleagues. It facilitates a solution-focused approach that helps people reflect upon their knowledge, skills and other personal attributes in order to identify resolutions to current difficulties. As well as enhancing learning opportunities, peer coaching has strong potential to promote psychological wellbeing and resilience and the qualities that underpin it, such as self-knowledge, self-efficacy and feelings of personal accomplishment (Adamson et al., 2012; Kinman and Grant, 2011). A further advantage of the peer-coaching approach is its mutually beneficial nature. Rather than one person providing assistance and the other receiving it, colleagues can simultaneously adopt the role of a coach when supporting a co-worker, as can a coachee when receiving support themselves.

This chapter aims to help social workers develop an appreciation of the peer-coaching process and its many benefits. The roles and responsibilities of both coach and coachee are discussed and the importance of establishing trust and maintaining confidentiality considered. Practice examples and guidance are provided to illustrate how the coach facilitates the peer-coaching process and how the coachee indentifies and achieves personal goals. In order to appreciate the potential of peer coaching, it is initially important to establish how it differs from other support mechanisms typically used to assist social workers in their development, such as supervision and mentoring.

What is peer coaching, and why is it different from existing support initiatives?

Support for social work practitioners is currently available through supervision and, in some settings, informal peer-mentoring or 'buddying' schemes. Supervision is the principal means of providing support for growth and development within social work (See Chapter 4). In supervision, practitioners are encouraged to review their practice and focus on emerging concerns in order to learn from experience. Supervision also provides an opportunity to discuss workload and accountability, as well as raise awareness of recent practice innovations, research and opportunities for professional development (Carroll, 2007). Supervision is therefore an effective way to support the development of social workers and ensure best practice. Nonetheless, as highlighted above and previously in Chapter 4, the inherent power imbalance within the supervisory relationship means that social workers may find it difficult to share their worries or concerns.

Mentoring can also facilitate supportive workplace relationships and promote learning and personal growth. Although mentoring and coaching approaches are often referred to synonymously, there are some important differences (Kutilek and Earnest, 2001). In mentoring, the mentor is seen as the 'expert' who draws on their knowledge and experience to guide and support their mentee (Greene and Grant, 2003). Mentoring can help social workers develop their skills, but may be less effective in facilitating a constructive, solution-focused approach to solving problems or building the competencies that underlie resilience.

Like supervision and mentoring, peer coaching can facilitate problem-solving and reflection, but it has many additional benefits. It is a collaborative relationship based on equality, mutual support and co-operation. Within the peer-coaching relationship, both parties (that is, the coach and coachee) are of equal status. Rather than 'teach or tell', the coach acts as a facilitator to help their coachee develop realistic solutions and options for change (Bresser and Wilson, 2006; Megginson and Clutterbuck, 2005). Peer coaching provides a supportive, but challenging framework to help people interrogate a problem from multiple perspectives, identify their personal strengths, and generate goals that are stretching, yet achievable. The importance of 'stretch' goals and identifying personal strengths and resources has been identified in Chapters 4 and 5 in the context of supervision and goal-setting. Such an approach can help change negative thinking patterns and foster an optimistic, strengths-focused perspective that develops self-awareness, reflective ability and self-efficacy. Thus, building resilience could be considered integral to the peer-coaching process.

Mutual respect, trust and confidentiality are fundamental to peer coaching, as the coachee may feel vulnerable as they disclose their thoughts, feelings and fears. It is therefore imperative that the coachee is assured that whatever is said within the relationship is confidential and will not be shared with others. The practice example below considers the importance of establishing clear ground rules before commencing a peer-coaching relationship.

PRACTICE FOCUS 8.1: MARGARET

Margaret is highly respected within her team, particularly with regard to her exceptional understanding of the wishes and feelings of the children she works with. Unfortunately, Margaret is poor at documenting assessments for court work and both she and her manager have identified this as an area which she needs to develop. This is causing her considerable stress and anxiety as well as impacting negatively on her job performance. Margaret's manager suggested that she establish a peer-coaching relationship with a colleague, David, whose report-writing skills are generally considered excellent. Initially, Margaret was wary of explaining her difficulties to David, as she felt that it could damage her reputation if he disclosed her weaknesses to other team members. During their first meeting, David reassured Margaret that everything that was said within the coaching sessions would remain confidential, and he would not share any information with her colleagues or her line manager. David understood that peer coaching is reciprocal in nature, and involves clarity regarding role and a reciprocal understanding about purpose. To this end, he explained to Margaret that he was looking forward to learning personally from her strengths in building relationships with children. On this basis, trust was established and Margaret and David were able to build a solution-focused relationship based on mutual trust and respect.

Peer coaches provide non-judgemental feedback in order to help the coachee reflect on their progress towards goals (Ladyshewsky, 2010). In everyday life, people commonly use *evaluative* feedback when talking with their friends and colleagues. This tends to be vague and judgemental: for example, 'you were great!' or 'you did a good job!' While such praise might boost confidence initially, it fails to give the person feedback about what was 'great' or 'good' about their performance and therefore does little to help their development. Non-evaluative feedback, on the other hand, is descriptive and detailed and focuses on specific behaviours. For example, feedback given to a fellow social worker along the lines of 'you weren't very empathic when you spoke to that service user' could be seen as negatively judgemental and may make them feel defensive. Using a more descriptive, non-evaluative approach such as 'I noticed that your facial expression didn't change when the service user was describing her unhappiness. I think she may not have known whether or not you empathized with her experiences' is more likely to encourage constructive reflection on behaviours and skills and how they might be improved. It is therefore crucial that the coach provides non-evaluative feedback and is sensitive to how the information may be perceived by the coachee.

As discussed in Chapter 5, research has shown a clear link between the pursuit of goals and increased self-confidence, job satisfaction, stress-management skills and psychological wellbeing (Linley et al., 2007; Kauffman and Scoular, 2004; Seligman, 2002). The importance of reflection in building resilience has been noted throughout this book; an additional benefit of peer coaching is that it can enhance the coachee's self-reflection abilities by encouraging them to observe their progress towards self-generated goals (Grant, 2008). The provenance of the goal is integral to improving performance and wellbeing (Emmons, 1986). The coachee, therefore, needs to feel that the goal is self-generated, rather than imposed upon them, so that they fully embrace it and generate and implement solutions to achieve it (Sheldon et al., 2004). In the practice example of Margaret above, the goal was clearly established prior to the start of the coaching session.

Another practice example, that of Sean, illustrates the importance of the goal-setting process to successful coaching relationships.

Although people can sometimes be evangelical in recommending interventions that have worked well for them, Sean's example highlights the importance of a coach developing effective listening skills and not imposing their own ideas or solutions on their coachee.

To identify acceptable solutions, the coach should use open questions to help the coachee reflect on the values, skills and resources that have helped them to resolve problems in the past. In Sean's case, open questions could be 'which methods have you used previously to achieve work–life balance?' and 'what type of things do you find relaxing?' By using this technique, the coachee may also uncover skills that have not previously been recognized as beneficial for coping with difficult situations and identify personal preferences for achieving change (Neenan, 2009). Through a consideration of the coachee's strengths, creative

PRACTICE FOCUS 8.2: SEAN

When working with a colleague, Sean explained that he was finding it difficult generating a realistic goal that could help him develop a better work–life balance. The coach (who had previously experienced similar difficulties) was extremely empathic and suggested that Sean become involved in community activities, as this had helped her improve her own work–life balance. Sean accepted the suggestion, as he had been unable to come up with a goal of his own. On further reflection, however, Sean felt uncomfortable about this idea, as he felt he needed to do something more relaxing during his free time. As a result, Sean failed to engage with the goal and made little attempt to identify suitable off-the-job activities. His work–life balance remained poor, and his feelings of self-efficacy in making changes in his life were further eroded.

solutions can be developed that help achieve the identified goals (Kauffman and Scoular, 2004). For example, Sean might remember that he enjoyed playing football when he was in college, and joining a football team would not only help him relax but also extend his social network: thus enhancing his work–life balance. The capacity to identify personal strengths and skills that can resolve specific situations creatively is also likely to improve coping flexibility, which is a fundamental component of resilience (see Chapter 9).

Peer coaching in action

Like the ground rules mentioned above, the structure of the peer-coaching sessions should be agreed in advance between the coach and coachee. They are likely to involve one-to-one meetings and/or regular telephone calls. The frequency of the sessions will depend on the coachee's needs, or the nature of the particular coaching relationship. Some relationships may be short-term in order to resolve a specific problem whereas, in other cases, regular peer-coaching sessions may be required to achieve the coachee's specified goals (Kauffman and Scoular, 2004). Mutually supportive peer-coaching relationships may also be maintained over the longer term, where partners take turns to be coach and coachee in order to monitor progress towards goals and consider other issues such as managing relationships with particular service users and ways to respond to organizational demands. Whatever the nature of the coaching relationship, it is important that times and structure are mutually convenient, and it is essential that coach and coachee are fully committed to the coaching process.

A peer-coaching relationship can be instituted formally and informally. For instance, peer coaching might be suggested by a line manager if a social worker becomes 'stuck' with a particular issue. Managers may recommend an appropriate colleague to work with. As in Margaret's case discussed above, this could be a co-worker who possesses skills or knowledge that would be beneficial in helping the social worker move forward. Martin's situation offers a further example of how formal peer coaching might work.

PRACTICE FOCUS 8.3: MARTIN

Although Martin had the same number of cases as before, he was struggling with his caseload. He no longer felt 'on top' of things, but could not pin down what was different. Martin's manager recommended the peer-coaching approach to help him find a way forward. She advised him to work with a colleague from a different team who might have been able to offer a different perspective. Martin suggested Winston, a colleague he had previously found to be supportive. The manager asked Martin to contact Winston to see whether he would be interested in peer coaching. If Winston agreed, the manager recommended they meet face-to-face once a week for six weeks in a small meeting room. This would mean that the peer-coaching sessions were private and Martin would feel able to speak openly about his difficulties and explore possible solutions. The manager requested that Martin meet with her following each peer-coaching session to feed back on progress and explore any issues arising.

Colleagues may also initiate a more informal peer-coaching relationship between themselves. For instance, Patricia talked to her colleague Alyeesha about how she was struggling with completing her assessments and writing analytically. Patricia explained that she had been taking the assessments home to complete and felt she was spending less time with her children. Rather than just talking about how distressing and frustrating the problem was, Alyeesha suggested that peer coaching might help Patricia work out ways of achieving her goal of writing more analytically. Patricia readily agreed. To ensure that the peer-coaching sessions remained focused on Patricia's goal, Alyeesha and Patricia decided to write a formal agreement, detailing when and where they would meet and for how long. The agreement also emphasized mutual commitment to the peer-coaching relationship and the need for confidentiality. Rather than meet at work, which might have been distracting or might have engendered curiosity from colleagues, Patricia and Alyeesha agreed to have their coaching sessions at a local coffee shop, during a quiet period, for 30 minutes twice a week. Patricia felt this was more achievable than 60 minutes once a week and it would allow her to try out more options for change and report back on her progress.

When talking with a colleague, it is easy to be diverted from the main purpose of the coaching relationship. It is essential, therefore, that peer-coaching sessions have a structured agenda and are not used for a general 'catch-up' session, or an opportunity to let off steam or gossip. This structure will help the coachee remain focused on their goals (Greene and Grant, 2003; Kutilek and Earnest, 2001). A simple but useful structure for problem-solving or goal-setting within a peer-coaching environment is the TGROW framework (Downey, 1999), outlined in Figure 8.1.

When starting peer coaching, the coachee may have clear ideas about the help they need or the skills they wish to acquire. It is common, however, for people to approach peer coaching with general feelings of dissatisfaction rather than a specific goal for change. As a consequence, the coachee may initially require some help to identify the specific issue that is causing them discomfort or hindering their progress. For example, Theresa had begun to feel anxious when working with particular service users, which was beginning to undermine her confidence. Theresa noticed that she was more likely to feel anxious when she interacted with service users that she believed were hostile towards her. Theresa decided to talk to her colleague Adam about her concerns, and asked if they could forge a peer-coaching relationship to help her find a way forward. The following extract works through the steps of the

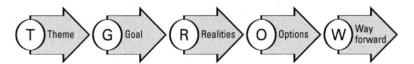

Figure 8.1 The TGROW framework

TGROW model using Theresa and Adam as an example. This example will also highlight the potential for peer coaching to build resilience via reflective ability, self-knowledge and enhanced stress-management skills.

Theme – A theme is an area or topic that reoccurs when discussing the areas that are causing concern or the skills that would be helpful to develop. Themes can be broad, such as improving work–life balance (as in Sean's case above), or focused on a specific issue. For example, after discussing her problems with Adam, Theresa realized that her anxiety arose from a lack of confidence in assessing service users that she found challenging. As a result, Theresa identified the theme for coaching: she needed support to improve her assessment skills to enhance her wellbeing and personal effectiveness.

Goal – The coachee may have a specific issue that needs to be addressed, but they can sometimes find the problem complex and overwhelming. Through discussions with the coach, the coachee will gradually be able to reflect on their concerns and become aware of the overall theme and the different components of the problem that needs addressing. For instance, when Theresa explained her difficulties to Adam, she self-identified that she wished to improve her assessment skills in working with complex and challenging cases. Adam was careful not to judge Theresa for lacking confidence in assessing service users' needs, although he personally felt competent in this area of practice. Instead he encouraged Theresa to share her thoughts openly and provided non-judgemental feedback. When Theresa reflected about the aspects of assessment that she found most stressful, she realized that her problems were due to her lack of experience in working with families who are reluctant to engage with social work services. As a result, Theresa expanded her initial theme and set herself the goals of improving her expertise in assessing complex cases, and enhancing her assertiveness and communication skills.

As mentioned earlier in this chapter (and in Chapter 5 in the context of time management and personal organization), for people to fully engage with their goals and achieve personal growth, they need to be challenging but achievable. Goals also need to be specific: if they are too vague, the coachee will not know if they have achieved their objective. Moreover, they will not experience the feelings of accomplishment and self-efficacy that accompany success. To avoid feeling overwhelmed by the enormity of a particular goal, it is important for the coach to encourage a positive attitude and maximize feelings of achievement. It is often helpful to break a goal down into small steps; by progressing through these smaller sub-goals, the larger, overarching goal feels more achievable. Feedback and encouragement offered by the coach each time one of the sub-goals is achieved will help motivate the coachee to continue the coaching process and achieve the larger goal. Theresa and Adam will need to keep this in mind as they progress through their coaching relationship.

Reality – Before committing to a goal, it is important to spend some time considering how practical and attainable the goal is. With the support of the coach, the coachee will need to evaluate the following issues: (a) whether the goal is achievable; (b) whether they have the resources to achieve the goal; (c) whether they possess the autonomy required to make the changes to fulfil the goal; (d) the extent to which the goal is aligned with their values and beliefs and (e) whether the goal can be attained within a reasonable time-frame.

When considering these issues, sometimes the coachee will recognize that the goal is unrealistic, or aspects of achieving it are beyond their control. As mentioned earlier, ownership of the goal and control of the process by which it can be achieved are integral to the peer-coaching process. It may therefore be necessary to reframe the goal, so that the course of action and associated strategies can be owned by the coachee. When the coachee is satisfied that the goal is realistic, they will need to think about the resources they can draw on to help them achieve their aims. For example, with Adam's help, Theresa carefully considered whether she would be able to achieve her aims and explored the resources she had available to her to enable her to do so.

Options – Identifying options for change can be challenging, and the coachee may become stuck. For instance, when talking through the resources available to achieve her goals, Theresa found it difficult to identify ways to improve her assertiveness and communication skills. She believed that her lack of confidence in her skills compounded her difficulties and, as a result, caused her to experience stress and anxiety.

As discussed above in the case of Sean, occasionally the coach may feel that they have the ideal solution to a coachee's problem. This is typically driven by empathy and a drive to alleviate the discomfort the coachee is experiencing. For example, to ease her colleague's distress, Adam suggested that they could work together in role-plays to improve Theresa's communication and assertiveness skills. Theresa tentatively agreed to try this idea, but seemed reluctant to set a date for the first peer-coaching session, despite encouragement from Adam.

For the coachee to commit fully to change and invest the effort required to attain the goal, it is imperative that they identify and develop their own strategies for reaching it. To help the coachee generate their own solutions, the coach could use open or Socratic questioning to help the coachee reflect and self-evaluate (see Chapter 4 for a more in-depth explanation of these techniques in relation to supervision). After the coachee has identified the actions they are willing to take to achieve their goal, the coach needs to ensure that they are fully committed to their goal. Realizing that he was imposing her opinions on Theresa (albeit with the best of intentions), Adam used open questions to help Theresa to identify the options for change to which she could realistically commit.

Way forward – For peer coaching to be effective, both the coach and coachee will need to agree a way forward. The coachee should commit to take specific actions to work towards their goals. By doing so, they are likely to develop and maintain the will, determination and motivation to succeed. In addition, it is necessary for the coach to commit to preparing for future sessions and supporting the coachee in achieving their self-identified aims.

The next section examines the techniques commonly used in peer coaching.

Peer-coaching techniques

Problem-focused versus solution-focused approaches

Problem-focused and solution-focused approaches to coping and their implications for wellbeing and resilience are discussed in Chapter 9. Using a solution-focused approach in coaching sessions has been shown to help people attain goals, as well as enhance their feelings of self-efficacy and wellbeing (Grant, 2012). This approach uses positive questions to help people pinpoint actions that have been effective previously and incorporate them into self-identified goals (Spence and Grant, 2007). Raising awareness of the strategies that have been successfully implemented in the past also reinforces confidence in problem-solving abilities and increases flexibility, with clear potential for building resilience (Neenan, 2009). Box 8.1 illustrates the difference between problem-focused and solution-focused questions.

BOX 8.1 DIFFERENCES BETWEEN SOLUTION-FOCUSED AND PROBLEM-FOCUSED QUESTIONS (GRANT, 2012)

Problem-focused questions aim to facilitate the exploration of thoughts, emotions and behaviours related to the problem.
  Solution-focused questions focus on ways of overcoming obstacles and generating positive feelings.

Problem-focused questions	Solution-focused questions
How long has this been a problem?	Think about a possible solution for the problem you just described. Now imagine the solution has 'magically' come about. Describe the solution.
How did it start?	Describe some ways you could move towards creating a solution.
What are your thoughts about the problem?	What are your thoughts about the solution?
How do you react when you have these thoughts?	How do you react when you have these thoughts?
What impact is having this issue having on you?	What impact is thinking about the solution having on you?

Solution-focused questions for coaching:
On a scale of 1 to 10, with 1 = *the problem* is totally in control and 10 = *you* are in control of the problem, where are you today?
  Where would you like to be tomorrow?
  What one thing could you do to increase your control, or move one point up the scale?
  How have you managed the problem so far?

There is evidence that people tend to demonstrate a negativity bias, in that they typically recall more negative problems than positive solutions (Baumeister et al., 2001). For example, when social work colleagues get together they may be more likely to talk about their problems than consider how they might best be addressed. Comparing and contrasting problem-focused and solution-focused questions in peer-coaching sessions may help the coachee extend their repertoire of

> ### PRACTICE FOCUS 8.4: STEVE
>
> Steve is an experienced social worker in a discharge team at a busy general hospital. He regularly meets the discharge planning deadlines and is known within the hospital for his strong decision-making skills and his ability to challenge other professionals to achieve the best outcome for patients. A recent influx of new social workers prompted Steve to re-evaluate his practice. On reflection, Steve felt he might have become complacent in his approach to patient discharge. He was particularly concerned that he might not be sufficiently taking into account the views of patients and their families when making decisions about their care. Steve concluded that he would like to explore how he might integrate an enhanced patient focus into his everyday work and asked his colleague Sue to be his peer coach.
>
> Sue used solution-focused questions to help Steve move towards his goals.
>
> Initially, Sue asked Steve to describe ways that she could start to move towards creating a solution.
>
> – Steve decided that, primarily, he needed to listen to patients and their families more and consider their wishes when identifying packages of care to support them on discharge.
>
> ➡

coping behaviours. Practice focus 8.4 illustrates how a solution focus can work in a social work context.

Solution-focused questioning is undoubtedly beneficial in helping the coachee generate creative strategies to achieve their goals. Nonetheless, identifying solutions can often feel like the hardest part of the coaching process. As mentioned above, people rarely have difficulties in sharing their worries and disappointments, but thinking of a positive solution to stubborn problems can be daunting. Reflecting on previous achievements can often expedite this process.

Peak moments

People often feel uncomfortable and embarrassed when sharing their successes with others. When asked to describe their talents and strengths, many will resist and say 'but I haven't got any', or seek to minimize those that they do disclose. Nonetheless, everyone can think

Sue then asked Steve how she felt about this solution.
- Steve said she felt positive about including the patients' views as this felt like a more holistic approach to patient care. Nonetheless, he felt it might be quite challenging to include others fully in the decision-making process, as this could impinge on planning deadlines. This caused Steve concern, as he had previously met these deadlines.

Sue acknowledged Steve's concerns and asked him to identify one thing he could do to increase her control over this situation.
- Steve felt that it might be beneficial to develop stronger working relationships with other members of the multi-disciplinary team. In the past, he had challenged other team members so as to gain the best care for his patients. Steve felt that if he improved the quality of his working relationships and emphasized collaboration the team might be more willing to accommodate his patients' needs.

Finally, Sue asked Steve to describe the impact that thinking about the solution was having on him.
- Steve said that, surprisingly, thinking about the solution had made him feel invigorated and motivated to make the changes. He said he now realized that refocusing on the patients' needs, instead of prioritizing deadlines, was long overdue.

of at least one situation where they felt proud of their achievements; a time when they felt their 'real self'. These are known as peak moments (Stanier et al., 2010) and normally occur when a person has been challenged to step outside their 'comfort zone'. They become aware that they are doing something well and that this is recognized by others. People generally prefer to keep their accomplishments close to them, like rare and precious treasures. For instance, social workers are rarely encouraged to celebrate their success, which can lead to a focus on the things that have gone wrong rather than those that have worked well. While reflective practitioners undoubtedly learn from negative experiences, reflecting on and sharing achievements provide the opportunity to enhance professional development. Indeed, a supportive peer-coaching relationship can give people the confidence to unpack their past triumphs and achievements: to share their treasure.

In peer-coaching sessions, themes may emerge when talking about behaviours or skills that were utilized when experiencing peak

BOX 8.2 SHARING TREASURES

Occasionally coachees may find it difficult to identify successful strategies to make progress. To facilitate positive thinking, it may be helpful to ask them to think of one or two peak moments.

To help the coachee share their peak moments, try asking some probing questions:
What did you do?
In which way were you 'at your best'?
How did you feel?
Where did this happen?
What was your role/part in the situation?
Who else was involved, if anyone?
What skills did you use?
How did you overcome any challenges or difficulties?
What was the key moment that made a difference?
What are you particularly proud of?

Alternatively,
If your coachee finds talking about their achievements difficult, ask them to write down their feelings and actions:
First, ask them to describe how they were feeling and thinking at the time.
Next, ask them to describe where they were and how they were behaving.
The coachee should aim write down any words that come into their head in response to the questions.

Now reflect back some of the answers.
How did the peak experience begin?
What choices or decisions did you make in order to achieve it?
Are you more likely to achieve peak experiences on your own, or when working with others?
Are there any key themes or behaviours that emerge from this experience?
What steps could you take to maximise the opportunity for more peak experiences?
(Bungay Stainer, 2010)

moments. The skills or behaviours that are used repeatedly are likely to be personal strengths; understanding these can enhance reflective abilities, aid professional and personal development, maximize opportunities for satisfaction and cultivate the qualities that underpin resilience.

Using strengths

A strengths-focused approach concentrates on the things people do well, that energize them and that they find enjoyable. Social workers demonstrate many strengths in their everyday practice (such as compassion, empathy, active listening and rapport-building) but they may not always recognize such behaviours in themselves, see them as positive features, or draw on them during times of adversity. The strengths associated with resilience are discussed in Chapter 2, but they include self-belief, self-acceptance, humour, flexibility, curiosity, obtaining support from others, problem-solving and finding meaning (Neenan, 2009). Conscious awareness of strengths and confidence in personal abilities enhances satisfaction, engagement and happiness. This self-knowledge

BOX 8.3 IDENTIFYING STRENGTHS

When you are at you best and using your strengths, how do you appear to others?
What would they see and hear in the tone of your voice, in your body language, and in the words you use? When people think about their peak moments they go beyond what they achieved. They also show what they felt at the time.

Think of the theme or strength that has been identified and ask: on a scale of 1 to 10, with 10 being 'using it to the fullest' and 1 being 'not using it at all', indicate the extent to which you are using the strength right now.
If you were using the strength more frequently, what would that feel like?
What would you be doing differently?

Notice how you feel when you use strengths.
When does the tone of your voice indicate energy and enjoyment?
What do you do that provides (rather than depletes) energy?
What do you instinctively pay attention to?
What things do you think are easy because you pick them up quickly?
When do you feel like the 'real you'?
(Linley, 2010)

PRACTICE FOCUS 8.5: SALLY

Sally is in a front-line team, working with service users over the age of 65. Sally has been in this team since she qualified five years ago; she is popular and considered by colleagues to be one of the most experienced members. Indeed, colleagues frequently ask her for advice about their cases, considering her to be very approachable and knowledgeable. Sally's workload is extremely demanding. She often feels stressed and is unable to complete her work, even though her caseload is equivalent to many of her colleagues.

Supporting Sally
During a peer-coaching session, Sally was given the time and space to discuss her problems and identify themes. The peer coach provided non-evaluative feedback on her concerns. From hearing her words reflected back to her, Sally became aware of her strong need to please other people; she also likes being distracted by other people's problems as this helps her avoid elements of her job that she finds less appealing. Sally decided that, in order to manage her current workload more effectively, she needs to focus on her own caseload rather than distracting herself by helping others.

Focusing on solutions and using strengths
As Sally's self-confidence and self-efficacy had been compromised by her high stress levels, the peer coach utilized a strength-based coaching approach. Rather than helping her to address her weaknesses, Sally was encouraged to identify the skills and attributes that energized her and

➡

is a further way to build resilience, as people are reassured that they possess the resources needed to help them overcome setbacks and cope with change (Trenier, 2010). Indeed, studies have shown that individuals who have been given the opportunity to identify their own personal strengths and use them effectively are less likely to experience stress and report higher levels of self-esteem, wellbeing and personal fulfilment (Govindji and Linley, 2007). The activity above is designed specifically to enable a coach and coachee to identify strengths to boost solution-focused behaviour.

In Practice focus 8.5, Sally uses peer coaching to identify her strengths and build resilience, which enhances her ability to manage adverse situations at work when they arise.

had been beneficial in previous situations. Sally's coach asked her to think about times when she became aware that she was enjoying what she was doing. The coach also prompted Sally to think about the things that she found easy in her job and the tasks she naturally paid attention to. After thinking carefully about the answers, Sally realized that she had many strengths, such as openness, compassion, empathy, tenacity, courage and emotional awareness. She also became aware that she uses an open communication style and is able to build effective relationships with colleagues and service users, and resolve other people's problems and difficulties.

Through the coaching process, Sally was able to draw upon many of these attributes to discuss her predicament with her colleagues. They were empathic and supportive and, although grateful for the guidance Sally had given previously, they encouraged her to prioritize her own caseload. Sally felt valued and realized that her relationships with her colleagues had not been weakened by her new approach.

Positive outcomes
Following peer coaching, Sally felt supported by her colleagues, more in control and more self-aware. As a result of peer coaching, Sally was optimistic about her ability to balance the demands of the role more effectively in future. Sally therefore felt that the peer-coaching process had helped her manage stress, enhanced her resilience and made her more confident to manage future problems more effectively.

Gains for the coach as well as the coachee

As seen above, peer coaching is likely to lead to considerable gains for the coach, but there will also be benefits for the coach. Research has shown that helping a coachee achieve their goals can enhance the coach's interpersonal skills, socio-emotional development and self-awareness (Grant, 2008; Ladyshewsky, 2004; Laske, 2006). These qualities are fundamental to a wide array of social work competencies such as empowering service users to instigate change, negotiating and establishing boundaries, demonstrating understanding, and communicating with authority and compassion. Expanding knowledge of other people's experiences and the strengths required to address difficulties effectively can, therefore, build resilience in the coach as well as the coachee.

Clarifying misconceptions

There can be some misconceptions about peer coaching. A brief examination of some of these may help the novice coach and coachee appreciate the boundaries of the coaching relationship and develop realistic expectations of what can be achieved.

- *Peer coaching is not magic*
  It does not offer an easy solution for problems, but provides a constructive framework that operates within a supportive relationship to help people achieve their goals. It is a challenging process which requires a change in behaviour, as well as consistent commitment and effort.
- *Peer coaching is not a cosy chat with friends*
  It is not the same as chatting with colleagues, friends or family, but is a structured way of helping. As outlined in this chapter, peer coaching offers a more focused, strengths-based approach to reaching solutions to difficult problems and aiding personal development.
- *Peer coaching is not directive*
  It is based on an equal relationship and does not involve telling, guiding or advising. In a coaching relationship, the role of the coach is to listen carefully, provide space and time to think, offer non-evaluative feedback on achievements, and give constructive support when challenges arise.
- *Peer coaching is not rescuing or persecuting*
  The coach's role is not to 'save' the coachee from a difficult situation (see Chapter 9 for a discussion of the implications of rescuing tendencies). The coach will work with the coachee to help them determine how to address the problem in a way that is intrinsically right for the coachee. The coach should not show disapproval or disappointment if the coachee does not reach their goals within the agreed time-frame. Instead, they should help the coachee determine why they have not yet achieved the specified goal and help them consider alternative ways to achieve success.
- *Peer coaching is not counselling*
  When working with a coachee, it is important that the coach is mindful of working not only within the coaching boundaries but

also within their competencies. Most importantly, it should be recognized that peer coaching is not a counselling relationship. Indeed, a coach should be aware that if the coachee becomes overly focused on past problems, or if they show evidence of mental health issues, the coaching session should be terminated. Under such conditions, coachees should be advised to consult a professional to obtain the support and assistance required.

Conclusion

As this chapter has established, peer coaching can be an effective strategy to enhance professional development and wellbeing as it aims to cultivate confidence in personal attributes and skills. Building self-awareness, reflecting on personal strengths and developing peer support are intrinsic to the peer-coaching process, and have all been highlighted as important factors in enhancing resilience (Jensen et al., 2008). A considerable strength of the peer-coaching approach is the equal status within the relationship, which can increase engagement with the process and effect real and sustainable change. This strengths-based approach has real potential to enable social workers to manage adversity in the workplace and build resilience to help them face future challenges.

ADDITIONAL RESOURCES

Bungay Stainer, M. (2010). *Do More Great Work*. New York: Workman.

Downey, M. (2003). *Effective Coaching*. London: Texere.

Linley, A. (2008). *Average to A+: Realising Strengths in Yourself and Others*. Coventry: CAPP Press.

Neenan, M. (2009). *Developing Resilience: A Cognitive Behavioural Approach*. Hove: Routledge.

Whitmore, J. (2002). *Coaching for Performance*. 3rd edn. London: Nicholas Brealey.

CHAPTER 9

Enhancing self-knowledge, coping skills and stress resistance

Gail Kinman, Isabella McMurray and Jo Williams

CHAPTER OVERVIEW

In order to build resilience, it is vital for social workers to gain insight into the aspects of the job that they find stressful, their personal stress reactions and the resources they have to help them manage stress. An overview of research that has examined stressors and strains in social work was provided in Chapter 1. This chapter focuses on some of the key internal and external stressors that have the potential to threaten the wellbeing of social workers. Several frameworks of workplace stress that are relevant to social work contexts are considered. Particular focus is placed on the transactional approach, which emphasizes the importance of individual appraisal and the effective use of personal and professional resources to not only help manage stress but build emotional resilience. The implications of different coping styles and strategies for wellbeing are also explored. Exercises are included to help social workers consider specific risk factors, map out their personal stress responses, and gain insight into how they appraise stressful situations, their coping strategies and their resilience resources.

The importance of self-knowledge

Awareness of one's beliefs, desires, motives, strengths and limitations are key qualities for professional practice (Ruch, 2000); they are also the foundations upon which emotional resilience is built. Resilient social workers will be aware of the working conditions and situations that threaten their wellbeing and have a keen insight into their personal reactions to stress and the coping strategies they utilize. They will be able to draw on an array of internal and external stress-resistance resources to help them manage the demands they face. Managing the expectations that other people have of us and those we have of ourselves in a realistic and effective manner is a key stress resistance resource. The next section considers this issue.

Managing expectations

External expectations are those made by other people or situations, such as service users, managers and colleagues, as well as expectations related to roles and responsibilities in the personal domain (See Chapter 3 for a discussion of role stress and its implications). An interview study conducted by Graham and Shier (2010) showed that the expectations that people have of social workers can be stressful. The negative portrayal of social workers in the news and entertainment media has also informed public perceptions of the profession (Zugazaga et al., 2006). Social workers may, therefore, come to believe that excessively high standards are required and their feelings of self-worth may become contingent upon fulfilling these expectations. Research with different occupational groups has found that this 'socially prescribed perfection-ism' can engender feelings of inadequacy and enhance the risk of burnout (e.g. Childs and Stoeber, 2010).

Internal demands relate to our own expectations of maintaining our personal values and standards of performance. Studies of social workers show that trying to adhere to personal standards and ideals in the face of high work demands and constraints on effectiveness can cause distress and burnout (Lloyd et al., 2002; Graham and Shier, 2010). The 'rescuer syndrome' is a personality characteristic (and internal stressor) that is particularly relevant to people in the helping professions. It is character-ized by a strong sense of social responsibility, a high level of empathy, an inner-directed action-orientated approach to work, and (like perfectionists discussed above) a drive to maintain exceptionally high standards of performance (Mitchell and Bray, 1990). While such qualities are undoubtedly required in helping roles, rescuers have problems differentiating between their own needs and those of service users and may take personal responsibility for resolving service users' problems; they are consequently at greater risk of over-involvement and burnout (Kets de Vries, 2010).

Rescuers mean well and can be effective, but it should be noted that rescuing behaviour can be used to bolster the helping professional's personal self-esteem and self-image rather than empower service users. Rescuers may also expect service users to be grateful for the time, effort and care they expend on them and become angry and resentful if their advice is not heeded. Indeed, social workers have acknowledged that the need to rescue can influence their perceptions of service users and the ways in which they interact with them (McMurray et al., 2008). As the need to rescue has strong potential to impair professional functioning and wellbeing, insight is required on how to recognize it and the ways in which it can be managed.

The questions in Exercise 9.1 are based on the work of Kets de Vries (2010) and are designed to help you find out whether you have rescuing tendencies.

EXERCISE 9.1

Are you a rescuer?
- Do you find it hard to ignore people's requests for help?
- Do you often find it difficult to stop thinking and worrying about other people and their problems?
- Do you feel responsible when unable to resolve another person's difficulties?
- Do you find it difficult to say no and create boundaries when people ask you to do things?
- Do you feel lost or anxious when there is no difficult situation to solve?
- Do you ever feel bitter when others are appreciative of your efforts in helping them or solving their problems?
- Do you feel uncomfortable when asking for or receiving help from others?
- Did you grow up in a family with a lot of emotional demands? As you were growing up, did you think it was your responsibility for effective family functioning?

If you answered 'yes' to more than three of these questions, you are likely to have rescuing tendencies. Self-examination, possibly facilitated by reflective supervision (see Chapter 4), can help social workers gain insight into their motives to do the job and the expectations they have of service users, as well as any early family dynamics that might have cultivated a rescuing orientation (Barak, Cherin and Berkman, 1998). Such knowledge can help social workers reduce over-involvement and develop more realistic expectations of themselves and service users. In turn, this will help them develop more effective boundaries, which will enhance personal resilience. Cognitive behavioural strategies (Chapter 6) can also be used to challenge maladaptive thinking patterns that might drive a compulsive need to rescue. The next section provides an overview of key frameworks of work-related stress that can help social workers gain insight into how working conditions might threaten or enhance their wellbeing.

Frameworks of work-related stress: an overview

Insight into the features of work that are considered stressful and satisfying can inform interventions to help social workers enhance their resilience. Warr (1987) has developed a novel perspective on stress, proposing that job characteristics have an effect on mental health that is analogous to the way that vitamins work in the human body. For example, like Vitamins C and E, some features of work (such as pay, physical safety, respect and meaningfulness) will enhance wellbeing up to a point, after which an increased 'dose' has no added benefit. Other job characteristics (such as control, variety and externally generated goals) are like Vitamins A and D in that they are beneficial at moderate levels, but too much or too little can be harmful. In other words, too much money or physical security will not be damaging, but jobs that provide too much autonomy and require the fulfilment of many different roles may be. Just as people differ in the extent to which they need different vitamins to achieve optimum health, individuals will differ in their need for particular job characteristics. For example, one social worker may have a strong need for control, whereas another may prefer to have clear goals set by others and their progress towards them monitored. Nonetheless, the vitamin model can help social workers reflect upon the features of their work that might threaten their wellbeing and those that have the potential to strengthen their resilience.

A resilient social worker will work in an environment that is congruent with their personal characteristics and requirements. A common source of work-related stress is a mismatch between a person's knowledge, skills, values, goals, needs and resources and the features of their job (French, 1973; Edwards, Caplan and Harrison, 1998). A lack of 'person–environment fit' can have many negative consequences, such as psychological distress, job dissatisfaction and lack of motivation (Greguras and Diefendorff, 2009). For example, a social worker who enjoys building long-term, mutually trusting relationships with service users, but is currently working in an overstretched intake team, may perceive a poor fit which could threaten their wellbeing and commitment. It is likely that a children and families team would be more compatible with this social worker's personal strengths and aspirations which, in turn, would help them build the resilience required to manage the demands of such work.

In order to foster resilience, social workers need to gain insight into the fit between their personal strengths, needs, values, capacities and aspirations. Focus could be placed on the match between:

- Your personal goals and those of the organization.
- Your personal values and those of team members and managers.
- The skills and abilities you have and those that are required to do the job effectively.
- The emotion-management skills needed to do the job successfully and those which you possess.
- The extent to which you need variety in your work and the opportunities you currently have to do different things with different groups of people.
- Your personal aspirations and the opportunities you have for career development.
- The support you receive from team members and managers and that which you require.
- The degree of control you have over when and how you do your job and your ideal situation.
- The extent to which you would like interact with service users and their families and those offered.
- The opportunities you have to confide in others and access emotional support and those available.

Achieving a perfect fit between your ideal situation and your working environment is not only unlikely, but inadvisable. Congruence is only needed for aspects of the job that are important to you: some social workers may prefer a close match with their personal goals and values, whereas others may prioritize variety or career development. Reflective supervision (Chapter 4) and peer coaching (Chapter 8) could help you gain insight into the 'goodness of fit' between your preferences and your current working environment. This process will also help you identify the aspects of your job where congruence with your personal goals and values is essential and those on which you are prepared to compromise. It should be recognized, however, that professionals who work in an environment that is entirely congruent with their current goals, skills and needs may stagnate rather than flourish. The concept of 'flow' (Csikszent, 1991), introduced in Chapter 3, argues that goals should be stretching, but manageable to maximize enjoyment, creativity, flexibility and adaptability – which are key aspects of resilience.

The person–environment fit framework can also help social work managers support resilience in their staff. The value of matching people who are proficient at managing specific stressors to jobs that require such skills has been emphasized (Jordan, 2003). To accomplish this, managers need to appreciate the competencies required to cope effectively with the emotional demands of particular roles, and consider how best to recruit and develop staff to achieve an optimum fit with scope for personal development. In order to accomplish this, it is useful to consider: (a) *needs–supplies fit*, which is characterized by how well the working environment fulfils individuals' personal goals and values, and (b) *demands–abilities fit*, which reflects the compatibility between employees' knowledge, skills and abilities and the characteristics of the job (Ostroff and Judge, 2007).

Resilient social workers will be aware of the aspects of their job that can protect their wellbeing when job demands are high. The next section draws on two key frameworks of job-related stress – the Job–Demand–Control–Support model (Karasek, 1990; Johnson and Hall, 1988) and the Effort–Reward imbalance model (Siegrist, 1996) – to discuss three workplace resources that may be particularly beneficial for social workers: job control, social support and rewards.

Key resilience resource: control and support

Even jobs that are very demanding will not necessarily threaten wellbeing, provided employees believe they have some control over what they do and feel supported (Spector, 2009). Job control refers to the degree to which employees can choose the skills they develop and utilize in their job, decide which tasks to do, and determine when and how to do them. Social support is defined as the perceived quality of relationships with colleagues, within teams and with supervisors or managers. Several studies of social workers have identified a strong sense of control and a high degree of social support as key stress-resistance resources (e.g. Adamson et al., 2012; Collins, 2013; Lloyd et al., 2002). The role played by a combination of control and support in protecting wellbeing is also highlighted in a study conducted by Wilberforce et al. (2012). Social workers who experienced high work demands but had insufficient control and support to fulfil them effectively were more dissatisfied with their job, whereas those with more control and support reported greater satisfaction regardless of how demanding their job was. Other research has found that specific aspects of control, such as involvement in decision making and strategic planning, are particularly likely to alleviate stress and burnout in social care contexts (Shier and Graham, 2011).

The benefits of social support at work for wellbeing and resilience were discussed in Chapter 8. Mutually supportive relationships foster feelings of belongingness and connectedness with others (Thoits, 2011). Furthermore, people who feel more supported tend to be healthier, both physically and psychologically (Cohen, 2004). There are many different kinds of support that are likely to be beneficial for social workers, such as *emotional support* (esteem, attachment and reassurance), *informational support* (the provision of advice, guidance and feedback), *companionship* (a sense of belonging) and *instrumental support* (tangible help and financial assistance) (Uchino, 2004).

A key skill underpinning resilience is identifying the type of support that is required and where it can be found. For support to be beneficial, however, it must closely 'match' what is required at the time (Cutrona and Russell, 1990). For example, a social worker may need informational support (such as advice or guidance) to help resolve a service user's problems, but is offered emotional support (such as sympathy or nurturance) to deal with the distress caused by being a target of the service user's frustration. This may alleviate the distress initially, but does nothing to solve the problems that caused it in the first place. Some problems, however, may require several types of support. For example, group supervision to discuss a complex case may give a social worker a sense of companionship, and the sharing of similar experiences between colleagues will also be likely to provide instrumental support and engender new approaches.

Key resilience resource: rewards

The effort–reward model of job stress developed by Siegrist (2002) proposes that people who believe that the efforts that they put into their work are counter-balanced by appropriate rewards tend to be healthier and happier. Rewards are not only financial, but gained from other factors such as respect, job security and career opportunities. Although extrinsic rewards, such as a fair salary, are undoubtedly important, helping professionals tend to be more strongly motivated by intrinsic rewards such as doing meaningful work and developing a rapport with service users (Stalker et al., 2007). For example, a social worker who puts a great deal of time and energy into their job but feels appreciated by service users is likely to be more healthy and satisfied than one who perceives an effort–reward imbalance. In order to build resilience, social workers might reflect upon the rewards they gain from their work, in their broadest sense, and consider those that are most likely to compensate them psychologically for their efforts.

The frameworks discussed in this section have highlighted the features of work and the individual that can impair wellbeing and those that can enhance it. The need for social workers to gain insight into their attitudes, preferences and behaviours has also been emphasized. Some of the strategies described in this book, particularly reflective supervision (Chapter 4) and peer coaching (Chapter 8), could be used to identify opportunities to enhance control and support in the workplace. Insight into what is perceived to be a 'fair' balance between efforts and rewards and ways to redress any inequity could also be explored through these techniques. Control can also be enhanced through the strategies outlined in the chapter on personal organization (Chapter 5).

In order to build resilience, social workers also need insight into their stress reactions. The next section focuses on the widespread impact that stress can have on wellbeing, health and personal and professional functioning. An exercise will help you map out your personal stress response and recognize the early warning signs that you are struggling to cope.

The wide-ranging impact of stress

Stress-related illness is the second most frequently reported work-related disorder (after musculoskeletal symptoms) (HSE, 2013). Stress can impair most areas of functioning, but its effects can be categorized into: *physical health*; *social and relational health*; *working health* and *psychological health*. Each of these categories will be discussed below, together with their implications for the wellbeing and job performance of social workers. Particular focus is placed on psychological health, as it has a strong influence on all other areas of functioning (Jones and Bright, 2001).

Physical health

Stress is not, in itself, a medical disorder, but when prolonged it can cause or exacerbate many physical health problems, ranging from minor symptoms (such as headaches, musculoskeletal pain and digestive disorders) to more serious illnesses (such as hypertension and coronary heart disease) (Schnall, Dobson and Rosskam, 2009). Chronic stress can also 'down-regulate' the immune system, increasing susceptibility to infectious disease and impairing wound healing (Daruna, 2012). People suffering from stress are also likely to have sleeping problems, resulting in fatigue that can compromise health and job performance (Knudsen, Ducharme and Roman, 2007).

Work-related stress also impacts on physical health via damaging health-related behaviours. A review of the literature by Payne et al. (2012) reported that people who are highly stressed frequently 'self-medicate' by drinking alcohol and/or smoking. Stress also tends to encourage other unhealthy behaviours, such as lack of exercise and 'comfort' eating. A heavy workload and a preoccupation with work may mean that healthy eating and physical activity are not prioritized. Unsurprisingly, people who experience high levels of work-related stress are at greater risk of obesity and associated disorders such as diabetes (Heraclides et al., 2009).

Social and relational health

Work-related stress can manifest itself as feelings of injustice, resentment and hostility (Spielberger and Sarason, 1996). Such feelings can escalate into interpersonal conflict, bullying and victimization, with high costs for individuals and organizations (Fox and Spector, 2005). As discussed in Chapter 3 in the context of work–life balance, people may also withdraw from others in an attempt to recoup their emotional and physical resources, or in response to feelings of vulnerability or low self-esteem. Both interpersonal conflict and social withdrawal will impair the quality of relationships inside and outside work which, in turn, will reduce opportunities to gain social support. As discussed above, supportive relationships are essential to buffer the negative effects of stress and build resilience. There is also evidence that job-related stress can diminish engagement with service users, which is likely to undermine the development of empathic, therapeutic relationships and consequently impair performance as well as personal wellbeing (Kahill, 1988).

Working health

Experiencing work-related stress can breach the 'psychological contract' which refers to employees' beliefs about reciprocal obligations between themselves and their employers (George, 2009). If people feel they are being treated unfairly, or that their distress is not taken seriously by others, they are likely to reduce their motivation and commitment (Guest and Conway, 2004). This is likely to have negative consequences for organizations, service users and employees. Research with safety-critical occupations has also found that stress can lead to error-making via fatigue and impaired concentration, and reduced problem-solving and decision-making abilities (Matthews et al., 2013). The wide-ranging implications of chronic stress for the working health of helping professionals were highlighted in an early study by Motowidlo, Packard and Manning (1986). Data obtained from nurses and their supervisors found that the degree of stress experienced was consistently related to aspects of interpersonal job performance (such as levels of sensitivity, warmth, consideration and tolerance) and cognitive/motivational performance (such as levels of concentration, perseverance and adaptability).

Work-related stress has also been associated with absenteeism. A report published in 2007 estimated that found that 20 percent of UK social workers had been signed off work for more than 20 consecutive days in the previous five years for stress-related conditions (CPCSW, 2007). Conversely, stress can also encourage 'presenteeism', where people continue to work when they are sick. There is evidence that presenteeism is more common among social workers than many other professional groups (Aronsson, Astvik and Gustafsson, 2013), implying that the health problems experienced within social work are greater than might be inferred from the absence figures reported above. Presenteeism may initially seem more attractive to organizations than absenteeism, but it is likely to be considerably more costly (Sainsbury Centre for Mental Health, 2007). While social workers may resist taking sick leave for fear of overloading colleagues or letting down service users, the long-term impact of such behaviour on health and job performance can be serious. It is therefore important for managers to encourage sick employees to recover at home and model such behaviour themselves (Demerouti et al., 2009).

Psychological health

Work-related stress is strongly linked with mental health problems. People in emotionally demanding occupations are at greater risk of developing depression and anxiety disorders than those in less stressful jobs (Johannessen, Tynes and Sterud, 2013). Stress can also engender other negative emotional states such as frustration and discontentment, as well as feelings of apprehension and fear (Kinman and Jones, 2005). Over the longer term, stress can also foster a pessimistic outlook. Optimism is key resource that can help people remain healthy and resilient. The implications of optimism and pessimism for the wellbeing of social workers and their professional practice are discussed in Box 9.1.

People employed in the helping professions are at particular risk of the burnout syndrome: a state of mental and/or physical exhaustion caused by excessive and prolonged work stress (Maslach, Jackson and Leiter, 1996). Burnout comprises three dimensions: emotional exhaustion, depersonalization/cynicism and reduced personal accomplishment. It is cyclical, whereby trying to fulfil the emotional demands of helping work can lead to compassion fatigue and *emotional exhaustion*. Professionals may react by distancing themselves emotionally from service users as a self-protection strategy. While this may conserve emotional energy, reducing their emotional investment in relationships with service users means that helping professionals are unable to make empathic connections with them and may see them as impersonal objects (*depersonalization*). A combination of emotional exhaustion and depersonalization can subsequently engender feelings of *reduced personal accomplishment* and a lack of professional effectiveness.

BOX 9.1 ACCENTUATING THE POSITIVE

Optimists generally expect that more good things will happen than bad, whereas pessimists anticipate the opposite. Optimists have the qualities associated with resilient people: they have higher self-esteem and utilize more flexible coping strategies (Carver, Scheier and Weintraub, 1989), whereas pessimists use a restricted range of coping mechanisms and tend to be in poorer health (Rasmussen, Scheier and Greenhouse, 2009).

Rather than fixed traits, it is useful to see optimism and pessimism as explanatory styles that influence how people interpret events (Seligman et al., 1990). Someone with an optimistic style will see themselves as causing positive events to happen (*internal*), will believe that good things will occur subsequently (*permanent*) and that other aspects of their life will be positive (*universal*). When negative events occur, optimists typically blame external circumstances (*external*), that are atypical (*temporary*) and irrelevant to other life areas (*specific*). For example, if an optimistic social worker is promoted, they will typically see it as a reward for good work and they will continue to receive such recognition in the future. If they are not promoted, they will tend to blame extenuating circumstance and expect promotion to occur in the future.

Pessimists have negative expectations about themselves, the world and other people. When positive events occur they are typically viewed as a stroke of luck (*specific*), caused by circumstances outside their control (*external*) and unlikely to occur again (*temporary*). Conversely, pessimists believe that they cause negative events (*internal*); they will always make mistakes (*permanent*), which is inevitable (*universal*). For example, if a pessimistic social worker has a negative experience with a service user, they will tend to blame this on their poor performance or unsuitable personality, they expect that they will inevitably let down service users in future and, therefore, feel they are unsuited to the job.

Social work is an intrinsically optimistic profession. A belief in service users' ability to change is fundamental, as is striving to help them overcome problems. The cognitive behavioural techniques outlined in Chapter 6, in particular, can foster a more optimistic outlook through positive reappraisal or reframing. Reflective supervision (see Chapter 4) can also help overcome a negative approach. Nonetheless, you should not endeavour to see a silver lining in every cloud. The accurate estimation of risk is central to social work practice and it should be recognized that 'unrealistic optimism' distorts perceptions of risk (Klein & Weinstein, 1997), which may lead to collusion. A regular 'optimism/pessimism check' is therefore essential to ensure that perceptions are realistic and flexible.

As discussed throughout this book, emotional resilience can protect social workers against burnout. It is nonetheless vital for helping professionals, particularly those with a 'rescuing' orientation (see above), to manage early signs of emotional exhaustion. Enhancing aspects of work such as job control and social support, providing reassurance of individual worth, and improving self-care strategies in response to these early warning signs are thought to be particularly effective (Felton, 1998). 'Full-blown' burnout, however, can be a serious problem with devastating implications for health, interpersonal relationships, career and quality of life (Schaufeli, Leiter and Maslach, 2009). Recovery from burnout can be a long and arduous process involving several stages: admitting the problem; distancing oneself from work; restoring health; questioning values; exploring future work possibilities and making objective changes to the working environment (Bernier, 1998). A combination of individual interventions, such as cognitive behavioural therapy (see Chapter 6,) and workplace-oriented interventions, such as restoring equity, enhancing support and improving communication, are considered most likely to restore health and facilitate return to work (Karlson et al., 2010; Van Dierendonck, Schaufeli and Buunk, 1998).

Your personal stress reactions

The many different ways that stress can impact on wellbeing have been documented above. It is important to recognize, however, that people

EXERCISE 9.2

Recognize your early warning signs
Think about how you feel when you first start to become stressed and write these symptoms down, adding to the list over the next week or two. We may initially find it difficult to identify our own stress reactions, especially if we have lost perspective, so you could ask your partner or a friend for their opinion. Often, the people we are closest to can spot early warning signs of stress in us that we may not register ourselves. Use your list of symptoms to raise awareness of the messages your body gives you to let you know that you are becoming stressed. This technique will help you take action to pre-empt more serious health problems.

Table 9.1 Symptoms of stress

Physical symptoms	Emotional symptoms
Tiredness and lethargy	Feeling out of control; mood swings, tearfulness
Aches and pains (e.g. back, neck, jaw)	Low mood, feelings of worthlessness
Tension headaches	Anxiety or apprehension
Grinding teeth	Failure to 'connect' with others
Breathlessness, dizziness, palpitations	Loneliness, feelings of isolation, lack of intimacy
Indigestion, heartburn, nausea	Excessive rumination or worrying
Bowel disturbances	Apathy, easily discouraged, lack of direction
High blood pressure	Loss of meaning, lack of enjoyment of life
Dry mouth or throat	Intolerance, resentment, cynicism
Feelings of emptiness	Suspicion, distrust of others' motives
Allergies	Low self esteem, lack of self-efficacy

Behavioural symptoms	Cognitive symptoms
Altered sleep patterns	Making mistakes, becoming forgetful
Frustration, irritability or aggression	Poor decision making
Increased drinking or smoking	Inability to prioritize, indecisiveness
Carelessness, accident proneness	Racing thoughts, inability to focus
Nervous tics (such as finger-drumming)	Over-reacting to minor setbacks
Altered eating habits, comfort eating	Impaired performance, low productivity
Social withdrawal	
Need for reassurance of worth	

respond to stress in different ways (see Table 9.1). Physically, one individual may develop headaches whereas another may have digestive problems. Emotionally, one person may become apathetic and tearful while another may ruminate excessively about work-related problems. Behaviourally, one individual may become irritable and seek out arguments, whereas another may withdraw from social contact entirely. As discussed above, cognitive symptoms can also range from memory impairment to minor accidents. It is useful to see these early warning signs as the equivalent of a light coming on in your car to warn you that there may be a breakdown if action is not taken. In order to build resilience, you must pay attention to your personal early warning signs: i.e. changes in physical and psychological health, feelings, attitudes and behaviours that are telling you that you are not coping well.

The strategies outlined in this book can be used to help you manage the stress symptoms you experience and build resilience for the future. For example, mindfulness practice (Chapter 7) can be useful in alleviating emotional and psychosomatic symptoms and compassion fatigue; CBT (Chapter 6) can help manage maladaptive health behaviours and interpersonal difficulties; and personal organization skills (Chapter 5) can attenuate feelings of anxiety by enhancing perceptions of control. The strategies included in Chapter 3 to improve work–life balance can help social workers identify opportunities for recovery. Reflective supervision (Chapter 4) can be used to explore the underlying reasons for chronic stress reactions and generate realistic options for change, and peer support and coaching (Chapter 8) can address feelings of isolation and alienation, and restore self-worth and self-efficacy. (Please note, however, that if you are worried about any symptoms you are experiencing over the longer term you should see your doctor.)

The importance of appraisal

As discussed above, what is considered stressful will vary from person to person, as will the impact of stress. The transactional approach to stress developed by Lazarus and Folkman (1984) recognizes the importance of individual differences in the stress process. From this perspective, stress is defined as 'a particular relationship between the person and the environment that is appraised by the person as taxing or exceeding his or her resources and endangering his or her wellbeing' (p.19). Two types of appraisal are involved that underpin coping responses and successful adaptation to stress:

- *Primary appraisal* relates to whether somebody believes that a particular event, situation or demand is potentially harmful to them. If the situation is considered unimportant, the coping process is terminated and the issue ignored, whereas if it is meaningful and possibly threatening, the person moves on to the next stage.
- *Secondary appraisal* is where the person evaluates the resources they have available to cope with this situation. This process is based on judgements of previous experiences of similar events, beliefs about

oneself and one's environment, and the availability of appropriate resources. How much control a person believes they have over the situation is of particular importance: the less control they perceive, the more threatening the situation and the greater the risk of harm.

- *Coping* is where the person takes whatever actions seem appropriate to manage the threat.

Appraising your resources

The example below demonstrates how people can appraise the same event in different ways according to how they perceive their personal resources. The situation involves a social worker being asked to work with a service user who has a history of challenging behaviour. Josh appraises the situation as threatening and decides that he does not have the resources required to deal with it effectively, whereas Patience feels she has only limited resources to do so. Both will experience distress. Diane and Sam, on the other hand, appraise the situation as challenging, believing that they may have the internal resources (i.e. problem-solving skills) or external resources (i.e. instrumental social support) to help them cope. They will therefore experience less stress. Marc appraises the situation as benign: i.e. it does not affect him in any way. While he will experience no stress, there is a risk of over-confidence, meaning that he makes little effort to pre-empt any problems if things do not go according to plan.

Josh: 'There's no way I can possibly manage this: I won't know what to do.'
(*threat + no resources = stress*)
Patience: 'This will be really hard: sometimes I'm not very good with challenging people.'
(*threat + limited internal resources = stress*)
Diane: 'Maybe I can manage this if I carefully consider the best approach.'
(*challenge + possible internal resources = less stress*)
Sam: 'I could maybe manage this if I get some support from my colleagues.'
(*challenge + external resources = less stress*)
Marc: 'This isn't a problem; I find it easy to manage challenging people.'
(*benign, no stress*)

Coping with stress

Coping is an important part of the appraisal process. People cope with stress in many different ways. As discussed above, the extent to which coping is effective depends on: (a) the type of demand that is experienced and (b) whether the person believes they have the appropriate resources. Self-knowledge is a key aspect of coping, as it helps people make more accurate judgements about potential threats to their well-being, their internal and external resources, and their ability to utilize the coping response that best fits the situation. With reference to the example above, effective coping requires people to be neither excessively pessimistic nor overly optimistic. Other qualities that underpin successful coping (such as self-efficacy, emotional literacy, a sense of meaningfulness and purpose, autonomy, social support and well developed problem-solving skills) are also key elements of resilience (see Chapter 2).

Resilient people are also adaptable, with the ability to utilize a wide repertoire of coping strategies. Lazarus and Folkman (1984) have highlighted two main coping styles: problem-focused and emotion-focused. *Problem-focused coping* aims to tackle the problem at source, and is used when a situation is seen as changeable. *Emotion-focused coping* aims to change people's negative feelings about stressful situations and is typically used when we believe that attempting to solve the problem itself is futile. There is no 'correct' way of coping with stress: both problem-focused and emotion-focused coping can be adaptive or maladaptive, depending on the circumstances. For example, trying to use a problem-focused coping style in situations that cannot be changed can lead to emotional exhaustion. Acceptance or attempting to interpret the situation more positively is likely to be more effective (see below). On the other hand, people who favour emotion-focused coping may resist using a problem-solving approach, even when a situation is potentially changeable. In such circumstances, cognitive behavioural and peer-coaching techniques could be useful in helping people reframe events as challenges rather than threats, and engender a problem-solving, goal-oriented coping style (Santiago-Rivera, Bernstein and Gard, 1995).

The COPE Scale (Carver et al., 1989), shown below, measures a wide range of strategies that people use to cope with stressful events. It comprises 15 coping styles that could be broadly categorized as active or avoidant. Active coping strategies are similar to problem-focused ones in that they are behavioural or psychological responses designed to change the nature of the problem or how one thinks about it (such as planning and seeking instrumental support). Avoidant coping strategies involve activities (such as the use of alcohol) or psychological responses (such as denial) that stop people from addressing the problem directly. The coping styles are:

- *Active coping*: taking active steps or initiating direct action;
- *Planning*: thinking about how to deal with a problem; developing strategies;
- *Seeking social support for instrumental reasons*: seeking advice or information;
- *Seeking emotional social support*: getting moral support, sympathy or understanding;
- *Suppression of competing activities*: avoiding being distracted;
- *Turning to religion*: seeking spiritual help and finding comfort in religion;
- *Positive reinterpretation and growth*: viewing a situation in a more positive light;
- *Restraint*: waiting for the right moment to act;
- *Resignation/acceptance*: accepting a challenging situation;
- *Focusing on and venting emotion*: expressing distress;
- *Denial:* refusing to believe the problem exists;
- *Mental disengagement*: using distracting activities;
- *Behavioural disengagement*: reducing efforts to deal with a problem;
- *Alcohol/drug use*: using drugs to avoid the problem, or for self-medication purposes;
- *Humour*: laughing and joking about the situation.

Generally speaking, active coping strategies are more effective ways to deal with problems than avoidant ones. Research findings show that social workers draw upon a wide range of coping styles, but are particularly likely to use active strategies such as planning and positive reframing (Kinman and Grant, 2011). This study also found that other strategies, such as seeking emotional and instrumental support, self-distraction, venting emotion and acceptance, were commonly used. Social workers who used active coping methods tended to report less distress and more resilience, whereas avoidant coping was related to poorer wellbeing and lower levels of resilience.

People are likely to favour particular coping strategies, but trying to solve every problem in the same way will not be effective. For example, a social worker who prefers to cope with stress by drawing on social support may gain sympathy and opportunities to let off steam, which could lead to positive interpretation and growth. Nonetheless, if they draw on them too often, they risk depleting their sources of support, and the use of more active coping strategies is likely to be more effective. The importance of a flexible repertoire of coping styles for psychological wellbeing has been recognized (Kato, 2012). It would be useful for social workers to use the COPE categories shown above to reflect upon their habitual ways of coping with stress. If a particular coping strategy is proving to be ineffective, this framework can also be used to determine a more appropriate response. For example, it may be that taking time out to 'unpack' a stressful or emotionally charged situation has been effective in the past, but on this occasion you are continuing to worry about the issue. It may be more productive to use an alternative strategy, such as reframing or accepting an unchangeable situation without self-blame, and move on. Reflective supervision and peer coaching can help social workers reflect upon the type and effectiveness of their coping responses. Moreover, a stress diary is a simple but powerful reflective tool to build resilience by helping identify adaptive and maladaptive patterns of thoughts, feelings, symptoms and behaviours (Clarkson and Hodgkinson, 2007). This format can be used to record stressful experiences, document stress reactions and coping styles and identify their short-term and longer-term consequences.

Stress inoculation training

This chapter concludes by outlining stress inoculation training (SIT). This technique was developed by Meichenbaum and Deffenbacher (1988) to help people cope more effectively with potentially stressful situations by reducing the potential for negative reactions. SIT is a type of cognitive behavioural intervention (see Chapter 6) and is based on the assumption that people find situations stressful because they think about them in catastrophizing ways. The technique has been used successfully in a range of workplace settings to help people manage stress (Meichenbaum, 2004; Flaxman and Bond, 2010). SIT has three stages:

1. *Cognitive preparation* involves exploring the ways in which we think about stressful situations. We often react to stress with negative self-statements such as 'I can't cope with this', which makes the situation

worse. This stage involves raising awareness of the relationship between such maladaptive thoughts and behaviour patterns so that we realize that we are not helpless and can cope well.

2. *Skill acquisition and rehearsal* helps us confront stressful situations by drawing on existing coping skills, or learning more appropriate strategies. This stage aims to replace negative coping self-statements with positive ones, which are subsequently learned.

3. *Application and follow-through* involves applying these newly developed skills. This may involve increasing our exposure to situations that are progressively more threatening.

Examples of how positive coping self-statements at each of the three SIT stages are shown below, along with an example of a reinforcing self-statement that will transfer learning to future stressful situations.

Preparing for a stressful situation: 'Don't worry, as that won't help. What can I actually *do* about it?'

Confronting and handling a stressful situation: 'Relax, I'm in control. What skills do I have to help me manage this situation? What has helped in similar situations? Do I need to learn new coping skills?'

Coping with the feeling of being overwhelmed: 'Make the fear manageable. When it comes, just pause and keep focusing on the present.'

Reinforcing self-statements: 'It worked, I controlled my fears and I will do it again next time. I just need to be well prepared.'

Stressful experiences that are perceived to be challenging but not overwhelming have been found to enhance resilience (Lyons et al., 2009). SIT has strong potential to help social workers build their resilience by improving self-knowledge and understanding and fostering mastery and coping flexibility, thus increasing the perceived manageability of future stressful events.

Conclusion

Self-knowledge is a fundamental aspect of resilience. This chapter has provided a range of tools to help social workers gain greater understanding of the aspects of work that they find most threatening and satisfying. It has also highlighted the significance of considering the ways in which they respond to stress and some of the individual difference factors that might diminish or enhance wellbeing and resilience.

The tools outlined in the present chapter, and those that came earlier, have strong potential to help social workers not only manage the challenges of social work practice, but also build resilience to sustain a long, satisfying and productive career.

ADDITIONAL RESOURCES

Antony, M., and Swinson, R. (2010), *When Perfect Isn't Good Enough*, 2nd edn. Oakland, CA: New Harbinger.

Bamber, M. R. (2011), *Overcoming Your Workplace Stress: A CBT-based Self-help Guide*. London: Routledge.

Cooper, C., and Kahn, H. (2013), *50 Things You Can Do Today to Manage Stress at Work*. Chichester: Summersdale.

Donaldson-Feilder, E., Lewis, R., and Yarker, J. (2011), *Preventing Stress in Organisations*. Oxford: Wiley-Blackwell.

Lamia, M., and Krieger, M. (2009), *The White Knight Syndrome: Rescuing Yourself from Your Need to Rescue Others*. Oakland, CA: New Harbinger.

Seligman, M.E.P. (2011), *Learned Optimism*. New York: Vintage.

CHAPTER 10

Resilient individuals and organizations: an integrated approach

Gail Kinman and Louise Grant

CHAPTER OVERVIEW

This chapter considers the role played by the organization in supporting resilient social work practitioners. The policies, structures and support systems that have the potential to protect wellbeing and practice and build resilience are explored. The need to develop multi-level interventions that comprise national and organizational initiatives as well as seek to enhance the competencies of individual social workers is emphasized. Ways in which these perspectives might work together to promote a culture of personal and organizational wellbeing are discussed. Particular focus is placed on the risk-assessment approach developed by the UK Health and Safety Executive (HSE) to monitor the work-related wellbeing of employees. Also considered is how the HSE manager-competency framework can be used to identify the behaviours required by social work managers and leaders to help their employees manage stress and develop an organizational culture that supports individual resilience. The chapter concludes by outlining priorities for organizational practice and future research.

The role of the organization in promoting resilience

This book provides social workers with a range of evidence-based strategies to help them alleviate work-related stress and build resilience.

Nonetheless, even the most resilient practitioners will be unable to survive, let alone flourish, in conditions where the demands of their work regularly exceed their coping resources. Although it is crucial for social workers and other helping professionals to prioritize self-care and develop a toolbox of coping skills and strategies, employers have a legal and moral duty of care to safeguard the wellbeing of their employees. It is therefore essential that social workers' personal resilience-building skills are supported by evidence-based organizational policies and practices. This chapter considers how this might be accomplished.

The high levels of stressors and strains found in studies of social workers that have been discussed in this book indicate that attention to the nature, organization and management of social workers' roles is essential in order to make improvements in wellbeing. In turn, this will ensure that services delivered to vulnerable people are assured, with wide-ranging benefits. A body of evidence shows that organizational-level interventions, where work-related stressors are ameliorated at source, are the most successful way to protect the health and performance of employees (Van der Klink et al., 2001; LaMontagne et al., 2007; Nielsen et al., 2010). Such interventions focus on adapting the working environment to meet the needs of employees, rather than expecting them to accommodate to challenging or untenable working conditions. Examples of organizational-level interventions include increasing role clarity, job control and training opportunities; improving the quality of support, communication and working relationships and enhancing respect and recognition. Organizations can also draw on the models of work-related stress outlined in Chapter 9 to increase, for example, person–environment fit, reduce effort–reward imbalance and enhance aspects of autonomy. Introducing equitable work–life balance policies is a further example of how an organization-level intervention can improve the wellbeing of employees and safeguard their practice (see Chapter 3).

An integrated approach

In order to build a culture of resilience, it is useful to adopt a holistic approach that considers how the wellbeing of social workers is conceptualized, prioritized and protected at different levels. This information can then be used to develop well-integrated interventions and support structures to meet the needs of social workers at different stages of their career. Knowledge is required at the following levels:

- *The national level*: the legislation, regulations and guidance that are in place to safeguard the occupational health of employees in general; the best practice currently adopted by other helping professions such as nurses.
- *The sector level*: the policies and guidelines that are currently in place within professional social work associations (such as the College of Social Workers and the British Association for Social Workers) and trade unions that represent social workers; how professional networks can best be used to share information and innovative practice.
- *The organizational level*: how national policies and guidelines are implemented by social work employers, and the strength and pervasiveness of the wellbeing culture within organizations; the use of case-study organizations to promote best practice in the sector rather than 'naming and shaming' employers who may be seen to be performing poorly.
- *The team level:* the quality of interpersonal relationships and the degree of support within and between work teams.
- *The individual level*: the competencies that underpin resilience and how they can be enhanced in different social work contexts.

Knowledge of personal competencies and effective support structures is also required at the *educational level* to prepare social work students for the realities of practice. A study conducted by Grant, Kinman and Baker (2014) explored social work course leaders' views about the concept of resilience, the strategies currently used to support self-care in their students, and their opinions on how wellbeing and resilience might best be cultivated via the pre-qualifying curriculum. Educators generally acknowledged that social work education currently tends to prioritize the cognitive (knowing and thinking) domain over the affective (emotional) realm. They were nonetheless unanimous in the belief that resilience is a crucial survival mechanism in an emotionally demanding and potentially stressful job; it was therefore considered vital for students to develop an appreciation of the need for resilience, and the ways in which it can be enhanced, early on in their training. Some innovative practices to enhance self-care and resilience were identified, but the majority of educators stressed the need to improve their own knowledge (and that of their team) of the competencies that underpin resilience and how these could best be integrated into the curriculum. Although the development of resilience competencies during training was considered important, the organization's duty of care to protect the wellbeing of employees was widely emphasized. As discussed in Chapter 4, the need for students to develop the assertiveness required to access high-quality reflective supervision and support in their subsequent practice was underlined particularly strongly.

As highlighted above, organizations need to introduce proactive, evidence-based policies and practices to safeguard the wellbeing and professional practice of their employees. The next section describes two key frameworks developed by the UK Health and Safety Executive (HSE: the UK body responsible for policy and operational matters related to occupational health and safety) that have strong potential to help organizations protect the wellbeing of social workers and develop a culture of resilience.

The HSE Management Standards approach: tackling stressors at source

The HSE has formulated a process to help employers manage the work-related wellbeing of their staff. A risk-assessment approach is adopted whereby work-related stress is viewed as a serious health and safety issue and stressors are measured and managed like any other type of workplace hazard. The process is based around a set of standards of good management practice (or benchmarks) for measuring employers' performance in preventing work-related stress from occurring at source. Based on extensive consultation with key stakeholders (such as occupational psychologists, human resources professionals and trade unions), the HSE selected several elements of work activity (known as psychosocial hazards) that are: (a) considered relevant to the majority of employees in the UK and (b) have a strong evidence base as the 'most critical predictors' of employee wellbeing and organizational performance (MacKay et al., 2004, p. 101). The specified hazards are demands, control, social support (from managers and peers), interpersonal relationships, role clarity and involvement in organizational change. The importance of these factors to the wellbeing of social workers has previously been highlighted in research reviewed in Chapters 1 and 9 of this book.

The HSE has developed a self-report survey instrument to help employers measure the levels of these key hazards within their organizations. The HSE Indicator Tool (Cousins et al., 2004) comprises 35 items within the seven hazard categories. Box 10.1 gives details of the factors included under each of these headings.

BOX 10.1 THE HSE HAZARD CATEGORIES

Demands: workload, pace of work and working hours;
Control: levels of autonomy over working methods, pacing and timing;
Peer support: assistance and respect received from colleagues;
Managerial support: supportive behaviours from line managers and the organization itself, including encouragement and the availability of feedback;
Relationships: interpersonal conflict within the workplace, including bullying behaviour and harassment;
Role: role clarity and the extent to which employees believe that their work fits into the overall aims of the organization;
Change: how well organizational changes are managed and communicated.

The questionnaire, together with guidance on administration and scoring, can be found at http://www.hse.gov.uk/stress/standards/pdfs/indicatortool.pdf.

The HSE risk-assessment approach is widely used by organizations, occupational groups and sectors to diagnose the most stressful aspects of work (Houdmont, Kerr and Randall, 2012; Kinman and Wray, 2013). It has recently been incorporated into occupational health guidelines developed by professional associations such as the Royal College of Nursing and the Association of Chief Police Officers. The management standards process allows employers to assess how well they are managing each of the hazard categories within their workforce, and helps them develop precisely targeted interventions to improve the work-related wellbeing of their staff. The approach can be adopted to determine the wellbeing profile of employees in general, but comparisons can also be made between employees in terms of function and demographics (for example, job type, gender or experience) which allow interventions to be specifically targeted to groups that are at particular risk. Moreover, the strategies utilised by any groups of employees who are found to have particularly high levels of wellbeing in relation to any of the hazard categories could be used to promote best practice. The HSE also provides normative data from different occupational groups, enabling employers to compare their scores for each of the hazards against national benchmarks. Where scores for any of the categories are compared unfavourably, the HSE suggests interim and longer-term target scores to help organizations improve their performance. This requires the administration of the questionnaire at regular intervals to assess the effectiveness of interventions that have been implemented.

The HSE approach has strong potential to help organizations enhance the wellbeing of social workers and build a culture that supports resilience. At the time of writing, however, it has been little used in social work contexts. A notable exception is a study conducted by Kerr, McHugh and McCrory (2009), who used the HSE indicator tool to explore levels of hazards in a community-based Health and Social Services Trust in the UK. Also examined was the relationship between each of the hazard categories and job-related depression and anxiety, job satisfaction and errors/near-misses. In combination, the hazards were powerful predictors of each of the outcomes, but job demands had the most powerful impact on job-related mood, manager support had the strongest association with job satisfaction and relationships had the strongest links with errors/near-misses.

Studies of various occupational groups indicate that job-specific stressors can be particularly potent sources of strain (e.g. Van der Doef and Maes, 1999). Although the HSE approach is undoubtedly useful, the questionnaire does not include stressors that are specific to the social work role, such as emotional demands, bureaucracy, threats of violence, and poor public image of the profession (see Chapter 1 for a discussion of these factors.) Social work employers might also find it helpful to supplement the HSE tool with additional measures that assess outcomes such as psychological distress, burnout and work–life conflict; these can provide valuable information on the job-related stressors that pose the greatest threat to wellbeing and, as such, help organizations prioritize interventions (Houdmont et al., 2012). The advantages of this broader approach are illustrated by the findings of the study conducted by Kerr et al. (2009) described above. Moreover, identifying the features of the social work role that predict positive as well as negative outcomes such as job satisfaction and flourishing may also be advantageous. This method is likely to be particularly effective in helping organizations translate their findings into practical, acceptable and effective interventions to minimize job-related stress and build a resilient culture.

Line-manager competencies: identifying the behaviours that protect employee wellbeing

Many studies have found that characteristics of managers, such as leadership style, support, consideration and empowerment, exert a strong impact on the wellbeing and performance of their staff and other key outcomes such as absenteeism and retention (Michie and Williams, 2003; Skakon et al., 2010). Line managers, therefore, play a vital role in identifying and managing work-related stress.

In terms of *prevention*, line managers should be able to identify signs of stress in their team members at an early stage; fully support risk assessments or stress audits; work with teams, occupational health and human resources to develop appropriate and acceptable interventions and adjustments to working conditions; and champion changes that aim to improve the wellbeing of staff.

In relation to *training and development*, line managers should possess the knowledge required to identify appropriate training to reduce stress and provide their employees with the opportunity to attend such sessions; they should also identify and support interventions at the group level that can equip team members with the skills to cope with the demands of their work more effectively.

In terms of *support*, managers should be aware of the various ways that stress can manifest itself (see Chapter 2 for a discussion of the impact of stress on physical, psychological, working and social health) and be able to identify ways to alleviate this. It is nonetheless important that managers appreciate the need to work within their competencies, and have the knowledge required to refer their employees to other agencies within and external to the organization. Managers also need to be prepared to work with employees to identify work adjustments to reduce their exposure to work-related stress and protect their wellbeing.

The HSE (in association with the Chartered Institute of Personnel and Development and Investors in People) have developed a framework to help managers, and those that recruit them, assess the extent to which they possess the behaviours found to be effective for preventing and reducing stress at work (Donaldson-Feilder, Lewis and Yarker, 2011). The aim is to help managers reflect on their behaviour and management style and identify areas for further development. The framework emerged from research with several hundred managers and employees from sectors with the highest prevalence of work-related stress (including local and central government, health care and education). Two

BOX 10.2 MANAGEMENT COMPETENCIES FOR PREVENTING OR REDUCING WORK-RELATED STRESS

The framework comprises four broad themes with twelve sub-themes that set out the required manager behaviours.

1. Managing emotions and possessing integrity
   - Integrity (e.g. being a good role model; being honest; not talking about team members behind their backs)
   - Managing emotions (e.g. acting calmly during crises; being consistent rather than unpredictable; not passing personal stress onto the team)
   - Considerate approach (e.g. showing respect and thoughtfulness; providing positive as well as negative feedback; not imposing unrealistic deadlines; prioritizing work–life balance)
2. Managing and communicating workload
   - Proactive work management (e.g. communicating objectives clearly; developing action plans; managing current and future workloads to minimize stress)
   - Problem-solving (e.g. being rational and decisive, tackling and following up work problems)
   - Participative (e.g. delegating work equally; involving team members in decision making; enabling and empowering the team; encouraging participation)
3. Managing the individual within the team
   - Personally accessible (e.g. being available; communicating face-to-face rather than by email; responding to requests promptly)
   - Sociable (e.g. being friendly and having a sense of humour)
   - Empathic engagement (e.g. being a good listener; showing an interest in others and concern for their problems; taking the perspective of team members)
4. Reasoning/managing difficult situations
   - Managing conflict (e.g. remaining objective; dealing with conflict at an early stage rather than 'keeping the peace')
   - Use of organizational resources (e.g. seeking advice and support from others in order to resolve problems)
   - Taking responsibility for resolving issues (e.g. following up issues and supporting employees).

See http://www.hse.gov.uk/stress/mcit.htm for further details and to download the competency indicator tool.

measures have been developed from this process: (a) a self-assessment tool for managers to assess their own behaviour and (b) a tool designed for managers to receive feedback from others (such as their staff, peers and senior managers) about their behaviour. The management competencies are shown in Box 10.2.

This framework has great potential to help organizations manage stress proactively by informing recruitment, selection and training and development policies for managers. It is likely to be a useful starting point in identifying the manager behaviours that are conducive to supporting the wellbeing of social workers and building a culture of resilience. Although managers have a key role to play in preventing and reducing work-related stress in their employees, they also have to protect their own wellbeing (College of Social Work, 2012). It is acknowledged, however, that this may be a challenge under current working conditions. Line managers may be constrained by the need to manage a team with a large caseload or an entire service. They may also work within an organizational culture that stigmatizes stress and help-seeking, encourages long working hours and presenteeism and turns a blind eye to the adverse impact on wellbeing, work–life balance and job performance.

The way forward

Organizations are responsible for accurately diagnosing work-related stressors, implementing precisely targeted interventions, and monitoring their success over time. They should also provide personal development opportunities for line managers to develop the competencies required to protect the wellbeing of their staff, whilst also ensuring that there are mechanisms in place to support managers' personal wellbeing. The benefits of an integrated approach to managing the work-related wellbeing of social workers are wide-ranging. Work-related stress is extremely costly to the economy as well as the health and quality of life of individual employees (Donaldson-Feilder et al., 2011; HSE, 2013). Perceptions of social work as a satisfying profession that has effective support systems in place to alleviate the emotional demands that are intrinsic to the profession will have many advantages. This will attract better-qualified applicants, reduce attrition and extend the working life of social workers beyond the current average of eight years to normal retirement age. Improved wellbeing and resilience will also help reduce sickness absence and the cognitive impairments that stem from chronic work-related stress. This can only benefit service users as well as social workers.

Research on the individual and organizational factors that promote resilience is still in its infancy, and there are many areas that require further attention. Although some insight has been gained into the individual competencies that underpin resilience in social workers, the extent to which they protect wellbeing over time should be assessed by longitudinal studies. The ways in which organizations can support the development of individual resilience should also be explored. The factors that might facilitate or hamper organizational support for resilience are also worthy of examination, as they will be key factors in building a culture of resilience that is sustainable over the long term. Such factors might include time constraints, demands, difficulty in prioritizing self-care over service users' needs and feelings of guilt in doing so, as well as the stigma attached to disclosing work-related stress and failure to cope. The manager-competency framework discussed above was developed to be applicable to all types of job. Nonetheless, many of the line manager behaviours that have the potential to protect the wellbeing of social workers are likely to be specific to the job context. The validity of the HSE manager-competency approach should be tested in social work contexts, and the knowledge, skills and attributes that protect the wellbeing of employees in this environment should be carefully considered.

Conclusion

Social work is an exciting and fulfilling career that presents many emotional and intellectual demands. In order to ensure that social workers are able to protect their wellbeing while ensuring the best possible outcomes for people with whom they work, well-developed and carefully integrated personal and organizational resilience resources are required. It is hoped that this book will inspire social workers, educators, managers and leaders to prioritize the development of a truly resilient culture so that social workers can thrive rather than merely survive.

References

ADAMSON, C., BEDDOE, L. & DAVYS, A. 2012. Building resilient practitioners: Definitions and practitioner understandings. *British Journal of Social Work*, bcs142.

ADCS. 2013. *Challenges facing social workers are more acute than ever before.* Association of Directors of Children's Services. Available at http://www.adcs.org.uk/download/press-release/2013/ADCS-PR_Pressures_on_Social_Workers.pdf.

ALLEN, T. D. & ARMSTRONG, J. 2006. Further examination of the link between work–family conflict and physical health: The role of health-related behaviors. *American Behavioral Scientist*, 49, 1204–21.

ALQAHTANI, M. & HISTON, J. M. 2012. Improving the management of interruption through the Working Awareness Interruption Tool: WAIT. *Proceedings of the Human Factors and Ergonomics Society Annual Meeting*, 56, 393–7.

ANDERSSON, L., KING, R. & LALANDE, L. 2010. Dialogical mindfulness in supervision role-play. *Counselling and Psychotherapy Research*, 10, 287–94.

ANTHONY, E. J. 1974. The syndrome of the psychologically invulnerable child. *In:* ANTHONY, E. J. & KOUPERNIK, C. (eds) *The Child in his Family: Children at Psychiatric Risk.* New York: John Wiley.

ARONSSON, G., ASTVIK, W. & GUSTAFSSON, K. 2013. Work conditions, recovery and health: A study among workers within pre-school, home care and social work. *British Journal of Social Work*, doi: 10.1093/bjsw/bct036.

AUKES, L. C., GEERTSMA, J., COHEN-SCHOTANUS, J., ZWIERSTRA, R. P. & SLAETS, J. P. 2007. The development of a scale to measure personal reflection in medical practice and education. *Medical Teacher*, 29, 177–82.

AYRE, P. & CALDER, M. 2010. The de-professionalisation of child protection: Regaining our bearings. *In:* AYRE, P. & PRESTON-SHOOT, M. (eds) *Children's Services at the Crossroads: A Critical Evaluation of Contemporary Policy for Practice.* Lyme Regis, Dorset: Russell House.

AYRE, P. & PRESTON-SHOOT, M. 2010. *Children's Services at the Crossroads: A Critical Evaluation of Contemporary Policy for Practice.* Lyme Regis, Dorset: Russell House.

BARAK, M., NISSLY, J. & LEVIN, A. 2001. Antecedents to retention and turnover among child welfare, social work, and other human service employees: What can we learn from past research? A review and metanalysis. *Social Service Review*, 75, 625–61.

BARAK, M. E. M., CHERIN, D. A. & BERKMAN, S. 1998. Organizational and personal dimensions in diversity climate: Ethnic and gender differences in employee perceptions. *Journal of Applied Behavioral Science*, 34, 82–104.

BARAK, M. E. M., TRAVIS, D. J., PYUN, H. & XIE, B. 2009. The impact of supervision on worker outcomes: A meta-analysis. *Social Service Review*, 83, 3–32.

BARLOW, C. & HALL, B. L. 2007. 'What about feelings?': A study of emotion and tension in social work field education. *Social Work Education*, 26, 399–413.

BARUCH, G. K. & BARNETT, R. C. 1986. Role quality, multiple role involvement, and psychological well-being in midlife women. *Journal of Personality and Social Psychology*, 51, 578.

BASW. 2011. BASW/CoSW England research on supervision in social work, with particular reference to supervision practice in multi disciplinary teams. Available at http://cdn.basw.co.uk/upload/basw_13955–1.pdf.

BAUMEISTER, R. F., BRATSLAVSKY, E., FINKENAUER, C. & VOHS, K. D. 2001. Bad is stronger than good. *Review of General Psychology*, 5(4), 323.

BEDDOE, L. 2010. Surveillance or reflection: Professional supervision in 'the risk society'. *British Journal of Social Work*, 40, 1279–96.

BEDDOE, L. & DAVYS, A. 2010. *Best Practice in Professional Supervision: A Guide for the Helping Professions*. London: Jessica Kingsley.

BEDDOE, L., DAVYS, A. & ADAMSON, C. 2013. Educating resilient practitioners. *Social Work Education*, 32, 100–17.

BENNETT, P., EVANS, R. & TATTERSALL, A. 1993. Stress and coping in social workers: A preliminary investigation. *British Journal of Social Work*, 23, 31–44.

BERCELI, D. & NAPOLI, M. 2006. A proposal for a mindfulness-based trauma prevention program for social work professionals. *Complementary Health Practice Review*, 11, 153–65.

BERNERTH, J. B., WALKER, H. J. & HARRIS, S. G. 2011. Change fatigue: Development and initial validation of a new measure. *Work & Stress*, 25, 321–37.

BERNIER, D. 1998. A study of coping: Successful recovery from severe burnout and other reactions to severe work-related stress. *Work & Stress*, 12, 50–65.

BETZ, A. L. & SKOWRONSKI, J. J. 1997. Self-events and other-events: Temporal dating and event memory. *Memory & Cognition*, 25, 701–14.

BION, W. R. 1984. *Second Thoughts: Selected Papers on Psychoanalysis*. London: Karnac Books.

BIRNIE, K., SPECA, M. & CARLSON, L. E. 2010. Exploring self-compassion and empathy in the context of mindfulness-based stress reduction (MBSR). *Stress and Health*, 26, 359–71.

BOBER, T. & REGEHR, C. 2006. Strategies for reducing secondary or vicarious trauma: Do they work? *Brief Treatment and Crisis Intervention*, 6:1, 1–9.
BOLTON, G. 2010. *Reflective Practice: Writing and Professional Development*. London: Sage.
BOND, F. W., HAYES, S. C. & BARNES-HOLMES, D. 2006. Psychological flexibility, ACT, and organizational behavior. *Journal of Organizational Behavior Management*, 26, 25–54.
BOWERS, B. J., LAURING, C. & JACOBSON, N. 2001. How nurses manage time and work in long-term care. *Journal of Advanced Nursing*, 33, 484–91.
BRESÓ, E., SCHAUFELI, W. B. & SALANOVA, M. 2011. Can a self-efficacy-based intervention decrease burnout, increase engagement, and enhance performance? A quasi-experimental study. *Higher Education*, 61, 339–55.
BRESSER, F. & WILSON, C. 2006. What is coaching? *In*: PASSMORE, J. (ed.) *Excellence in Coaching: The Industry Guide*. London: Kogan Page.
BRIDE, B. E. 2007. Prevalence of secondary traumatic stress among social workers. *Social Work*, 52, 63–70.
BRINKBORG, H., MICHANEK, J., HESSER, H. & BERGLUND, G. 2011. Acceptance and commitment therapy for the treatment of stress among social workers: A randomized controlled trial. *Behaviour Research and Therapy*, 49, 389–98.
BROWN, K. W. & RYAN, R. M. 2003. The benefits of being present: Mindfulness and its role in psychological well-being. *Journal of Personality and Social Psychology*, 84, 822.
BROWN, K. W., RYAN, R. M. & CRESWELL, J. D. 2007. Mindfulness: Theoretical foundations and evidence for its salutary effects. *Psychological Inquiry*, 18, 211–37.
BRUNERO, S., COWAN, D. & FAIRBROTHER, G. 2008. Reducing emotional distress in nurses using cognitive behavioral therapy: a preliminary program evaluation. *Japan Journal of Nursing Science*, 5, 109–15.
BUEHLER, R., GRIFFIN, D. & PEETZ, J. 2010. Chapter one – the planning fallacy: Cognitive, motivational, and social origins. *Advances in Experimental Social Psychology*, 43, 1–62.
BUEHLER, R., GRIFFIN, D. & ROSS, M. 1994. Exploring the 'planning fallacy': Why people underestimate their task completion times. *Journal of Personality and Social Psychology*, 67, 366.
BUNGAY STAINER, M. 2010. *Do More Great Work*. New York: Workman.
BURT, C. D. & KEMP, S. 1994. Construction of activity duration and time management potential. *Applied Cognitive Psychology*, 8, 155–68.
CALLAN, V. J., TERRY, D. J. & SCHWEITZER, R. 1994. Coping resources, coping strategies and adjustment to organizational change: Direct or buffering effects? *Work & Stress*, 8, 372–83.

CAMPINHA-BACOTE, J. 2002. The process of cultural competence in the delivery of healthcare services: A model of care. *Journal of Transcultural Nursing*, 13, 181–4.

CARROLL, M. 2007. One more time: What is supervision? *Psychotherapy in Australia*, 13, 34.

CARVER, C. S., SCHEIER, M. F. & WEINTRAUB, J. K. 1989. Assessing coping strategies: A theoretically based approach. *Journal of Personality and Social Psychology*, 56, 267.

CHASKALSON, M. 2011. *The Mindful Workplace: Developing Resilient Individuals and Resonant Organizations with MBSR.* Oxford: Wiley-Blackwell.

CHILDREN'S WORKFORCE DEVELOPMENT COUNCIL 2009. *NQSW: Guide for Supervisors: Newly Qualified Social Worker Pilot Programme 2009–2010.* London: Children's Workforce Development Council.

CHILDS, J. H. & STOEBER, J. 2010. Self-oriented, other-oriented, and socially prescribed perfectionism in employees: Relationships with burnout and engagement. *Journal of Workplace Behavioral Health*, 25, 269–81.

CHISHOLM, C. D., COLLISON, E. K., NELSON, D. R. & CORDELL, W. H. 2000. Emergency department workplace interruptions: Are emergency physicians 'interrupt-driven' and 'multitasking'? *Academic Emergency Medicine*, 7, 1239–43.

CLAESSENS, B. J., VAN EERDE, W., RUTTE, C. G. & ROE, R. A. 2004. Planning behavior and perceived control of time at work. *Journal of Organizational Behavior*, 25, 937–50.

CLAESSENS, B. J., VAN EERDE, W., RUTTE, C. G. & ROE, R. A. 2007. A review of the time management literature. *Personnel Review*, 36, 255–76.

CLARKSON, G. P. & HODGKINSON, G. P. 2007. What can occupational stress diaries achieve that questionnaires can't? *Personnel Review*, 36, 684–700.

CLEMENTS, A. J., KINMAN, G. & GUPPY, A. 2014. 'You could damage somebody's life': Student and lecturer perspectives on commitment. *Social Work Education*, 33, 91–104.

COFFEY, M., DUGDILL, L. & TATTERSALL, A. 2004. Stress in social services: Mental wellbeing, constraints and job satisfaction. *British Journal of Social Work*, 34, 735–46.

COHEN, B.-Z. 1999. Intervention and supervision in strengths-based social work practice. *Families in Society: The Journal of Contemporary Social Services*, 80, 460–6.

COHEN, S. 2004. Social relationships and health. *American Psychologist*, 59, 676.

COHEN-KATZ, J., WILEY, S., CAPUANO, T., BAKER, D. M., DEITRICK, L. & SHAPIRO, S. 2005a. The effects of mindfulness-based stress reduction on nurse stress and burnout: A qualitative and quantitative study, part III. *Holistic Nursing Practice*, 19, 78–86.

COHEN-KATZ, J., WILEY, S. D., CAPUANO, T., BAKER, D. M. & SHAPIRO, S. 2005b. The effects of mindfulness-based stress reduction on nurse stress and burnout, Part II: A quantitative and qualitative study. *Holistic Nursing Practice*, 19, 26–35.

COJOCARU, S. 2010. Appreciative supervision in social work: New opportunities for changing the social work practice. *Revista de Cercetare şi Intervenţie Socială*, 29, 72–91.

COLLARD, P., AVNY, N. & BONIWELL, I. 2008. Teaching mindfulness based cognitive therapy (MBCT) to students: The effects of MBCT on the levels of mindfulness and subjective well-being. *Counselling Psychology Quarterly*, 21, 323–36.

COLLEGE OF SOCIAL WORK. (2012) *Professional Capabilities Framework*, College of Social Work. Available at http://www.tcsw.org.uk/pcf.aspx.

COLLINGS, J. A. & MURRAY, P. J. 1996. Predictors of stress amongst social workers: An empirical study. *British Journal of Social Work*, 26, 375–87.

COLLINS, S. 2007. Social workers, resilience, positive emotions and optimism. *Practice*, 19, 255–69.

COLLINS, S. 2008. Statutory social workers: Stress, job satisfaction, coping, social support and individual differences. *British Journal of Social Work*, 38, 1173–93.

COLLINS, S. 2013. Alternative psychological approaches for social workers and social work students dealing with stress in the UK: Sense of coherence, challenge appraisals, self-efficacy and sense of control. *British Journal of Social Work*, bct103.

COLLINS, S., COFFEY, M. & MORRIS, L. 2010. Social work students: Stress, support and well-being. *British Journal of Social Work*, 40, 963–82.

COLTRANE, S., MILLER, E. C., DEHAAN, T. & STEWART, L. 2013. Fathers and the flexibility stigma. *Journal of Social Issues*, 69, 279–302.

COOPER, A. 2005. Surface and depth in the Victoria Climbié inquiry report. *Child & Family Social Work*, 10, 1–9.

COOPERRIDER, D. L., WHITNEY, D. K. & STAVROS, J. M. 2003. *Appreciative Inquiry Handbook*. Toronto, ON: Lakeshore Communications.

COUSINS, R., MACKAY, C. J., CLARKE, S. D., KELLY, C., KELLY, P. J. & MCCAIG, R. H. 2004. 'Management standards' work-related stress in the UK: Practical development. *Work & Stress*, 18, 113–36.

COVEY, S. R. 1997. *The 7 Habits of Highly Effective Families*. New York: St. Martin's Press.

COX, T., KARANIKA, M., GRIFFITHS, A. & HOUDMONT, J. 2007. Evaluating organizational-level work stress interventions: Beyond traditional methods. *Work & Stress*, 21, 348–62.

CPCSW, C. P. 2007. No More Blame Game: The Future for Children's Social Workers. *Report of the Conservative Party Commission on Social Workers*.

London, Conservative Party. Available at www.conservatives. com/~/media/ Files/Downloadable% 20Files.

CRANE, R. 2009. *Mindfulness-based Cognitive Therapy: Distinctive Features.* London: Routledge.

CROPLEY, M. & ZIJLSTRA, F. 2011. Work and rumination. *In:* LANGAN-FOX, J. & COOPER, C. L. (eds) *Handbook of Stress in the Occupations.* Cheltenham: Edward Elgar.

CROSSFIELD, S., KINMAN, G. & JONES, F. 2005. Crossover of occupational stress in dual-career couples: The role of work demands and supports, job commitment and marital communication. *Community, Work and Family,* 8, 211–32.

CSIKSZENT, M. 1991. *Flow.* London: HarperCollins.

CUNNINGHAM, M. 2004. Teaching social workers about trauma: Reducing the risks of vicarious traumatization in the classroom. *Journal of Social Work Education,* 40, 305–17.

CUTRONA, C. E. & RUSSELL, D. W. 1990. Type of social support and specific stress: Toward a theory of optimal matching. *In:* SARASON, B. R., SARASON, I. G. & PIERCE, G. R. (eds) *Social Support: An Interactional View.* New York: John Wiley.

DAHL, M. S. 2011. Organizational change and employee stress. *Management Science,* 57, 240–56.

DARUNA, J. H. 2012. *Introduction to Psychoneuroimmunology,* San Diego: Academic Press.

DAVIS, D.M. & HAYES, J.A. 2011. What are the benefits of mindfulness? A practice review of psychotherapy-related research. *Psychotherapy,* 48(2), 198.

DAVIS, M. H. 1983. Measuring individual differences in empathy: Evidence for a multidimensional approach. *Journal of Personality and Social Psychology,* 44, 113.

DEMEROUTI, E., LE BLANC, P. M., BAKKER, A. B., SCHAUFELI, W. B. & HOX, J. 2009. Present but sick: A three-wave study on job demands, presenteeism and burnout. *Career Development International,* 14, 50–68.

DE VOS, A., & SOENS, N. 2008. Protean attitude and career success: The mediating role of self-management. *Journal of Vocational Behavior,* 73(3), 449–56.

DICKSTEIN, L. J., STEPHENSON, J. J. & HINZ, L. D. 1990. Psychiatric impairment in medical students. *Academic Medicine,* 65, 588–93.

DIERDORFF, E. C. & ELLINGTON, J. K. 2008. It's the nature of the work: Examining behavior-based sources of work-family conflict across occupations. *Journal of Applied Psychology,* 93, 883.

DIMAURO, J., DOMINGUES, J., FERNANDEZ, G. & TOLIN, D. F. 2013. Long-term effectiveness of CBT for anxiety disorders in an adult outpatient clinic sample: A follow-up study. *Behaviour Research and Therapy,* 51, 82–6.

DONALDSON-FEILDER, E., LEWIS, R. & YARKER, J. 2011. *Preventing Stress in Organizations: How to Develop Positive Managers*. Chichester: Wiley.

DOWNEY, M. 1999. *Effective Coaching*. London: Orion Business Books.

DOXTDATOR, M. L. 2012. Mindfulness: Helping Social Workers' Bring Themselves Home'. Open Access dissertations and theses. Available at http://digitalcommons.mcmaster.ca/cgi/viewcontent.cgi?article=8406& context=opendissertations.

DRACH-ZAHAVYA , A., EREZ, M. 2002.Organizational challenge versus threat effects on the goal–performance relationship. *Behavior and Human Decision Processes*, 88, 667–82.

DRISCOLL, M. 2011. Christian yoga: it's a stretch. Available at http://pastormark.tv/2011/11/02/christian-yoga-its-a-stretch.

DRUCKER, P. F. 1967. *The Effective Executive*. London: HarperCollins.

DUGGLEBY, W., COOPER, D. & PENZ, K. 2009. Hope, self-efficacy, spiritual well-being and job satisfaction. *Journal of Advanced Nursing*, 65, 2376–85.

DZIEGIELEWSKI, S. F., TURNAGE, B. & ROEST-MARTI, S. 2004. Addressing stress with social work students: A controlled evaluation. *Journal of Social Work Education*, 40, 105–19.

EBORALL, C., GARMESON, K. & BRITAIN, G. 2001. *Desk Research on Recruitment and Retention in Social Care and Social Work*. London: Department of Health.

EBY, L. T., CASPER, W. J., LOCKWOOD, A., BORDEAUX, C. & BRIN-LEY, A. 2005. Work and family research in IO/OB: Content analysis and review of the literature (1980–2002). *Journal of Vocational Behavior*, 66, 124–97.

EDWARDS, J. R., CAPLAN, R. D. & HARRISON, R. V. 1998. Person-environment fit theory: Conceptual foundations, empirical evidence, and directions for future research. *In:* COOPER, C. L. (ed.) *Theories of Organizational Stress*. Oxford: Oxford University Press.

EDWARDS, J. R. & ROTHBARD, N. P. 1999. Work and family stress and well-being: An examination of person-environment fit in the work and family domains. *Organizational Behavior and Human Decision Processes*, 77, 85–129.

EMMONS, R. A. 1986. Personal strivings: An approach to personality and subjective well-being. *Journal of Personality and Social Psychology*, 51, 1058.

EVANS, S., HUXLEY, P., WEBBER, M., KATONA, C., GATELY, C., MEARS, A., MEDINA, J., PAJAK, S. & KENDALL, T. 2005. The impact of 'statutory duties' on mental health social workers in the UK. *Health & Social Care in the Community*, 13, 145–54.

FELTON, J. 1998. Burnout as a clinical entity – its importance in health care workers. *Occupational Medicine*, 48, 237–50.

FERGUSON, H. 2009. Performing child protection: home visiting, movement and the struggle to reach the abused child. *Child & Family Social Work*, 14, 471–80.

FERGUSON, H. 2011. *Child Protection Practice*. Basingstoke: Palgrave Macmillan.

FERRIE, J. E., SHIPLEY, M. J., MARMOT, M. G., STANSFELD, S. & SMITH, G. D. 1998. The health effects of major organisational change and job insecurity. *Social Science & Medicine*, 46, 243–54.

FIGLEY, C. R. 2002. Compassion fatigue: Psychotherapists' chronic lack of self care. *Journal of Clinical Psychology*, 58, 1433–41.

FLAXMAN, P. E. & BOND, F. W. 2010. A randomised worksite comparison of acceptance and commitment therapy and stress inoculation training. *Behaviour Research and Therapy*, 48, 816–20.

FLETCHER, D. & SARKAR, M. 2013. Psychological resilience: A review and critique of definitions, concepts, and theory. *European Psychologist*, 18, 12.

FOOK, J. & GARDNER, F. 2007. *Practising Critical Reflection: A Resource Handbook*. Maidenhead: McGraw-Hill International/Open University Press.

FOUCHÉ, C. & MARTINDALE, K. 2011. Work–life balance: practitioner well-being in the social work education curriculum. *Social Work Education*, 30, 675–85.

FOX, S. & SPECTOR, P. E. 2005. *Counterproductive work behavior: Investigations of actors and targets*, Washington, DC: American Psychological Association.

FRENCH, J. R., Jr. 1973. Person Role Fit. *Occupational Mental Health*, 3, 15–20.

FRIED, Y., BEN-DAVID, H. A., TIEGS, R. B., AVITAL, N. & YEVERECHYAHU, U. 1998. The interactive effect of role conflict and role ambiguity on job performance. *Journal of Occupational and Organizational Psychology*, 71, 19–27.

FROMAN, L. 2010. Positive psychology in the workplace. *Journal of Adult Development*, 17, 59–69.

FRONE, M. R., RUSSELL, M. & COOPER, M. L. 1992. Antecedents and outcomes of work–family conflict: testing a model of the work-family interface. *Journal of Applied Psychology*, 77, 65.

GAZZOLA, N. & THÉRIAULT, A. 2007. Super-(and not-so-super-) vision of counsellors-in-training: Supervisee perspectives on broadening and narrowing processes. *British Journal of Guidance & Counselling*, 35, 189–204.

GEO 2009. Flexible working: benefits and barriers: Perceptions of working parents. Available at http://sta.geo.useconnect.co.uk/PDF/294951_GEO_flexible_working_acc.pdf.

GEORGE, C. 2009. *The Psychological Contract: Managing And Developing Professional Groups: Managing and developing professional groups*. Maidenhead: McGraw-Hill Education.

GERDES, K. E. & SEGAL, E. 2011. Importance of empathy for social work practice: Integrating new science. *Social Work*, 56, 141–8.

GIBB, J., CAMERON, I., HAMILTON, R., MURPHY, E. & NAJI, S. 2010. Mental health nurses' and allied health professionals' perceptions of the role of the Occupational Health Service in the management of work-related stress: how do they self-care? *Journal of Psychiatric and Mental Health Nursing*, 17, 838–45.

GIBBS, G. 1988. *Learning by Doing: A Guide to Teaching and Learning Methods*. Oxford: Further Education Unit, Oxford Polytechnic.

GOCKEL, A., CAIN, T., MALOVE, S. & JAMES, S. 2013. Mindfulness as Clinical Training: Student Perspectives on the Utility of Mindfulness Training in Fostering Clinical Intervention Skills. *Journal of Religion & Spirituality in Social Work: Social Thought*, 32, 36–59.

GOH, E. C. 2012. Integrating mindfulness and reflection in the teaching and learning of listening skills for undergraduate social work students in Singapore. *Social Work Education*, 31, 587–604.

GOLDIN, P. R., ZIV, M., JAZAIERI, H., WERNER, K., KRAEMER, H., HEIMBERG, R. G. & GROSS, J. J. 2012. Cognitive reappraisal self-efficacy mediates the effects of individual cognitive-behavioral therapy for social anxiety disorder. *Journal of Consulting and Clinical Psychology*, 80, 1034.

GOLEMAN, D. 1996. *Emotional Intelligence: Why It Can Matter More Than IQ*. London: Bloomsbury.

GOVINDJI, R. & LINLEY, P. A. 2007. Strengths use, self-concordance and well-being: Implications for strengths coaching and coaching psychologists. *International Coaching Psychology Review*, 2, 143–53.

GRAHAM, J. R. & SHIER, M. L. 2010. The social work profession and subjective well-being: The impact of a profession on overall subjective well-being. *British Journal of Social Work*, 40, 1553–72.

GRANT, A. 2010. *Cognitive Behavioural Interventions for Mental Health Practitioners*. London: Sage.

GRANT, A. M. 2008. Personal life coaching for coaches-in-training enhances goal attainment, insight and learning. *Coaching: An International Journal of Theory, Research and Practice*, 1, 54–70.

GRANT, A. M. 2012. Making positive change: A randomized study comparing solution-focused vs. problem-focused coaching questions. *Journal of Systemic Therapies*, 31, 21–35.

GRANT, J., SCHOFIELD, M. J. & CRAWFORD, S. 2012. Managing difficulties in supervision: Supervisors' perspectives. *Journal of Counseling Psychology*, 59, 528.

GRANT, L. 2013. Hearts and minds: aspects of empathy and wellbeing in social work students. *Social Work Education*, 1–15.

GRANT, L. & KINMAN, G. 2012. Enhancing wellbeing in social work students: building resilience in the next generation. *Social Work Education*, 31, 605–21.

GRANT, L. & KINMAN, G. 2013. 'Bouncing back?' Personal representations of resilience of student and experienced social workers. *Practice*, 25, 349–66.

GRANT, L., KINMAN, G. & ALEXANDER, K. (2014). What's all this talk about emotion? Developing emotional intelligence in social work students. *Social Work Education*, DOI:10.1080/02615479.2014.891012

GRANT, L., KINMAN, G. & BAKER, S. 2013. Developing an 'emotional curriculum' for social workers. York. Higher Education Academy. Available at http://www.heacademy.ac.uk/assets/documents/disciplines/hsc/SW-SP/Developing_emotional_curriculum_Grant_Oct_2013.pdf.

GREEN, L., OADES, L. & GRANT, A. 2006. Cognitive-behavioral, solution-focused life coaching: Enhancing goal striving, well-being, and hope. *Journal of Positive Psychology*, 1, 142–9.

GREEN, S., GRANT, A. & RYNSAARDT, J. 2007. Evidence-based life coaching for senior high school students: Building hardiness and hope. *International Coaching Psychology Review*, 2, 24–32.

GREENBERG, M. A., WORTMAN, C. B. & STONE, A. A. 1996. Emotional expression and physical heath: Revising traumatic memories or fostering self-regulation? *Journal of Personality and Social Psychology*, 71, 588.

GREENE, J. & GRANT, A. M. 2003. *Solution-focused coaching: Managing people in a complex world*. Harlow: Pearson Education.

GREENHAUS, J. H. & BEUTELL, N. J. 1985. Sources of conflict between work and family roles. *Academy of Management Review*, 10, 76–88.

GREGURAS, G. J. & DIEFENDORFF, J. M. 2009. Different fits satisfy different needs: Linking person-environment fit to employee commitment and performance using self-determination theory. *Journal of Applied Psychology*, 94, 465.

GREUBEL, J. & KECKLUND, G. 2011. The impact of organizational changes on work stress, sleep, recovery and health. *Industrial Health*, 49, 353–64.

GUEST, D. & CONWAY, N. 2004. *Employee Well-being and the Psychological Contract: A Report for the CIPD*. London: Chartered Institute of Personnel and Development.

HAMAMA, L. 2012. Burnout in social workers treating children as related to demographic characteristics, work environment, and social support. *Social Work Research*, 36, 113–25.

HAMMER, L. B., KOSSEK, E. E., ZIMMERMAN, K. & DANIELS, R. 2007. Clarifying the construct of family-supportive supervisory behaviors (FSSB): A multilevel perspective. *Research in Occupational Stress and Well-being*, 6, 165–204.

HANSON, R. 2009. *Buddha's Brain: The Practical Neuroscience of Happiness, Love, and Wisdom*. Oakland, CA: New Harbinger.

HERACLIDES, A., CHANDOLA, T., WITTE, D. R. & BRUNNER, E. J. 2009. Psychosocial stress at work doubles the risk of Type 2 diabetes in middle-aged women Evidence from the Whitehall II Study. *Diabetes Care*, 32, 2230–5.

HERSHCOVIS, M. S. & BARLING, J. 2010. Comparing victim attributions and outcomes for workplace aggression and sexual harassment. *Journal of Applied Psychology*, 95, 874.

HEWSON, J. & SHOHET, R. 2008. Passionate supervision: A wider landscape. *Passionate Supervision*, 34–47.

HICK, S. F. 2009. *Mindfulness and Social Work*. Chicago: Lyceum Books.

HIGGINS, E. T., KLEIN, R. & STRAUMAN, T. 1985. Self-concept discrepancy theory: A psychological model for distinguishing among different aspects of depression and anxiety. *Social Cognition*, 3, 51–76.

HOCHSCHILD, A. R. 1983. *The Managed Heart: Commercialization of Human Feeling*. Berkeley: University of California Press.

HOFMANN, S. G., ASNAANI, A., VONK, I. J., SAWYER, A. T. & FANG, A. 2012. The efficacy of cognitive behavioral therapy: A review of meta-analyses. *Cognitive Therapy and Research*, 36, 427–40.

HOLMES, T. H. & MASUDA, M. 1973. Life change and illness susceptibility. *In:* SCOTT, J. P. & Senay, E. C. (eds) *Separation and Depression*. Washington, DC: American Association for the Advancement of Science.

HOUDMONT, J., KERR, R. & RANDALL, R. 2012. Organisational psychosocial hazard exposures in UK policing: Management Standards Indicator Tool reference values. *Policing: An International Journal of Police Strategies & Management*, 35, 182–97.

HOUSTON, G. 1990. *The Red Book of Gestalt*. Open & Distance Education Statistics.

HOWE, P. D. 2008. *The Emotionally Intelligent Social Worker*: Basingstoke: Palgrave Macmillan.

HSE 2009. Self-reported Work-related Illness and Workplace Injuries in 2007/08: Results from the Labour Force Survey. Available at www.hse.gov.uk/statistics/lfs/lfs0708.pdf.

HSE 2010. Management Standards for Work Related Stress. Available at www.hse.gov.uk/stress/standards/.

HSE 2013. Stress and Psychological Disorders in Great Britain 2013. Available at www.hse.gov.uk/statistics/causdis/stress/stress.pdf.

HUGHES, L. & PENGELLY, P. 1997. *Staff Supervision in a Turbulent Environment: Managing Process and Task in Front-Line Services*. London: Jessica Kingsley.

HÜLSHEGER, U. R., ALBERTS, H. J., FEINHOLDT, A. & LANG, J. W. 2013. Benefits of mindfulness at work: The role of mindfulness in emotion regulation, emotional exhaustion, and job satisfaction. *Journal of Applied Psychology*, 98, 310.

HUNOT, V., CHURCHILL, R., SILVA DE LIMA, M. & TEIXEIRA, V. 2007. Psychological therapies for generalised anxiety disorder. *Cochrane Database System Review*, 1.

HUSSEIN, S., MANTHORPE, J., RIDLEY, J., AUSTERBERRY, H., FARRELLY, N., LARKINS, C., BILSON, A. & STANLEY, N. 2013. Independent Children's Social Work Practice Pilots: Evaluating Practitioners' Job Control and Burnout. *Research on Social Work Practice*, 1049731513492859.

HUXLEY, P., EVANS, S., GATELY, C., WEBBER, M., MEARS, A., PAJAK, S., KENDALL, T., MEDINA, J. & KATONA, C. 2005. Stress and pressures in mental health social work: The worker speaks. *British Journal of Social Work*, 35, 1063–79.

JACELON, C. S. 1997. The trait and process of resilience. *Journal of Advanced Nursing*, 25, 123–9.

JENSEN, P. M., TROLLOPE-KUMAR, K., WATERS, H. & EVERSON, J. 2008. Building physician resilience. *Canadian Family Physician*, 54, 722–9.

JOHANNESSEN, H. A., TYNES, T. & STERUD, T. 2013. Effects of occupational role conflict and emotional demands on subsequent psychological distress: a 3–year follow-up study of the general working population in norway. *Journal of Occupational and Environmental Medicine*, 55, 605–13.

JOHNSON, J. V. & HALL, E. M. 1988. Job strain, work place social support, and cardiovascular disease: a cross-sectional study of a random sample of the Swedish working population. *American Journal of Public Health*, 78, 1336–42.

JOHNSTON, P. & PATON, D. 2003. Environmental resilience: Psychological empowerment in high-risk professions. In PATON, D, VIOLANTI, J. & SMITH, L. (eds) *Promoting Capabilities to Manage Posttraumatic Stress: Perspectives on Resilience*. Springfield, IL: Charles C. Thomas.

JONES, F. & BRIGHT, J. 2001. *Stress: Myth, Theory and Research*. Harlow: Pearson Education.

JONES, F. & IBBESTON, K. 1991. Stressors and strains amongst social workers: Demands, supports, constraints, and psychological health. *British Journal of Social Work*, 21, 443–69.

JORDAN, J. 2003. *Beacons of Excellence in Stress Prevention*. London: HSE Books.

JORDAN, P. J., ASHKANASY, N. M. & HARTEL, C. E. 2002. Emotional intelligence as a moderator of emotional and behavioral reactions to job insecurity. *Academy of Management Review*, 27, 361–72.

JOYCE, B. & SHOWERS, B. 1982. The coaching of teaching. *Educational Leadership*, 40, 4–10.

KABAT-ZINN, J. 1994. *Wherever You Go, There You Are: Mindfulness Meditation in Everyday Life*. New York: Hyperion.

KAHILL, S. 1988. Symptoms of professional burnout: A review of the empirical evidence. *Canadian Psychology/Psychologie Canadienne*, 29, 284.

KAHN, R. L., WOLFE, D. M., QUINN, R. P., SNOEK, J. D. & ROSENTHAL, R. A. 1964. *Organizational Stress: Studies in Role Conflict and Ambiguity*. Hoboken, NJ: John Wiley.

KAHNEMAN, D. & TVERSKY, A. 1977. *Intuitive Prediction: Biases and Corrective Procedures*. DTIC Document.

KALLIATH, P., HUGHES, M. & NEWCOMBE, P. 2012. When work and family are in conflict: Impact on psychological strain experienced by social workers in Australia. *Australian Social Work*, 65, 355–71.

KALLIATH, P. & KALLIATH, T. 2006. Work Family Conflict and Facilitation among Social Workers: A Proposed Study. *In:* STASHEVSKY, S. (ed.) *Work Values and Behavior*. Shreveport, LA: International Society for the Study of Work and Organizational Values.

KANTER, R. M. 1989. Work and Family in the United States: A Critical Review and Agenda for Research and Policy. *Family Business Review*, 2, 77–114.

KARASEK, R. 1990. Lower health risk with increased job control among white collar workers. *Journal of Organizational Behavior*, 11, 171–85.

KARLSON, B., JÖNSSON, P., PÅLSSON, B., ÅBJÖRNSSON, G., MALMBERG, B., LARSSON, B. & ÖSTERBERG, K. 2010. Return to work after a workplace-oriented intervention for patients on sick-leave for burnout – a prospective controlled study. *BMC Public Health*, 10, 301.

KATO, T. 2012. Development of the Coping Flexibility Scale: Evidence for the coping flexibility hypothesis. *Journal of Counseling Psychology*, 59, 262.

KATZ, D. & KAHN, R. 1978. *Social Psychology of Organizations*, 2nd edn. New York: John Wiley.

KAUFFMAN, C. & SCOULAR, A. 2004. Toward a positive psychology of executive coaching. *Positive Psychology in Practice*, 287–302.

KEMERY, E. R., MOSSHOLDER, K. W. & BEDEIAN, A. G. 1987. Role stress, physical symptomatology, and turnover intentions: A causal analysis of three alternative specifications. *Journal of Organizational Behavior*, 8, 11–23.

KENG, S.-L., SMOSKI, M. J. & ROBINS, C. J. 2011. Effects of mindfulness on psychological health: A review of empirical studies. *Clinical Psychology Review*, 31, 1041–56.

KERR, R., MCHUGH, M. & MCCRORY, M. 2009. HSE Management Standards and stress-related work outcomes. *Occupational Medicine*, 59, 574–9.

KESSEN, C. & TURNER, K. 2012. Developing professional competence in graduate school: Student Experiences of the social work curriculum. *Public Voices*, 12, 10–18.

KETS DE VRIES, M. F. 2010. *Leadership Coaching and the Rescuer Syndrome: How to Manage both Sides of the Couch*. INSEAD Working Paper No.

2010/104/EFE/IGLC. http://papers.ssrn.com/sol3/papers.cfm?abstract_id=1722610.

KIM, H. & STONER, M. 2008. Burnout and turnover intention among social workers: Effects of role stress, job autonomy and social support. *Administration in Social Work*, 32, 5–25.

KINMAN, G. & GRANT, L. 2010. *Emotional Intelligence, Reflective Abilities and Wellbeing in Social Workers and Related Skills in Predicting Wellbeing and Performance in Social Work Practice*. Bedford: University of Bedfordshire, Report for CETL.

KINMAN, G. & GRANT, L. 2011. Exploring stress resilience in trainee social workers: The role of emotional and social competencies. *British Journal of Social Work*, 41, 261–75.

KINMAN, G. & JONES, F. 2001. The work–home interface. *In:* JONES, F., BRIGHT, J. & CLOW, A. (eds) *Stress: Myth, Theory and Research*. New York: Prentice Hall.

KINMAN, G. & JONES, F. 2005. Lay representations of workplace stress: What do people really mean when they say they are stressed? *Work & Stress*, 19, 101–20.

KINMAN, G. & WRAY, S. 2013. *Higher Stress: A Survey of Stress and Well-being among Staff in Higher Education*. London: University and College Union.

KINMAN, G., WRAY, S. & STRANGE, C. 2011. Emotional labour, burnout and job satisfaction in UK teachers: the role of workplace social support. *Educational Psychology*, 31, 843–56.

KLEIN, W. M. & WEINSTEIN, N. D. 1997. Social comparison and unrealistic optimism about personal risk. *In:* BUUNK, B. P. & GIBBONS, F. X., *Health, Coping, and Well-being: Perspectives from Social Comparison Theory*. Mahwah, NJ: Lawrence Erlbaum.

KNUDSEN, H. K., DUCHARME, L. J. & ROMAN, P. M. 2007. Job stress and poor sleep quality: Data from an American sample of full-time workers. *Social Science & Medicine*, 64, 1997–2007.

KOESKE, G. F. & KELLY, T. 1995. The impact of overinvolvement on burnout and job satisfaction. *American Journal of Orthopsychiatry*, 65, 282–92.

KOESKE, G. F. & KOESKE, R. D. 1989. Work load and burnout: Can social support and perceived accomplishment help? *Social Work*, 34, 243–8.

KOLB, D. A. 1984. *Experiential Learning: Experience as the Source of Learning and Development*. Englewood Cliffs, NJ: Prentice-Hall.

KORABIK, K., LERO, D. S. & WHITEHEAD, D. L. 2011. *Handbook of Work–Family Integration: Research, Theory, and Best Practices*. New York: Elsevier Science.

KOSSEK, E. E., LAUTSCH, B. A. 2008. *The CEO of Me: Creating a Life that Works in the Flexible Job Age*. Pennsylvania, PA: Wharton School Publishing.

KOSSEK, E. E., LAUTSCH, B. A. & EATON, S. C. 2006. Telecommuting, control, and boundary management: Correlates of policy use and practice, job control, and work–family effectiveness. *Journal of Vocational Behavior*, 68, 347–67.

KOSZYCKI, D., BENGER, M., SHLIK, J. & BRADWEJN, J. 2007. Randomized trial of a meditation-based stress reduction program and cognitive behavior therapy in generalized social anxiety disorder. *Behaviour Research and Therapy*, 45, 2518–26.

KOTZÉ, M. & VENTER, I. 2011. Differences in emotional intelligence between effective and ineffective leaders in the public sector: An empirical study. *International Review of Administrative Sciences*, 77, 397–427.

KOZLOWSKA, K., NUNN, K. & COUSENS, P. 1997a. Adverse experiences in psychiatric training. Part 2. *Australian and New Zealand Journal of Psychiatry*, 31, 641–52.

KOZLOWSKA, K., NUNN, K. & COUSENS, P. 1997b. Training in psychiatry: An examination of trainee perceptions. Part 1. *Australasian Psychiatry*, 31, 628–40.

KUTILEK, L. M. & EARNEST, G. W. 2001. Supporting professional growth through mentoring and coaching. *Journal of Extension*, 39, 3–13.

LADYSHEWSKY, R. 2004. The impact of peer-coaching on the clinical reasoning of the novice practitioner. *Physiotherapy Canada*, 56(1), 15–26.

LADYSHEWSKY, R. 2010. Peer coaching. *In:* COX, E., BACHKIROVA, T. & CLUTTERBUCK, D. (eds) *The Complete Handbook of Coaching.* London: Sage.

LAGERVELD, S. E., BLONK, R. W., BRENNINKMEIJER, V., WIJNGAARDS-DE MEIJ, L. & SCHAUFELI, W. B. 2012. Work-focused treatment of common mental disorders and return to work: A comparative outcome study. *Journal of Occupational Health Psychology*, 17, 220.

LAMBERT, E. G., PASUPULETI, S., CLUSE-TOLAR, T., JENNINGS, M. & BAKER, D. 2006. The impact of work-family conflict on social work and human service worker job satisfaction and organizational commitment: An exploratory study. *Administration in Social Work*, 30, 55–74.

LAMING, H. B. & COMMONS, G. B. P. H. O. 2009. *The Protection of Children in England: A Progress Report.* London: Stationery Office.

LAMONTAGNE, A. D., KEEGEL, T., LOUIE, A. M., OSTRY, A. & LANDSBERGIS, P. A. 2007. A systematic review of the job-stress intervention evaluation literature, 1990–2005. *International Journal of Occupational and Environmental Health*, 13, 268–80.

LARSEN, J. K., BRAND, N., BERMOND, B. & HIJMAN, R. 2003. Cognitive and emotional characteristics of alexithymia: A review of neurobiological studies. *Journal of Psychosomatic Research*, 54, 533–41.

LASKE, O. E. 2006. From coach training to coach education: Teaching coaching within a comprehensively evidence based framework. *International Journal of Evidence Based Coaching and Mentoring*, 4, 45–57.

LAZARUS, R. S. & FOLKMAN, S. 1984. *Stress, Appraisal, and Coping*. New York: Springer.

LEVITT, J. T., BROWN, T. A., ORSILLO, S. M. & BARLOW, D. H. 2004. The effects of acceptance versus suppression of emotion on subjective and psychophysiological response to carbon dioxide challenge in patients with panic disorder. *Behavior Therapy*, 35, 747–66.

LI, C.-Y. & SUNG, F.-C. 1999. A review of the healthy worker effect in occupational epidemiology. *Occupational Medicine*, 49, 225–9.

LINLEY, A. 2008. *Average to A+: Realising Strengths in Yourself and Others*. Coventry: CAPP Press.

LINLEY, P. A., NIELSEN, K. M., GILLETT, R., & BISWAS-DIENER, R. (2010). Using signature strengths in pursuit of goals: Effects on goal progress, need satisfaction, and well-being, and implications for coaching psychologists. *International Coaching Psychology Review*, 5(1), 6–15.

LIZZIO, A., WILSON, K. & QUE, J. 2009. Relationship dimensions in the professional supervision of psychology graduates: Supervisee perceptions of processes and outcome. *Studies in Continuing Education*, 31, 127–40.

LLOYD, C., KING, R. & CHENOWETH, L. 2002. Social work, stress and burnout: A review. *Journal of Mental Health*, 11, 255–65.

LOCKE, E. A. & LATHAM, G. P. 2006. New directions in goal-setting theory. *Current Directions in Psychological Science*, 15, 265–8.

LOFTUS, E. F. & MARBURGER, W. 1983. Since the eruption of Mt. St. Helens, has anyone beaten you up? Improving the accuracy of retrospective reports with landmarkevents. *Memory & Cognition*, 11, 114–20.

LOWINGER, R. J. & ROMBOM, H. 2012. The effectiveness of cognitive behavioral therapy for PTSD in New York City transit workers: A preliminary evaluation. *North American Journal of Psychology*, 14:3, 471.

LUTHANS, F., AVOLIO, B. J., AVEY, J. B. & NORMAN, S. M. 2007. Positive psychological capital: Measurement and relationship with performance and satisfaction. *Personnel Psychology*, 60, 541–72.

LUTHANS, F., NORMAN, S. M., AVOLIO, B. J. & AVEY, J. B. 2008. The mediating role of psychological capital in the supportive organizational climate–employee performance relationship. *Journal of Organizational Behavior*, 29, 219–38.

LUTHAR, S. S., CICCHETTI, D. & BECKER, B. 2000. The construct of resilience: A critical evaluation and guidelines for future work. *Child Development*, 71, 543–62.

LYONS, D. M., PARKER, K. J., KATZ, M. & SCHATZBERG, A. F. 2009. Developmental cascades linking stress inoculation, arousal regulation, and resilience. *Frontiers in Behavioral Neuroscience*, 3, 32.

MACAN, T. H. 1994. Time management: Test of a process model. *Journal of Applied Psychology*, 79, 381.

MACAN, T. H., SHAHANI, C., DIPBOYE, R. L. & PHILLIPS, A. P. 1990. College students' time management: Correlations with academic performance and stress. *Journal of Educational Psychology*, 82, 760.

MACEWEN, K. E. & BARLING, J. 1991. Effects of maternal employment experiences on children's behavior via mood, cognitive difficulties, and parenting behavior. *Journal of Marriage and the Family*, 635–44.

MACKAY, C., COUSINS, R., KELLY, P., LEE, S. & MCCAIG, R. 2004. 'Management Standards' and work-related stress in the UK: Policy background and science. *Work & Stress*, 18, 91–112.

MAIDMENT, J. 2003. Problems experienced by students on field placement: Using research findings to inform curriculum design and content. *Australian Social Work*, 56, 50–60.

MAJOR, D. A., GERMANO, L. M., JONES, F., BURKE, R. & WESTMAN, M. 2006. The changing nature of work and its impact on the work–home interface. *In:* JONES, F., BURKE, R. & WESTMAN, M. (eds) *Work–life Balance: A Psychological Perspective*. New York: Psychology Press.

MARC, C. & OȘVAT, C. 2013. Stress and burnout among social workers. *Social Work Review/Revista de Asistenta Sociala*, 12(3), 121–30.

MARCHAND, W. R. 2012. Mindfulness-based stress reduction, mindfulness-based cognitive therapy, and Zen meditation for depression, anxiety, pain, and psychological distress. *Journal of Psychiatric Practice* 18, 233–52.

MASLACH, C., JACKSON, S. E. & LEITER, M. P. 1996. *Maslach Burnout Inventory Manual*. 3rd edn. Palo Alto, CA: Consulting Psychologists Press.

MASTEN, A. S., BEST, K. M. & GARMEZY, N. 1990. Resilience and development: Contributions from the study of children who overcome adversity. *Development and Psychopathology*, 2, 425–44.

MASTEN, A. S. & GARMEZY, N. 1985. Risk, vulnerability, and protective factors in developmental psychopathology. *In:* LAHEY, B. B. & KAZDIN, A. E. (eds) *Advances in Clinical Child Psychology*, Vol. 8. New York: Plenum.

MATHIAS-WILLIAMS, R. & THOMAS, N. 2002. Great expectations? The career aspirations of social work students. *Social Work Education*, 21, 421–35.

MATTHEWS, G., DAVIES, R., WESTERMAN, S., & STAMMERS, R. 2013. *Human Performance: Cognition, Stress, and Individual Differences*. London: Psychology Press.

MCALLISTER, M. & MCKINNON, J. 2009. The importance of teaching and learning resilience in the health disciplines: a critical review of the literature. *Nurse Education Today*, 29, 371–9.

MCCANN, C. M., BEDDOE, E., MCCORMICK, K., HUGGARD, P., KEDGE, S., ADAMSON, C. & HUGGARD, J. 2013. Resilience in the health professions: A review of recent literature. *International Journal of Wellbeing*, 3(1), 60–81.

MCDONALD, G., JACKSON, D., WILKES, L. & VICKERS, M. H. 2012. A work-based educational intervention to support the development of personal resilience in nurses and midwives. *Nurse Education Today*, 32, 378–84.

MCGARRIGLE, T. & WALSH, C. A. 2011. Mindfulness, self-care, and wellness in social work: Effects of contemplative training. *Journal of Religion & Spirituality in Social Work: Social Thought*, 30, 212–33.

MCMILLAN, K. & PERRON, A. 2013. Nurses amidst change: The concept of change fatigue offers an alternative perspective on organizational change. *Policy, Politics, & Nursing Practice*, 14, 26–32.

MCMURRAY, I., CONNOLLY, H., PRESTON-SHOOT, M. & WIGLEY, V. 2008. Constructing resilience: social workers' understandings and practice. *Health & Social Care in the Community*, 16, 299–309.

MEGGINSON, D., & CLUTTERBUCK, D. 2005. *Techniques for Coaching and Mentoring*. London: Routledge.

MEICHENBAUM, D. 2004. Stress inoculation. *In:* O'DONOHUE, W. T., FISHER, J. E. & HAYES, S. C. (eds) *Cognitive Behavior Therapy: Applying Empirically Supported Techniques in Your Practice*. Hoboken, NJ: John Wiley.

MEICHENBAUM, D. H. & DEFFENBACHER, J. L. 1988. Stress inoculation training. *Counseling Psychologist*, 16, 69–90.

MENZIES, L. E. 2000. Social systems as a defence against anxiety. *In:* DU GAY, P., EVANS, J., REDMAN, P. & UNIVERSITY, O. (eds) *Identity: A Reader*. London: Sage.

MICHIE, S. & WILLIAMS, S. 2003. Reducing work related psychological ill health and sickness absence: A systematic literature review. *Occupational and Environmental Medicine*, 60, 3–9.

MIDDLETON, C. A. 2008. Do mobile technologies enable work–life balance? *In:* HISLOP, D. (ed.) *Mobility and Technology in the Workplace*. Abingdon: Routledge.

MILLS, S. M. 2012. Unconscious sequences in child protection work: case studies of professionals' experiences of child removal. *Journal of Social Work Practice*, 26, 301–13.

MITCHELL, J. T. & BRAY, G. P. 1990. *Emeregency Services Stress: Guidelines for Preserving the Health and Careers of Emergency Services Personnel*, Englewood Cliffs, NJ: Prentice Hall/ PTR.

MOEN, P. 1997. Women's roles and resilience: Trajectories of advantage or turning points. *In:* GOTLIB, I. H. & WHEATON, B. (eds) *Stress and Adversity Over the Life Course: Trajectories and Turning Points*. New York: Cambridge University Press.

MORENO-JIMÉNEZ, B., MAYO, M., SANZ-VERGEL, A. I., GEURTS, S., RODRÍGUEZ-MUÑOZ, A. & GARROSA, E. 2009. Effects of work–family conflict on employees' well-being: The moderating role of recovery strategies. *Journal of Occupational Health Psychology*, 14, 427.

MORRIS, J. A. & FELDMAN, D. C. 1996. The dimensions, antecedents, and consequences of emotional labor. *Academy of Management Review*, 21, 986–1010.

MORRISON, T. 2007. Emotional intelligence, emotion and social work: Context, characteristics, complications and contribution. *British Journal of Social Work*, 37, 245–63.

MORRISON, T., HATHAWAY, J. & FAIRLEY, G. 2005. *Staff Supervision in Social Care: Making a Real Difference for Staff and Service Users*, Brighton: Pavilion.

MOTOWIDLO, S. J., PACKARD, J. S. & MANNING, M. R. 1986. Occupational stress: Its causes and consequences for job performance. *Journal of Applied Psychology*, 71, 618.

MUNRO, E. 2002. *Effective Child Protection*. London: Sage.

MUNRO, E. 2011. *The Munro Review of Child Protection: Final Report, a Child-centred System*. London: Stationery Office.

NAPOLI, M. & BONIFAS, R. 2011. From theory toward empathic self-care: Creating a mindful classroom for social work students. *Social Work Education*, 30, 635–49.

NEENAN, M. 2009. *Developing Resilience: A Cognitive-Behavioural Approach*. London: Taylor & Francis.

NETEMEYER, R. G., BOLES, J. S. & McMurrian, R. 1996. Development and validation of work–family conflict and family–work conflict scales. *Journal of Applied Psychology*, 81, 400.

NEWSOME, S., WALDO, M. & GRUSZKA, C. 2012. Mindfulness group work: Preventing stress and increasing self-compassion among helping professionals in training. *Journal for Specialists in Group Work*, 37, 297–311.

NICE 2009. *Depression: The treatment and management of depression in adults*. London: National Institute for Health and Clinical Excellence.

NIELSEN, K., RANDALL, R., HOLTEN, A.-L. & GONZÁLEZ, E. R. 2010. Conducting organizational-level occupational health interventions: What works? *Work & Stress*, 24, 234–59.

NIELSEN, M. B. & EINARSEN, S. 2012. Outcomes of exposure to workplace bullying: A meta-analytic review. *Work & Stress*, 26, 309–32.

ONYETT, S. 2011. Revisiting job satisfaction and burnout in community mental health teams. *Journal of Mental Health*, 20, 198–209.

OSTROFF, C. L. & JUDGE, T. 2007. *Perspectives on Organizational Fit*. London: Psychology Press.

OXFORD DICTIONARIES & WAITE, M. 2012. *Paperback Oxford English Dictionary*. Oxford: Oxford University Press.

PADESKY, C. A. & MOONEY, K. A. 2012. Strengths-based cognitive–behavioural therapy: A four-step model to build resilience. *Clinical Psychology & Psychotherapy*, 19, 283–90.

PARTON, N. 1998. Risk, advanced liberalism and child welfare: The need to rediscover uncertainty and ambiguity. *British Journal of Social Work*, 28, 5–27.

PAYNE, N., KINMAN, G. & JONES, F. 2012. Work stress and health behaviour: Evidence and potential mechanisms. *In:* HOUDMONT, J., LEKA, S. & SINCLAIR, R. R. (eds) *Contemporary Occupational Health Psychology: Global Perspectives on Research and Practice.* Oxford: Wiley-Blackwell.

PERLS, F. 1973. *The Gestalt Approach & Eye Witness to Therapy.* Palo Alto, CA: Science & Behavior Books.

PETERSON, C. & SELIGMAN, M. E. 1984. Causal explanations as a risk factor for depression: Theory and evidence. *Psychological Review*, 91, 347.

PETERSON, C. & SELIGMAN, M. E. P. 2004. *Character Strengths and Virtues: A Handbook and Classification.* New York: Oxford University Press.

PINES, E. W., RAUSCHHUBER, M. L., NORGAN, G. H., COOK, J. D., CANCHOLA, L., RICHARDSON, C. & JONES, M. E. 2012. Stress resiliency, psychological empowerment and conflict management styles among baccalaureate nursing students. *Journal of Advanced Nursing*, 68, 1482–93.

POOLEY, J. A. & COHEN, L. 2010. Resilience: A definition in context. *Australian Community Psychologist*, 22, 30–7.

PUDDICOMBE, A. 2012. *Get Some Headspace: How Mindfulness Can Change Your Life in Ten Minutes a Day.* New York: St. Martin's Press.

RACHMAN, S. 1997. The evolution of cognitive behaviour therapy. *In:* CLARK, D. M. & FAIRBURN, C. G. (eds.) *Science and Practice of Cognitive Behaviour Therapy.* Oxford and New York: Oxford University Press.

RAMON, S. & MORRIS, L. 2005. Responding to perceived stress in a social services department: Applying a participative strategy. *Research Policy and Planning*, 23, 43–54.

RASMUSSEN, H. N., SCHEIER, M. F. & GREENHOUSE, J. B. 2009. Optimism and physical health: A meta-analytic review. *Annals of Behavioral Medicine*, 37, 239–56.

REPETTI, R. L. 1994. Short-term and long-term processes linking job stressors to father–child interaction. *Social Development*, 3, 1–15.

RILEY, H. & SCHUTTE, N. S. 2003. Low emotional intelligence as a predictor of substance-use problems. *Journal of Drug Education*, 33, 391–8.

ROBBINS, S. P. & DECENZO, D. A. 2004. *Fundamentals of Management: Essential Concepts and Applications.* Upper Saddle River, NJ: Prentice Hall.

ROLFE, G., FRESHWATER, D. & JASPER, M. 2001. *Critical Reflection for Nursing and the Helping Professions: A User's Guide.* Basingstoke: Palgrave Macmillan.

ROY, M. M., CHRISTENFELD, N. J. & McKenzie, C. R. 2005. Underestimating the duration of future events: Memory incorrectly used or memory bias? *Psychological Bulletin*, 131, 738–56.

RUCH, G. 2000. Self and social work: Towards an integrated model of learning. *Journal of Social Work Practice*, 14, 99–112.

RUCH, G. 2005. Relationship-based practice and reflective practice: Holistic approaches to contemporary child care social work. *Child & Family Social Work*, 10, 111–23.

RUCH, G. 2007. Reflective practice in contemporary child-care social work: The role of containment. *British Journal of Social Work*, 37, 659–80.

RUCH, G. 2008. *Post-Qualifying Child Care Social Work: Developing Reflective Practice*. London: Sage.

RUCH, G. 2012. Where have all the feelings gone? Developing reflective and relationship-based management in child-care social work. *British Journal of Social Work*, 42, 1315–32.

RUSSELL, T. 2012. St. Edmunds Church in Southampton bans yoga class for not being Christian. *Southern Daily Echo*. Available at www.dailyecho.co.uk/news/9949333.Church_bans_yoga_for__not_being_Christian_.

RUTHS, F. A., DE ZOYSA, N., FREARSON, S. J., HUTTON, J., WILLIAMS, J. M. G. & WALSH, J. 2013. Mindfulness-based cognitive therapy for mental health professionals – a pilot study. *Mindfulness*, 4, 289–95.

RUTTER, M. 1999. Resilience concepts and findings: Implications for family therapy. *Journal of Family Therapy*, 21, 119–44.

SAINSBURY CENTRE FOR MENTAL HEALTH 2007. *Mental Health at Work: Developing the Business Case*. London: Sainsbury Centre for Mental Health.

SALKOVSKIS, P. M. 1997. The Cognitive Approach to Anxiety: Threat Beliefs, Safety-Seeking Behaviour, and the Special Case of Health Anxiety and Obsessions. *In:* SALKOVSKIS, P. M. (ed.) *Frontiers of Cognitive Therapy*. New York: Guilford Press.

SANTIAGO-RIVERA, A. L., BERNSTEIN, B. L. & GARD, T. L. 1995. The importance of achievement and the appraisal of stressful events as predictors of coping. *Journal of College Student Development*, 36(4), 374–83.

SAPOLSKY, R. M. 2004. *Why Zebras Don't Get Ulcers: The Acclaimed Guide to Stress, Stress-Related Diseases, and Coping*. New York: Henry Holt.

SCHAUFELI, W. B., LEITER, M. P. & MASLACH, C. 2009. Burnout: 35 years of research and practice. *Career Development International*, 14, 204–20.

SCHNALL, P. L., DOBSON, M. & ROSSKAM, E. 2009. *Unhealthy Work: Causes, Consequences, Cures*, Amityville, NY: Baywood.

SCHÖN, D. A. 1983. *The Reflective Practitioner: How Professionals Think in Action*. New York: Basic Books.

SCHUTTE, N. S., MALOUFF, J. M., HALL, L. E., HAGGERTY, D. J., COOPER, J. T., GOLDEN, C. J. & DORNHEIM, L. 1998. Development and validation of a measure of emotional intelligence. *Personality and Individual Differences*, 25, 167–77.

SEGAL, Z. V., WILLIAMS, J. M. G., TEASDALE, J. D. & KABAT-ZINN, J. 2012. *Mindfulness-Based Cognitive Therapy for Depression*. New York: Guilford Press.

SELIGMAN, M. E., NOLEN-HOEKSEMA, S., THORNTON, N. & THORNTON, K. M. 1990. Explanatory style as a mechanism of disappointing athletic performance. *Psychological Science*, 1, 143–6.

SELIGMAN, M. E. P. 2002. *Authentic Happiness: Using the New Positive Psychology to Realize Your Potential for Lasting Fulfillment*. New York: Free Press.

SHAPIRO, S. L. & CARLSON, L. E. 2009. *The Art and Science of Mindfulness: Integrating Mindfulness into Psychology and the Helping Professions*. Washington, DC: American Psychological Association.

SHAPIRO, S. L., CARLSON, L. E., ASTIN, J. A. & FREEDMAN, B. 2006. Mechanisms of mindfulness. *Journal of Clinical Psychology*, 62, 373–86.

SHELDON, K. M., RYAN, R. M., DECI, E. L. & KASSER, T. 2004. The independent effects of goal contents and motives on well-being: It's both what you pursue and why you pursue it. *Personality and Social Psychology Bulletin*, 30, 475–86.

SHIER, M. L. & GRAHAM, J. R. 2011. Work-related factors that impact social work practitioners' subjective well-being: Well-being in the workplace. *Journal of Social Work*, 11, 402–21.

SIEGRIST, J. 1996. Adverse health effects of high-effort/low-reward conditions. *Journal of Occupational Health Psychology*, 1, 27.

SIEGRIST, J. 2002. Effort-reward imbalance at work and health. *In:* PERREWE, P. & GANSTER, D. (eds.) *Research in Occupational Stress and Well-being*. New York: JAI Elsevier.

SINGER, J. B. & DEWANE, C. 2010. Treating New Social Worker Anxiety Syndrome (NSWAS). *New Social Worker*, 17, 8–12.

SKAKON, J., NIELSEN, K., BORG, V. & GUZMAN, J. 2010. Are leaders' well-being, behaviours and style associated with the affective well-being of their employees? A systematic review of three decades of research. *Work & Stress*, 24, 107–39.

SONNENTAG, S. & FRITZ, C. 2007. The Recovery Experience Questionnaire: Development and validation of a measure for assessing recuperation and unwinding from work. *Journal of Occupational Health Psychology*, 12, 204.

SPECTOR, P. E. 2009. The role of job control in employee health and well-being. *In:* COOPER, C. L., QUICK, J. C. & J., S. M. (eds.) *International Handbook of Work and Health Psychology*. Chichester: Wiley-Blackwell.

SPENCE, G. B. & GRANT, A. M. 2007. Professional and peer life coaching and the enhancement of goal striving and well-being: An exploratory study. *Journal of Positive Psychology*, 2, 185–94.

SPIELBERGER, C. D. & SARASON, I. G. 1996. *Stress and Emotion: Anxiety, Anger, and Curiosity*. London: Taylor & Francis.

STALKER, C. A., MANDELL, D., FRENSCH, K. M., HARVEY, C. & WRIGHT, M. 2007. Child welfare workers who are exhausted yet satisfied with their jobs: How do they do it? *Child & Family Social Work*, 12, 182–91.

STANIER, M. B., GODIN, S., BABAUTA, L., GUILLEBEAU, C., PORT, M. & ULRICH, D. 2010. *Do More Great Work: Stop the Busywork. Start the Work That Matters*. New York: Workman.

STEINER, C. M. & PERRY, P. 1999. *Achieving Emotional Literacy*. London: Bloomsbury.

STOREY, J. & BILLINGHAM, J. 2001. Occupational stress and social work. *Social Work Education*, 20, 659–70.

SWENEY, M. 2009. Ads to fight stigma of social work after Baby P case. *Guardian*. Available at www.theguardian.com/media/2009/sep/01/social-workers-government-advertising-campaign.

TEASDALE, J. D., SEGAL, Z. & WILLIAMS, J. M. G. 1995. How does cognitive therapy prevent depressive relapse and why should attentional control (mindfulness) training help? *Behaviour Research and Therapy*, 33, 25–39.

THOITS, P. 2011. Revisiting the stigma of mental illness. *Social Psychology Quarterly*, 74, 6–28.

THOMAS, J. T. & OTIS, M. D. 2010. Intrapsychic correlates of professional quality of life: Mindfulness, empathy, and emotional separation. *Journal of the Society for Social Work and Research*, 1, 83–98.

TING, L., JACOBSON, J. M. & SANDERS, S. 2011. Current levels of perceived stress among mental health social workers who work with suicidal clients. *Social Work*, 56, 327–36.

TOASLAND, J. 2007. Containing the container: An exploration of the containing role of management in a social work context. Journal of *Social Work Practice*, 21, 197–202.

TOBIN, P. & CARSON, J. 1994. Stress and the student social worker. *Social Work and Social Sciences Review*, 5, 246–55.

TOTTERDELL, P., HERSHCOVIS, M. S., NIVEN, K., REICH, T. C. & STRIDE, C. 2012. Can employees be emotionally drained by witnessing unpleasant interactions between coworkers? A diary study of induced emotion regulation. *Work & Stress*, 26, 112–29.

TRENIER. E. 2010. Using strengths to guide career transition. *Assessment and Development Matters*, 2(2), 5.

TREVITHICK, P. 2005. *Social Work Skills: A Practice Handbook*. Maidenhead: McGraw-Hill.

TSUI, M.-S. 2004. Social Work Supervision: Contexts and Concepts. London: Sage.

TURNER, K. 2009. Mindfulness: The present moment in clinical social work. *Clinical Social Work Journal*, 37, 95–103.

UCHINO, B. N. 2004. *Social Support and Physical Health: Understanding the Health Consequences of Relationships*. New Haven, CT: Yale University Press.

UM, M.-Y. & HARRISON, D. F. 1998. Role stressors, burnout, mediators, and job satisfaction: A stress-strain-outcome model and an empirical test. *Social Work Research*, 22, 100–15.

UNGAR, M. & LIEBENBERG, L. 2011. Assessing resilience across cultures using mixed methods: Construction of the child and youth resilience measure. *Journal of Mixed Methods Research*, 5, 126–49.

VAN BREDA, A. D. 2011. Resilient workplaces: An initial conceptualization. *Families in Society: The Journal of Contemporary Social Services*, 92, 33–40.

VAN DER DOEF, M. & MAES, S. 1999. The job demand-control (-support) model and psychological well-being: A review of 20 years of empirical research. *Work & Stress*, 13, 87–114.

VAN DER KLINK, J., BLONK, R., SCHENE, A. H. & VAN DIJK, F. 2001. The benefits of interventions for work-related stress. *American Journal of Public Health*, 91, 270.

VAN DIERENDONCK, D., SCHAUFELI, W. B. & BUUNK, B. P. 1998. The evaluation of an individual burnout intervention program: The role of inequity and social support. *Journal of Applied Psychology*, 83, 392.

VAN HEUGTEN, K. 2011. *Social Work under Pressure: How to Overcome Stress, Fatigue and Burnout in the Workplace*. London: Jessica Kingsley.

VAN STEENBERGEN, E. F. & ELLEMERS, N. 2009. Feeling committed to work: How specific forms of work-commitment predict work behavior and performance over time. *Human Performance*, 22, 410–31.

VIRGILI, M. 2013. Mindfulness-based interventions reduce psychological distress in working adults: A meta-analysis of intervention studies. *Mindfulness*, 1–12.

VOYDANOFF, P. 2005. The differential salience of family and community demands and resources for family-to-work conflict and facilitation. *Journal of Family and Economic Issues*, 26, 395–417.

WARR, P. 1987. *Work, Unemployment, and Mental Health*. Oxford: Oxford University Press.

WASTELL, D., WHITE, S., BROADHURST, K., PECKOVER, S. & PITHOUSE, A. 2010. Children's services in the iron cage of performance management: Street-level bureaucracy and the spectre of Švejkism. *International Journal of Social Welfare*, 19, 310–20.

WERNER, E. E., GARMEZY, N. & SMITH, R. S. 1989. *Vulnerable But Invincible: A Longitudinal Study of Resilient Children and Youth*. New York: Adams, Bannister, Cox.

WESTBROOK, J. I., WOODS, A., ROB, M. I., DUNSMUIR, W. T. & DAY, R. O. 2010. Association of interruptions with an increased risk and severity of medication administration errors. *Archives of Internal Medicine*, 170, 683–90.

WHITAKER, T. 2012. Social workers and workplace bullying: Perceptions, responses and implications. *Work: A Journal of Prevention, Assessment and Rehabilitation*, 42, 115–23.

WILBERFORCE, M., JACOBS, S., CHALLIS, D., MANTHORPE, J., STEVENS, M., JASPER, R., FERNANDEZ, J.-L., GLENDINNING, C., JONES, K. & KNAPP, M. 2012. Revisiting the causes of stress in social work: Sources of job demands, control and support in personalised adult social care. *British Journal of Social Work*, bcs166.

WILLIAMS, L. & DAY, A. 2007. Strategies for dealing with clients we dislike. *American Journal of Family Therapy*, 35, 83–92.

WILLIAMS, M. & PENMAN, D. 2011. *Mindfulness: A Practical Guide to Finding Peace in a Frantic World*. London: Piatkus.

YELLOLY, M. & HENKEL, M. 1995. *Learning and Teaching in Social Work: Towards Reflective Practice*. London: Jessica Kingsley.

YOUSSEF, C. M. & LUTHANS, F. 2007. Positive organizational behavior in the workplace The impact of hope, optimism, and resilience. *Journal of Management*, 33, 774–800.

ZAPF, D. 2002. Emotion work and psychological well-being: A review of the literature and some conceptual considerations. *Human Resource Management Review*, 12, 237–68.

ZUGAZAGA, C. B., SURETTE, R. B., MENDEZ, M. & OTTO, C. W. 2006. Social worker perceptions of the portrayal of the profession in the news and entertainment media: An exploratory study. *Journal of Social Work Education*, 42, 621–36.

ZYSBERG, L. & RUBANOV, A. 2010. Emotional intelligence and emotional eating patterns: a new insight into the antecedents of eating disorders? *Journal of Nutrition Education and Behavior*, 42, 345–8.

Index